Rowena Murray graduated in  ɔm
the University of Glasgow. Sl ːed
States, gaining a PhD for a the he
is now Reader in the Departr ɲal
Studies and Associate Dean (Research) at the University of
Strathclyde. She has published extensively, on literature, on writing in
academic research, teaching and educational development.

Brian Murray read English at Glasgow University, and was a teacher in
the west of Scotland, Adviser in English for Ayrshire and a Head
Teacher. With Archie Bevan he has been editing the unpublished and
uncollected work of George Mackay Brown – twelve volumes to date,
with others projected. Like his daughter Rowena, he was a long-term
friend of the writer.

Also by Rowena Murray

Ethical Dilemmas in Healthcare
How to Write a Thesis
How to Survive Your Viva
Writing for Academic Journals
Teaching at University
    (with Kate Morss)
The Handbook of Academic Writing: A Fresh Approach
    (with Sarah Moore)

Also by Brian Murray (editor)

A Sense of Belonging: Six Scottish Poets of the Seventies
    (with Sydney Smyth)
Northern Lights: A Poet's Sources / George Mackay Brown
    (with Archie Bevan)
Travellers / George Mackay Brown
    (with Archie Bevan)
Collected Poems / George Mackay Brown
    (with Archie Bevan)

Interrogation of Silence

The Writings of George Mackay Brown

ROWENA MURRAY

&

BRIAN MURRAY

Steve Savage
LONDON AND EDINBURGH

Steve Savage Publishers Ltd
The Old Truman Brewery
91 Brick Lane
LONDON
E1 6QL

www.savagepublishers.com

Revised edition published by Steve Savage Publishers Ltd 2008

First published in Great Britain by John Murray (Publishers)
A division of Hodder Headline 2004

Maps courtesy of Dr John Flett Brown.
Photograph of George Mackay Brown at Glasgow University graduation
© *The Scotsman* www.scotsman.com.
Photograph of George Mackay Brown and the 'Pierhead Parliament'
courtesy of Orkney Library and Archive.

ISBN: 978-1-904246-32-9

Typeset by Steve Savage Publishers Ltd
Printed and bound by The Cromwell Press Ltd

This book is dedicated to our family and friends.

George Mackay Brown after receiving his honorary doctorate at the
University of Glasgow, 19 June 1985

Contents

Part Three: 1975–1996
'Keeping the roots alive'

List of Illustrations

Acknowledgments

We would like to thank the people who read this book in draft for their helpful and encouraging feedback: Archie Bevan, Julie Lang, Paul Maharg, Meg and Bill Mowat, Mary Newton and Morag Thow.

Lizzie Dipple, Grant McIntyre and Cathy Piggott at John Murray's provided support and encouragement.

The American Association of University Women funded an International Fellowship for PhD research on George Mackay Brown at the Pennsylvania State University.

We are grateful for help given by the following individuals and institutions: Archie Bevan for permission to quote from Brown's work; BBC Scotland; Jane Birkett; Maggie Body; Tricia Boyd; Dr John Flett Brown, particularly for the maps; Castlequoy Graphics; Linda Duncan; Sally Harrower; the Estate of Ted Hughes; Oula Jones; Claire Laurensen; Innes Leitch; Michael Moar; Gunnie Moberg; Gerald and Nora Meyer; John Murray; the Orkney Library (Robert K. Leslie, Karen Walker, Karen Miller, Alison Fraser, Phil Astley and Kathleen Hogarth); Sally Pagan; Colin Sinclair; the libraries of Aberdeen, Edinburgh, Glasgow, Pennsylvania State, Stirling and Strathclyde Universities; the British Library; the Carnegie Library, Ayr (Sheena Andrew); Edinburgh Central Library; the Mitchell Library, Glasgow; the National Library of Scotland; the Shetland Library and Stromness Public Library; Rebecca Ford and Carol Flett; Sigurd Towrie.

Preface

George Mackay Brown was utterly dedicated to his writing, beyond everything else. This book tells the story of his development from the point when he first started writing at the age of seven to his death at seventy-four. Each phase shows developing competence and confidence. We show how he developed his identity as a writer, how his motivation to write strengthened over time and how he came to find and hone his ideas and preoccupations.

Our aim in writing this literary biography is to provide an overview, for the first time, of all of his writing, including works published posthumously. We tell the story of his life as a writer, focusing on the composition process and the craft of writing. This book is not, then, a biography of Brown the man but of Brown the writer.

We draw on research – ours and others' – and on insights gained into George Mackay Brown's thinking and practices from many years of friendship with him. We refer to the extensive collections of the Orkney Library and Edinburgh University Library. In addition to textual scholarship, our story was shaped by discussions with Brown himself. We also considered his writing on writing as an important source.

In writing this book we aim to provide a resource for students and scholars. Equally importantly, we hope to lead readers back to Brown's books. We want to help people find a way into his writings. Those who already know his work will already have their favourite 'GMB' poem or story; we hope this book helps them to find new favourites.

For this new edition some minor errors have been corrected and a few items have updated the bibliography.

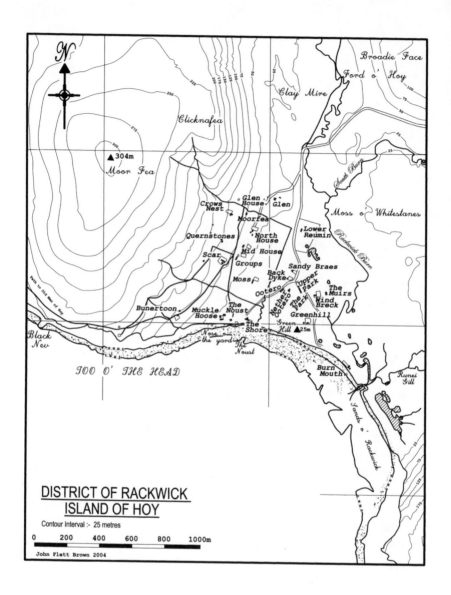

DISTRICT OF RACKWICK
ISLAND OF HOY

Contour Interval :- 25 metres

0 200 400 600 800 1000m

John Flett Brown 2004

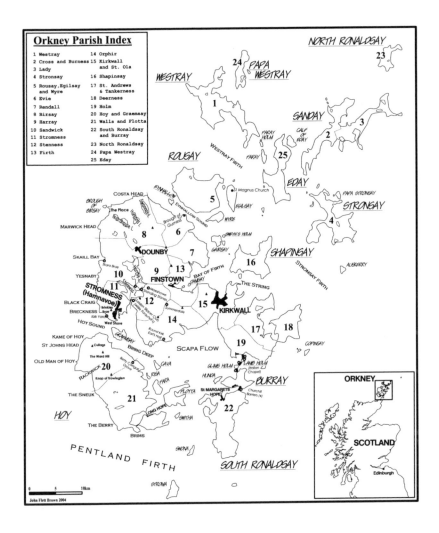

Orkney Parish Index

1 Westray
2 Cross and Burness
3 Lady
4 Stronsay
5 Rousay,Egilsay and Wyre
6 Evie
7 Rendall
8 Birsay
9 Harray
10 Sandwick
11 Stromness
12 Stenness
13 Firth
14 Orphir
15 Kirkwall and St. Ola
16 Shapinsay
17 St. Andrews & Tankerness
18 Deerness
19 Holm
20 Hoy and Graemsay
21 Walls and Flotta
22 South Ronaldsay and Burray
23 North Ronaldsay
24 Papa Westray
25 Eday

John Flett Brown 2004

0   5   10km

NORTH RONALDSAY   23

24 PAPA WESTRAY

WESTRAY   SANDAY   3

1   FARAY HOLM   CALF OF EDAY   2

ROUSAY   WESTRAY FIRTH   FARAY   25

EDAY   PAPA STRONSAY

Costa Head   St Magnus Church   STRONSAY

BROUGH OF BIRSAY   The Place   EYNHALLOW SOUND   EGILSAY   4

MARWICK HEAD   Brough of Gurness   WYRE   GAIRN'S HOLM

8   6   GAIRSAY   SHAPINSAY   AUKSKERRY

DOUNBY   7   16

SKAILL BAY   Skara Brae   9   13   BAY OF FIRTH   STRONSAY FIRTH

YESNABY   10   FINSTOWN   THE STRING

11   Maeshowe Standing Stones

STROMNESS (Hamnavoe)   12   15   KIRKWALL

BLACK CRAIG   BRECKNESS   Kirk Yard   West Shore   Round Kirk Earl's Holm   14   17   18

HOY SOUND   19   COPINSAY

KAME OF HOY   GRAEMSAY   SCAPA FLOW

ST JOHNS HEAD   BRING DEEP

OLD MAN OF HOY   The Ward Hill   Cuilags   GLIMS HOLM   LAMB HOLM (Italian Chapel)

20   CAVA   HUNDA   Churchill Barriers (4)   BURRAY

Knap of Trowieglen   FLOTTA   St Margarets Hope   22

THE SNEUK   21   LONG HOPE   SOUTH RONALDSAY

HOY   SWITHA

THE BERRY   BRIMS   SWONA

PENTLAND FIRTH   STROMA

ORKNEY   SCOTLAND   Edinburgh

xiii

The Poet

Therefore he no more troubled the pool of silence
But put on mask and cloak,
Strung a guitar
And moved among the folk.
Dancing they cried,
'See how our sober islands
Are gay again, since this blind lyrical tramp
Invaded the Fair!'

Under the last dead lamp
When all the dancers and maskers had gone inside
His cold stare
Returned to its true task, interrogation of silence.

George Mackay Brown

Fair copy of 'The Poet', ending with the words 'interrogation of silence'.
(Courtesy of the National Library of Scotland.)

Introduction: 'Interrogation of silence'

This book

The purpose of this book is to provide an introduction to George Mackay Brown's work that will stimulate readers to explore it further. It is also addressed to students, scholars and those with an interest in how writers develop the craft of writing and maintain their motivation to write.

Given the volume of writing Brown produced since the previous overview by Alan Bold, published in 1978, in which every poem and story was the subject of comment, we had to adopt a different approach. Yet a coherent overview of Brown's output has to include detailed examination of the formal variety and artistic accomplishment of certain key texts. We therefore cover all the genres in which Brown wrote, poetry, prose, drama, journalism, autobiography, children's story and essay.

We have constructed a narrative account to lead the reader through the whole body of the work. Our rationale for dealing with Brown's works chronologically is to provide a sense of his development of the craft of writing, showing the gradual emergence of his themes and increasing technical skills. For example, if we read the story of Brown's writing as a narrative in this way, we can see a gradual move away from treating character as archetype in his early writings towards more psychological complexity in his later works. We have consulted Brown's notebooks, letters and autobiographical writings – published and unpublished – before asserting continuity – or disruption – in this narrative of his writing life.

In addition we draw on interviews with Brown conducted by other writers and on our extended contact and dialogue with him. Through years of informal discussions we have developed – and tested – our understanding of his thinking and habits of work.

We take account also of critical responses, addressing, for example, the often-repeated strictures on Brown's alleged insularity, excessive preoccupation with Orkney's past, formulaic technique and the role of Catholicism in his work. We try to capture Brown's sense of his task as poet; he saw himself as having a social role, linked to social occasions and driven by social change.

This was Brown's habit of thought: his consistent preoccupation with themes, with many facets of what in some sense is the same subject. Frequently he used a variety of modes, or different perspectives, in one story, as if he were simply not prepared to accept one dimension of a subject.

At times, his experience of writing and his vision of writing were coloured by his sense of the inadequacy of thought and expression. It is as if, in his view, each published work could never be more than an incomplete version of his idea. Revising was, therefore, part of his method, as for any writer, yet at times, his repeated re-assembling of shifting perspectives is unsettling; the pursuit of 'silence' strikes a note of desperation.

We explore how events and experiences seem to have affected Brown's choice of theme and form: for example, school, illnesses, journalism, study at Newbattle Abbey College and Edinburgh University, observation of Stromness life and character and Roman Catholicism. Without wanting to make direct causal connections between life events and his writing, we do propose that there was a strong relationship, at certain times, between his experiences – or rather how he viewed them – and the writing he produced. In fact, over time, his writing became his life, in the sense that he dedicated more and more time and energy to writing than to anything else.

We have divided Brown's writing career into three phases:

Part One, 1921–1960, looks at his first writings, his early, ambivalent commitment to writing and his apprenticeship as an all-round journalist.

Part Two, 1961–1974, tells the story of how he became a full-time writer, Orkney chronicler and established figure in the Scottish Literary Renaissance.

Part Three, 1975–1996, shows him branching out in all literary forms, particularly the novel.

Each chapter opens with biographical notes to provide context. The main story-line is Brown's quest for 'the perfect poem', or perfect story, in what he saw as an increasingly imperfect world.

In the course of this book, we set out to demonstrate Brown's remarkable gifts as he pursued 'the poet's true task'. We take Brown's frequent references to his quest for silence and repeated revisions of even published and well received work to reflect an obsession with perfection of form and expression that he thought was beyond him. Our title, *Interrogation of Silence*, is intended to stimulate a wide range of interpretations for readers, as it stimulated Brown himself. Since he made it the central image for his work and craft, we have taken it as the focus for this book.

The idea of silence

The Poet

Therefore he no more troubled the pool of silence.
But put on mask and cloak,
Strung a guitar
And moved among the folk.
Dancing they cried,
'Ah, how our sober islands
Are gay again, since this blind lyrical tramp
Invaded the Fair!'

Under the last dead lamp
When all the dancers and masks had gone inside
His cold stare
Returned to its true task, interrogation of silence.[1]

This poem expresses a central idea in George Mackay Brown's writing: the power of poetry and the poet's route to it, through silence. Silence was both the source – the 'pool of silence' – and the goal. For him, the work of the poet was constant refining, endless revision, persistent striving for the perfect poem. Consequently, silence is a persistent motif throughout his writings. It is both a central idea and a symbol of his motivation.

'Interrogation' suggests a darker idea: persistent, cruel, even torturous questioning likely to produce more questions than answers. For Brown it was the 'true task' of the poet, returning again and again to his persistent questions in the hope of finding better, clearer answers, never completely satisfied with what he had written.

Understanding his notion of silence helps to make sense of Brown's continuing return to, for example, the story of Saint Magnus, the Orkney setting and the cycle of the seasons. These were, for him, among the most meaningful of subjects, but more than that, he returned to them again and again in order to improve on his previous work. What is fascinating about this process is that he almost always found something new to say: a new angle, a different form or a fresh perspective.

'A cold pure round of silence'

Silence was a theme in Brown's work throughout his life: 'The poem was, as never before, a cold pure round of silence; a fold; a chalice where, having tasted, a man may understand and rejoice.'[2]

Again, 'I think it best, speaking for myself, to leave a silence. Let "the wisdom and spirit of the universe" write in the number or the note; if such . . . is deemed necessary.'[3]

The meaning of silence, for Brown, was not inarticulacy, failure, withdrawal or complacency but acceptance, affirmation and humility. He used it to refer to death: 'Death, critics say, is a theme that nags through my work: the end, the darkness, the silence. So it must be with every serious artist, but still I think art strikes out in the end for life, quickening, joy. The good things that we enjoy under the sun have no meaning unless they are surrounded by the mysterious fecund sleep.'[4]

For Brown, silence, even in death, was associated with creativity. For some, this will seem like a form of special pleading. The inflated language suggests that he was rising to the challenge of the debate. Such passages also show him wrestling with antitheses and giving a healthy response to critics, provoked into explaining what he was doing, being drawn into wider discussions of the meaning and function of art. In the process, he was disclosing the view that all artistic creation is doomed to imperfection. Yet, his struggle to find meaning for poets and poetry in the modern world would continue for the rest of his life.

Source

Silence also represented the well of ideas, 'the pool of silence', from which meanings and images could be sought. In this connection Brown may have been influenced by Harold Monro's poem 'The Silent Pool', which we know Brown had read. Brown's poem has distinct echoes of Monro's:

> At night we often go
> With happy comrades to that real estate,
> Where dreams in beauty grow,
> And every man enjoys a common fate . . .
>
> Oh, that a man might choose
> To live unconsciously like beast or bird,
> And our clear thought not lose
> Its beauty when we turn it into word.[5]

There is here the same contrast between what Monro calls 'happy comrades' and Brown called the 'dancers and masks', on the one hand, and the impossibility of capturing the clarity and beauty of a thought, in Monro's poem, or the endless questioning evoked by 'interrogation' in Brown's.

Another Scottish poet, Hugh MacDiarmid, also wrote of silence as a reservoir and source: 'I regard silence as the great reservoir out of which articulation and expression come and as long as we are conscious of that enormous resource then we are not inclined to attach too much importance to any particular thing we may say in a given thing [*sic*]. We can always refer it back to the source and the source can accommodate anything.'[6]

Brown had an abiding fascination with the process of composition, from the earliest days all the way through to later works like 'Poet and Prince' in *The Island of the Women and Other Stories*.

Seeking

Brown's idea of silence was also the search for the perfect poem, whose perfection, paradoxically, could not be expressed in words: 'An imperfect poem goes on seeking the silence.'[7] Brown conveyed the pursuit of silence as a quest in this 'Note', written at a time when he was still looking for his key subjects. It represented a general and absolute standard: 'In a sense all writing – my own included – aspires to the same condition of silence.' Again, 'Verse is a golden ring, a gathered silence.'[8]

In another poem, also called 'The Poet', published only in the *New Statesman* (17 May 1974), Brown developed the theme of seeking along the same lines:

> Its secret is always beyond your deepest
> questionings,
> That rune.

What does silence signify? Is it the peace of mind the poet feels when a piece of writing has been completed – a fleeting sense of achievement? Is it unattainable perfection? Or is it the process of seeking that matters? A poetic ideal? Whatever we take it to mean, it has a rarefied, intense and abstract quality. It sits at the core of Brown's work.

On the one hand, he gave us a kind of running commentary on Orkney life; on the other, he pursued formal perfection for its own sake. What stops the works from moving into the territory of the absurd, or despair, is that they convey a sense that Brown was always moving a step along the road towards achieving the effect he was aiming for. He was only too ready to admit that writing was, from time to time, a dutiful exercise; but, at the same time, it meant for him the recovery of things that were in danger of being lost:

> I hoard, before time's waste
> Old country images[9] . . .

Brown's position was acceptance of the fact that no matter how hard he tried he would not achieve silence, the ideal union of subject, feeling and form. This acceptance struck a new, more positive, note: 'I think of the harp that sang by itself the music of innocence and death and ripeness but is only in truth a frame of wood and strings; a lark or a crow according as the player brings initiated or uncouth fingers to his tryst with silence.'[10] Seeking silence was a creative discipline for Brown; his imperfect work was part of the creative process.

Horizon

'. . . he has found another shore, where there is no need (as I believe) of song or story; for all who set foot there are enclosed within a horizon of pure silence; and are content that it should be so.'[11] This refers to the wanderer character who had never been out of Orkney, but it could also refer to Brown himself. The world of the imagination was sufficient for him. Perhaps 'no need . . . of song and story' suggests that he considered that the work stood for him; nothing more needed to be said, either about the work or about his life: 'In the morning I will bring a work of great beauty to the prince, a blank paper, silence. After the perfect poem – which no poet ever will write – the second-best poem is silence.'[12]

Perfection

Brown also used silence to signify perfection: 'If he's wise, he does what the poem wants: tears it up and gives it to the wind, burns it. A poem exists in its purity, as the perfect statue is hidden in the rock. Silence is best: poetry is forever striving for the unattainable perfection of silence.'[13]

A hundred Lents from now
Who will remember us?
What is a carved name, some numbers?

Sand sifts through the skulls.

Who shall know the skull of a singer?

Interrogation of Silence

Silence is best. Song
Should be rounded with silence.

Another tongue of dust will rejoice
A hundred springs from now.[14]

Sometimes silence signifies the rare occasion when the poet is, perhaps for a moment, content with his work.

Brown used the idea of silence in many, many more of his works than we have selected here. Many of his references to silence have echoes of established theological, philosophical, mystical and musical traditions in which silence has particular functions and meanings. This can be seen as the broader intellectual context within which Brown was working, a context that he was aware of through wide reading. He did not subscribe to any one existing tradition, but cleverly kept his particular aesthetic of silence open to a range of interpretations and to an interplay between them.

PART ONE: 1921–1960

Becoming a Writer

1

'A seeker after images':
Childhood and Adolescent Writing
1921–42

Introduction

> It was a dangerous world I had come into. I did not trust it. I would
> never wander far from my own doorstep. I would listen to the stories
> and poems and eat an apple on Sunday mornings, and that was all the
> travelling in this world I intended to do. Already I was a word-wanderer,
> a seeker after images.[1]

In this chapter we provide a context for Brown's first works. His
childhood writings, along with later essays in which he looked back on
early days, provide a sense of where the later writing came from. This is
the first time these early writings have been studied. Without going into
detailed biography, we can see links between the picture Brown drew of
his early years and the emerging world view that shaped his writing.
There are insights into his childhood and adolescence in his writing:

> A child in a sea-close, the salt on his tongue

> A boy on a pier, taut dripping line
> and twist of silver (a sillock)[2]

Again in 'A Work for Poets':

> To have carved on the days of our vanity
> A sun
> A ship
> A star
> A cornstalk

> Also a few marks
> From an ancient forgotten time
> A child may read

That not far from the stone
A well
Might open for wayfarers

Here is a work for poets –
Carve the runes
Then be content with silence[3]

These lines can be read as a kind of prospectus for the writing that was to come.

Biographical notes: 1921–42 (to age 21)

Brown was born on 17 October 1921, at 9.10 a.m., in Stromness, the Hamnavoe of his writing, youngest of six children, one of whom died in infancy. He drew the character of Stromness, second largest settlement in Orkney, with around 1,900 inhabitants, bonded to the sea, in prose that cleverly took on the rhythm of a walk along its main street:

> The whole seaward side of Hamnavoe consists of these stone fishing piers, a score of them, and the houses and sheds built on them. Above the piers is the street of the town, one long street paved with huge flagstones that twists and flows and surges and dodges along for a mile parallel to the shore, narrow between tall grey chasms of houses, and opening suddenly into little squares and gardens. On the upper side of the street a score of closes rise steeply to the higher houses and gardens built into the side of the hill. The whole town is a labyrinth, a warren, a crazy stone web.[4]

He lived for the first few years of his life at 80 Victoria Street: 'The first thing I remember is the blue flag-stones of the floor, and a white-maa looking in through the open door of our house. The close we lived in ended in a small stone pier, with a cobbled slip.'[5] The family moved to 3 Melvin Place, then to 6 Well Park (now 27 Guardhouse Park), and finally he lived alone at 3 Mayburn Court till his death.

Brown felt that his mother's Gaelic background – she grew up in Braal, Sutherland – gave him a link with the Scottish mainland. He said he had the Celtic instinct for 'decoration', with '"the Calvinist work ethic" . . . deeply grained'.[6] He stated on several occasions his belief that his sister's teaching of Scottish ballads to him, when he was still very young, was a key point in his development as a writer.

This period brought the start of Brown's serious health problems: agoraphobia, bronchitis, depression, measles (causing an eye condition for more than forty years). After leaving school in 1939 he worked full-time for a short period in the Post Office. When one of the journalists in post at *The Orkney Herald* was called up for active service in the Second World War, Brown, declared unfit on account of his tuber-culosis, was asked by the editor, Jack Twatt, to take over, and he started work as Stromness Correspondent in 1944, writing a regular column or two on local events and features on 'Stromness News'.

His first attack of tuberculosis forced him to give up activities like football and to turn in on himself in his reading and writing. Patterning, ritualising, mythologising language, structure and characters show him forming his own meaning from experience and his own vision and style. The illness affected his outlook: 'The summer of 1941 passed. It seems, looking back, to have been an empty time.'[7] It foreshortened his sense of his own lifespan: 'early in October 1941. In a few days' time I would be twenty. There were three more years left to me, I reckoned.'[8]

Much later, after a period of feeling isolated as an artist in Orkney, he found comfort in his reconstruction of his roots: 'I am not an isolated storyteller writing in the late twentieth century; I draw from a treasury of narrative written and unwritten out of the islands' past; many voices speak through me; I am part of a tradition.'[9]

His father was cynical about religion, interested in left-wing politics and intrigued by 'those on the fringes of society – tinkers, eccentrics, tramps, people with unusual skills and trades, fairground men and women, "all things counter, original, spare, strange"'.[10] These characters came to occupy an important position in Brown's writing: 'I mention these trivial events because later, when I first began to write, tinkers and drinkers entered frequently into my stories and poems.'[11]

By contrast, a long posthumously published poem describes his mother's reassuring presence and personality:

Gentleness, poverty, six children
(One died) in stone houses
Along Hamnavoe, at close and pier.[12]

She was a fluent writer of letters: 'She had this latent gift of image and rhythm, and I think this came from her purely Celtic blood. (In my own writing, a strong Celtic element is discernible, a mingling of mysticism and intricate image.)'[13] Referring to this Highland theme in his autobiography, Brown revealed something of his own psychology:

I yearned back towards my childhood, and dreaded what was to come. One symptom was that whenever my mother left the house to go shopping, I was convinced every time that she would never come home again. I would shadow her along the street, and dodge into doorways if she chanced to look back. I can't remember how long this state of affairs went on, but it's certain that a part of my mind was unhinged.[14]

In this period of his life Brown had to face up to accusations – real or imagined – that he was a layabout and a burden to his family. He saw no social or professional purpose for his life. From this position, he had to construct a place for himself, creating images of a socially integrated family and of himself as a much-loved child within that family.

What were the options for a young man of eighteen with literary leanings, and perhaps gifts, and adequate school qualifications, with the Second World War imminent? Congenial employment in Stromness Post Office was what he chose before two major events denied him the chance of a university education and put his health – and life – at serious risk: the sudden death of his father, who had retired early from the Post Office on health grounds, without pension, in 1940 and his own diagnosis with tuberculosis in 1941.

'Colditz on the heights'

For the young Brown, school was not a place of inspiration:

In the twenties and thirties, to be a schoolboy was rather like being in prison. The atmosphere was all fear and resentment and boredom. 'By hook or by crook you *will* learn this, and commit that to memory.

That is the way, and *the only way*, to improve yourself, and to *get on in the world*' . . .

Nobody in authority actually said this to us, but that was the atmosphere we breathed. The grim millstones thundered on, day after day. It was appalling . . .

There was a famous prize day when I was about 13 or 14. A leading townsman [J. G. Marwick, in 1937] gave the speech, and he ended with an immortal quatrain which (he claimed) had helped him through life:

> Go on, go on, go on, go on
> Go on, go on, go on
> Go on, go on, go on, go on
> Go on, go on, go on.[15]

Brown wrote about the absence of imagination in his own schooling and took this further as a criticism of Orkney itself, in 'Opinion', an unsigned leader we attribute to Brown in *The Orkney Herald*:

Intellectually we are poverty-stricken. We have of course produced many men of extraordinary mental gifts, some of them living among us today. But there is no sense of unity among the intellectuals of Orkney. Each man ploughs his lonely furrow, unaided.

There is no doubt that our education is partly to blame.[16]

He particularly lamented the neglect of indigenous culture in the school curriculum:

We send our children to school to learn Scottish history and English history; but never once is mention made of our far more fascinating Orkney history. They learn the superficial geography of the world, but half of them have no idea where Mull Head or Kierfea Hill is. Our children leave school as ignorant of their native islands as they went into it.

This is another dimension of the growing tension between Brown's idealised images of himself as a writer, dedicating himself to poetry, and his sense of standing alone by doing so, with no one to support him, no community of writers or artists, no culture. Depopulation, the disappearance of the Norse tradition and the Orcadian temperament, he believed, prevented Orcadians from producing good art.

Early encouragement to write

For Brown this became, for a time, a personal cultural crusade: having endured his share of sickness, morbidity and despair, he berated his community for its lack of support for the artist and intellectual. This was not simply the petulance of youth; isolation had for him become a very real predicament. It was seeping into his work, shaping his world view. This is why mentor figures, including other writers like John Cook, Ernest Marwick and Francis Scarfe and others, were to be so important to him.

As he progressed through school, Brown's experience of literature deepened. Primary school teachers' encouragement in stories and compositions had been left behind, but other teachers took an interest in the young writer: his Latin and English teachers, John Cook, himself a poet, and Ian Paterson. Cook's commendation of Brown's early poetic efforts, some of which he typed for him, and Paterson's introduction to modern literature – MacDiarmid and Eliot, particularly – stimulated Brown to read and write in ways that were a liberation from the perhaps unhealthy intensity with which he had abandoned himself to the Romantic poets:

> I kept *The Golden Treasury* on my locker. Keats, Shelley, Swinburne: I wallowed in them, more for the sound and tone than for the sense. What could be more romantic than withering slowly in a sanatorium, a temple of death, while in the fields around cattle and horses moved, and, beyond, in Kirkwall people went about the prosaic business of getting and spending?[17]

Brown was being taken seriously by teachers and others from an early stage, and contact with other poets would soon make the possibility of his own writing life seem more real.

Childhood writing

When he was seven Brown created a magazine which he called *The Celt* (1929), of which most of one issue survives, the 'fragment' Brown referred to in a later essay (*Under Brinkie's Brae*). This consists of twelve pages, lacking the covers, so each issue was probably sixteen pages long. The format resembles a child's comic, similar to ones he would have read, but there are more words than pictures. There are science fiction and football reports, including a Football Forecast Competition, but the main feature is his original stories. *The Celt* was hand-written, and he wrote out two or three copies to circulate among his classmates. 'The Conquerers from Mercury' is a science fiction story with two illustrations:

> The Men from Mercury were sailors as well as warriors, and when the news came that a fleet was to attack them they had, with the soft, golden, metal with which their helmets were made, quickly built four, queer-shaped ships to meet the French and British. The battle was about to begin. Would the Mercurians be stopped or the pride of Britain and France be conquered? That question was on everybody's lips.

[TO BE CONTINUED NEXT WEEK IN THE 'CELT'. DON'T MISS THIS THRILLING SERIAL NEXT WEEK, WHEN THE GREAT SEA-BATTLE WILL BE FOUGHT]

The story shows competence in language and narrative and a sense of structure. There is an interest in suspense and variation in sentence length and structure for effect. This is a crisp, confident narrative, with an early – perhaps the first – form of Brown's 'fishermen with ploughs' theme: 'sailors as well as warriors'. There are strong visual images – 'soft, golden, metal' – and arresting headlines.

The eight-year-old editor also used other formats and forms. In 'The Editor Calling' he invited feedback: 'How do you like the new stories and competitions in the "Celt" . . . I should be very glad if you write and let me know your views and news.' 'SMILE WITH THE JESTER!' is half-a-dozen jokes, short, neatly laid out. He invented a football team, the Swifts:

NEW STORY!
NO BOY SHOULD MISS IT!!
THE WORLD IS DOOMED!!!

'THE CONQUERERS
FROM MERCURY'

Chapter I - The Coming of the Conquerers

Jock Crawford grunted as she looked up into the sky, blazing with stars. "There's somethin' queer up there," he said aloud, "look at Mercury, there's been queer blue and green lights flashing there for nearly a week now. Even the animals are afraid".

Next morning Jock's horses refused to work. They sniffed up at the sky, as if they feared something terrible would happen, and within an hour that terrible thing happened!

Men had landed in Africa in strange rocket machines from Mercury, with the idea of conquering the earth. Their weapons, strange guns which shot electricity, had killed the N'kamba tribe and many British; the men from Mercury had faces of a golden colour, and queer helmets. They were advancing north to occupy Europe, and were nearing the Suez Canal. But they knew not that the British and French fleets combined were steaming at full speed to stop them from reaching the Mediterranean. But the war-ships were not in time to stop them from capturing the Suez Canal.

'The Conquerers from Mercury'.
A story from Brown's magazine *The Celt*, October 1929.

NEW STORY!
READ ABOUT THE RIVERSIDE SWIFTS.
STARTS TODAY!

Chapter one, 'The Sporting Millionaire's Arrival', was several pages of murder mystery with a cliffhanger ending: 'Tom Kelly, the Swifts' goalie, fell, but before he reached the ground he was dead, shot through the heart. [Who is the murderer, and what is his reason for killing Tom Kelly? Follow up this yarn next week].'

A 'complete adventure story about the Denton Street Gang' includes illustrations of the characters, brisk narrative and elements of what, in his later work, we would call the saga style – although he would not have read the sagas at this time – that Brown would later develop, in the grim humour and put-down of heroes: 'Their hands were tied behind their backs and a rope passed through each one's throat. Finally a placard was stuck on Wolf's jacket, saying that this was the King Street champions returning home. Thus the human chain returned to the hoots & jeers of their followers.' A trailer for the next issue promises continuation of the stories, competitions, a letter to the editor, an editorial, more jokes and free gifts.

We do not want to overstate the quality of these early writings, but for an eight-year-old, it is high and it is sustained over several pages, showing technical competence beyond his years, imaginative energy, a sense of narrative form and security in grammar and punctuation.

They also show awareness of the value of variety in the use of different forms. For all the influences of other writers we see in Brown's later work, these childhood writings show that long before he even heard of Thomas Mann, E. M. Forster, Dylan Thomas, Edwin Muir, James Joyce, Virginia Woolf or T. S. Eliot, his favourite ideas and subjects were there from the start. While Brown's autobiographical essays help us to reconstruct the origins of his ideas, these early works show his first expressions of them. What is intriguing about *The Celt* is that there are signs of the full range of subjects and voices that feature in his mature works.

The first poem

Brown's Commonplace Book, a notebook for the years 1946–48 (75 pages), gives insights into his thoughts at this time: his impressions of writers, folklore, local people, the relationship of art and religion, a selection of his reading of poets and other writers, along with early rough drafts of his own poems, some still unpublished. Writing about himself in the third person, he described the composition of his first poem:

> On a summer morning he sat, alone, on a slope of the narrow park, waiting for the boys to come and play football. The sun lay warm on the slate roofs of the town houses below him, he could see a segment of sea over the shoulder of the Salvation Army hall. He began to make loose rhyming quatrains about the town and its environs, praising their beauty. The phrases and stanzas, [jingling and artificial, scored out] formed themselves easily and naturally in his head: he brought them out delighted, repeated them, remembered them, and stored them back again in his head . . . Later, after football, he went home and wrote his poem down on a scrap of paper, carefully numbering the stanzas. He was perhaps nine years old, or ten, and this was his first poem. He shyly showed it to them [his parents] and they were pleased with it: he was very proud. But it was 6 years before he wrote another.[18]

Between the ages of eight and ten, therefore, Brown was writing poetry as well as the varied material of *The Celt*. He invented a character called 'Mazurin', whose experiences mirrored his own, again a device for distancing himself from his own story, perhaps to avoid self-pity and sentimentalism, perhaps to allow him to say more than he would in his own voice:

> Mazurin envied with a touch of bitterness the grace and energy of the swimmers, the lovers, and the footballers, because he was incapable of living in these strenuous physical ways. For he was ill, and the slightest exertion exhausted him. He felt often that he was 3 parts dead already – a rather disgusting rag blown about on the winds of life. One evening his good angel spoke to him. Though he could not participate in the gay physical life he could enjoy watching it through his eyes. And the footballers that ran so swiftly and kicked so surely –

what were Beethoven, Keats, Hilaire Belloc, and Lazarus but dull creatures in books to them? All their lives were long agonising searches for sweet wells in immense deserts of boredom. As for Mazurin, well, he came on wells rather oftener than his fellows, and they were sweeter and cooler, even though for him the desert hills quaked at noon day with appalling menace.[19]

We can be certain that this is autobiographical writing. Though written in the third person, it shows Brown's early ability in prose and his readiness to write about his own life and preoccupations, at one remove. Numerous pieces like this in the notebook explore subjects from different angles. It was not, therefore, a diary; he did not simply document daily activities, but developed his responses to his environment, his reading and his writing. More importantly, he was developing the writing habit.

Adolescent writing

Brown did not write poetry between the ages of eight or nine and fifteen-and-a-half, but from then he did so regularly.

We know his opinion of his earliest writings from letters he later wrote to Ernest Marwick, describing his sense of vocation for literature and his view that his 'first poem' was his best. We do not have that first poem, but his first published one was 'The Hills of Hoy at Sunset' which appeared in *The Orkney Herald* on 14 June 1939. In error, Brown said that his first – and best – poem was 'The Island', written when he was fifteen or sixteen, which was not published till 1943 in *The Orkney Herald* (under the title 'The Isle'), when he was twenty-two:

The Island

The purple night is hushed and calm
Save here, where crashing breakers roar,
And sigh again with ceaseless moan
　　On northern shore.

The velvet sky above, illumed
With myriad of silent stars.

Interrogation of Silence

How vast and bare its beauty is,
    Seen from afar.

Anon from out the darkness black
A crying seagull wings his flight,
And hovers ghostly o'er the foam
    By pale moonlight.

And o'er the heaving restless deep
The golden lights of harbour gleam.
There life goes on with endless roar
    No time to dream.

But give to me this lonely isle
Where sweet salt odours ever flow:
To live alone with bird and flower,
    And fear no foe.

Interesting themes here are the perspective of distance from the town and its people, the need to conquer fear of some 'foe', isolation in nature and the desire to shun human contact. Some elements of this poem seem like a formal exercise, as if Brown were more interested in form than expression.

Between the ages of fifteen and twenty-four we know, from his letters (27 April 1946), that he had eighteen poems in manuscript, 'ranging over nine years'. While in his later work he was noted for mining the history of Orkney, in some of his early writing he drew on personal experience, including memories of his father. For all Brown was rooted in Orkney, there was frequently an element of ambivalence towards the place in his writing. It was a time when he was very unhappy; his health was poor and a bout of measles had, he felt, affected his sight permanently.

There was always the oasis of reading. Brown discovered the early Penguin titles when he was fourteen. We are told that he stood and read them in the local bookshop:

The sheer, sensuous delight of simply holding those mint red-and-white paperback books with the comical Antarctic bird on the cover in one's hands, in the bookshop! It is certain that one's first love affair with literature is the most wildly thrilling of all; even though, with maturity, will come experiences more profound and lasting. But the outpouring of those early Penguins gave a richness and assurance to adolescence – a much-needed help in time of trouble, for in other respects adolescence is nothing but trouble, fear, uncertainty and mute suffering.[20]

Brown's first three Penguin titles were still on his shelves when he died: André Maurois's *Ariel*, Ernest Hemingway's *A Farewell to Arms* and Eric Linklater's *Poet's Pub*.

Autobiographical writings

Brown's autobiographical essays show the vision of his childhood he constructed for himself. In style, many of these pieces are quite patterned, with Brown working in rituals, mythologising characters and adapting language to different time settings and structures, while shaping his own meaning from his experiences. They are cleverly targeted at different audiences: for example, the 'Writers and Education' (1975) piece was written for school teachers, while 'Writer's Shop' (1976), although it covers some of the same subjects, is written for those interested in Brown's development as a writer.

Clearly, most writers target their audience in this way, but it is interesting to see how shifts in tone and point of view change the slant on his life. We need, therefore, to be careful in drawing conclusions about what actually happened in his life. The very personal unpublished works, in some ways more revealing than these, will be covered in Chapter Two.

Certain events in Brown's life are highlighted throughout the autobiographical articles and are probably therefore very important. There is a narrative core running through them all: idealised home life, sea setting of Stromness, darker tones when he goes to school, threat of the outside world, oasis of reading and writing that saved him, his father's depression and mother's warmth. The following selection shows Brown forming his vision and style on the pretext of writing about his life.

'Living in Orkney'

In this essay Brown reflected on what it was like to be an artist in Orkney. He lamented the impact of socio-economic change on art, values and local life generally:

> Language was once a rich and lovely thing in the Orkneys; the poetry fashioned from it was 'anonymous and communal', to use Thomas Mann's phrase; everyone knew the poem, and nobody worried about the author, for in a deep sense they knew that they all contributed to its making.
>
> But now we have culture, and the word is like an upheaval in nature, which drops a great chasm between poet and people. All communication is lost . . .
>
> For [Orkney people], poets and artists are an inferior breed. 'What', they ask with ruthless logic, 'is the *use* of pictures and verses?' And it is useless to explain that pictures and poems are made to keep their eyes bright and their blood flowing.
>
> Orkney nowadays is a comfortable well-off place. But there is a flaw somewhere, through which the imagination and the old country virtues are leaking away. Some think it would be better for us to be, like our fathers, superstitious, poor, and visionary. But of course it is impossible to beat the bell backwards; and out of the new conditions that time has imposed on us, new virtues and new faculties will spring, though at the moment our eyes are sealed.[21]

There are darker tones here again; the artist in Orkney can find no proper place in the community. Brown was beginning to connect this with the 'new conditions' of the world outside Orkney. He adopted the dogmatic proselytising, even aggressive, tone that became a characteristic of some of his journalism.

A more concrete threat was the subject of his essay 'Oilscene'.[22] With the discovery of oil Orkney was under siege from the outside world, the twentieth century, and what Brown saw as a side effect of material improvement, the erosion of local traditions. This threat strengthened his commitment to preserving Orkney's stories, traditions and characters.

'Writers and Education'

Brown used this essay to rant against the rote learning, content and delivery of the school curriculum as he had known it, with its failure to involve children actively. He described how children were given no introduction to important literary texts, such as *The Merchant of Venice*. As far as he was concerned, real education occurred outside school:

> Children grow and develop, whatever their circumstances. I'm sure the wholesome growth of mind and spirit, the slow widening of horizons, took place outside the school gates altogether. The old men told their stories in the tailor shop. The elements slowly grained their essences into us and shaped our minds. We came at last to love the islands . . .
>
> I think, looking back, that our education would have been infinitely sweeter and more rewarding if our imaginations had been appealed to; if the arts had had a greater part to play and if pupils had been free active participants, with musical instrument and mask and voice.
>
> This is what education should be, surely – 'the playtime of the spirit'.[23]

Writing about his own life was an opportunity for Brown not only to criticise education but also to make the case for the imagination. In doing so, he offered insights into not only his life experiences but also the origins of his personal beliefs and literary values.

'Writer's Shop'

'I first began to think I might have some ability as a writer when at the age of seven or eight we had to write compositions for our teacher . . . I found to my astonishment that I always wrote the best compositions.'[24] This essay tells us what Brown read as a boy – Grimm's fairy tales and the Old Testament – and what he read later in life – Thomas Mann, E. M. Forster, Bertolt Brecht, T. S. Eliot, Gerard Manley Hopkins, W. B. Yeats, John Keats, the Border ballads and the Icelandic sagas (in translation). This reading provided his education in narrative: 'I learned from these stories, without realising it, how narrative is shaped and given rhythm.'

'An Autobiographical Essay'

This essay is important because it contains so many of Brown's ideas about his own childhood and his evolution as a writer; it is less anecdotal than his other essays, more a statement of his purpose and progress in art.

> The first five years, it's said, is the important time in every life; the basic pattern is set then; what follows, into maturity and white hairs, consists of variations and elaborations of the pattern, repeated over and over . . .
>
> We arrive on the scene with a vast heritage of experience: the hunt, the battle, the voyage, the settlement, defeat and triumph and reconciliation: all our ancestors are present in us. The archetypes are set, that make us human.[25]

Brown argued that this was the writer's task: to write about archetypal moments. The challenge was to show their importance, while finding a way to connect with contemporary audiences. For example, when he wrote about the past he had to refresh its meaning for the modern reader. His impulse was not simply to preserve ritual and tradition, but to capture their meaning and value. He described how he experienced this process himself:

> I don't know when I began to think of him (there were several fishermen) as the essence of the town, the man bringing in the sea treasures, as the very first men on this shore had done. The fisherman became a symbol, but only much later. (Symbols are made when daily life is seen no longer as a mime, or a game, but as a perilous enduring between birth and death. Then the fisherman, as the original food-gatherer, the hunter in the sea, assumes an importance not usually accorded to him by men more safely circumstanced.)

Brown revealed how he shaped his symbolism into a dynamic involving other social groups:

> Fisherman and farmer are in a sense stark opposites. One is thirled to

a perilous unpredictable element, which is sometimes generous and sometimes stingy (always menacing). The other is bound to the slow sure wheel of agriculture . . . The Orkney crofters were poor in former generations; most of them had fishing yawls as well as plough-and-horse. Land and sea meshed in the one food-provider; a fish-oil lamp lit the table of bere-bannocks, cheese and ale.

Without that symbolical figure, the Orkney crofter with a boat, I think I could not have written a word of any significance.

These people, in their way of life, became emblems in, and perhaps for, Brown's writing. Cumulatively, they represent the fable, the web connecting different times, cutting across material and physical changes that occur over time: 'It is the writer's task to relate the legend (what Edwin Muir called "the fable") to this age of television, uranium, and planet-flight.'

Glimpses of Brown's early preoccupations emerge in these auto-biographical pieces, reconstructing the world of Brown's youth, or rather showing how he reconstructed it. What is astonishing is that what were to become his enduring preoccupations were given literary form in Brown's earliest childhood writing.

Conclusion

Brown's vision was firmly fixed, from the start, on Orkney. That focus would, for the rest of his writing life, be his strength and, some would argue, his weakness. However, like other writers who choose to focus on a 'postage stamp' of territory, like William Faulkner, Brown made his narrow focus creative and productive. More importantly, he was beginning to have a sense of himself as a writer, and this was taking a highly original form because of – rather than in spite of – the geographical and social constraints. He had developed a liking for reading and writing and had published poems in the local newspaper.

The next phase of his life brought serious health problems. He would write about these too, confronting his illness and disabilities, developing the quality of self-sufficiency, becoming self-contained at times, with a mixture of horror at and fascination with illness. He was to rely more and more on his own resources, his own imagination and his own writing processes.

Brown's memoir of his father ended with a longing for a writer who could record Orkney's 'conversations':

> A quintessence of dust, he lies in a field above Hoy Sound among all the rich storied dust of Stromness. The postman had left the last door, he had quenched the flame in his lantern. The tailor had folded the finished coat and laid it aside. He was at rest with fishermen, farmers, merchants, sailors and their women-folk – many generations.
>
> I wish there was a Thomas Hardy in Orkney to report the conversations of those salt and loam tongues in the kirkyard, immortally.[26]

By the time he was twenty-one he was about to take up that role himself as an Orkney journalist.

2

The Stromness Correspondent:
Journalism, Poems and Stories
1943–51

Introduction

> On the whole, I think the best thing I ever did for *The Orkney Herald*
> were the weekly paragraphs . . . in the Stromness News (1960).[1]

> All who worked on the *Herald* have fragrant memories of it. And I not
> least, because in its columns appeared my first poems and tales.[2]

Most readers know George Mackay Brown as a creative writer; few
will know that he was also a prolific journalist. Between 1944 and
1951, while he was beginning to produce more poetry and prose
poems, he also wrote approximately 300,000 words on 'Stromness
News', the equivalent of three substantial novels. If we include his
other journalism of this period the total is much higher, possibly as
much again. This is a phenomenal output. Although by 1983 he looked
back on this period with what seems like nostalgia, at the time, in 1946,
his feelings towards journalism were expressed more negatively: 'I take
this business of poetry very seriously. Journalism means nothing to me
at all, except as a means to gain a livlihood [*sic*].'[3]

While journalism gave Brown a writer's apprenticeship, the journey
he made in this period was from absolute professional commitment to
journalism to equally intense dedication to poetry.

Biographical notes: 1943–51 (aged 22–30)

In his autobiography Brown described this period as 'years that the
locust ate'.[4] Although he was developing as a writer he was still in
turmoil about where art – and artists – fitted into Orkney society, if
at all. More turmoil and distress came with the threat of death; he

thought he would be dead from tuberculosis by the age of twenty-three.

In August 1944, at a time of serious staff shortage, Jack Twatt, editor of *The Orkney Herald*, invited Brown to become his Stromness Correspondent. This gave Brown access to a reading public, from which he might have been expected to shrink in his earlier years. It meant also that he would be published regularly, could write about his own ideas and obsessions and would make a little money from writing.

The Second World War changed the Orkney Brown knew. Suddenly it was full of people. Brown knew he was not going to war; the war came to him. There were many theatrical events and personalities in Orkney to entertain the troops.

He had the *Penguin New Writing* series to keep up with other writers of the day. There was plenty to write about and he also began to publish an abundance of material of his own that he had been collecting. He had fifty contributions in *The New Shetlander* literary magazine between May 1947 and June 1951.

A typical month's journalism

From someone who had published almost nothing, Brown quickly became a prolific journalist. For an insight into his regular output we can look at his contributions to *The Orkney Herald* for September 1945, which included four columns of 'Stromness News', four reports, four articles, three book reviews, three essays and the first of a long series of his column 'Island Diary'. His journalism included not simply reports but also essays and leader columns. As his output grew, he began to move beyond apprenticeship, stretching his responsibility, escaping from its constraints, proving himself as a journalist and, in the process, maintaining close contact with the community's debates and just about all of its activities.

What we see in the writing itself is Brown's commitment to both the social role and the literary discipline of journalism:

> 'Island Diary' is just three years old. . . . It was born in very inauspicious circumstances. During those dreadful years of the war, the entire reporting staff of *The Orkney Herald* was in the forces. Copy was scarce,

and space hard to fill . . . conceived first of all as a stop-gap, a number of light gossipy paragraphs to occupy the greater part of a column . . . That first week 'Island Diary' was very flippant and very gossipy. It concerned itself . . . with the fact that ice cream was once more on sale, after five years of enforced absence. It required considerable ingenuity to weave a whole readable column out of that simple fact, but I managed it.[5]

In this 'celebration' of his own column, he was frank about his initial limitations, but not so modest as to fail to take credit for his achievements. What some might see as recycling is another form of effective journalism: drawing attention to his original column, revisiting previous controversies, possibly renewing them. Brown's journalism was not just a response to his muse; he was concerned to make his writing readable and was not afraid to write controversial articles, some provoking strong, even violent, responses from readers.

'Orkney has no culture'

It was in his regular columns that he developed his themes: 'Orkney has no culture', 'the glorification of Orkney' and 'Orkney at first hand'. He developed an approach that combined celebration of Orkney with first-hand observations:

We decided to see Orkney at first hand, and week by week we took bus and boat to all the available parts of the islands. We returned laden with observations and impressions, and churned out copy by the square yard. I learned that, to the humble columnist, the Orkney countryside in summer pays big dividends for the favour of a visit. 'Island Diary' no longer foolishly proclaimed that Orkney was the loveliest place in God's creation: but it learned, at the same time, to know and love Orkney with a saner and deeper passion.

I still believe that the Orkney people lack the creative vision without which no community can be really alive, and I will keep on believing it until it is proved to the contrary.[6]

Looking at the second paragraph, contrasting so dramatically with the first, we cannot help but wonder if he is using that journalistic staple of over-stating for effect. He had, in fact, been stating such views strongly in other pieces and the correspondence with those who raised objections was lively, to say the least. There is evidence that he took himself very seriously in this role. He had found that he was good at stirring up controversy, seeming at times to do his best to get his readers going, engaging in running fights, flyting (a traditional Scottish poetic form of skirmishing), and being deliberately provocative, to the point of rudeness.

His 'Stromness News' pieces in *The Orkney Herald* from September 1944, were lively, conscientious articles on local issues (like housing). He wrote on literary subjects (for example, Robert Burns), reflections on what makes good writing, hints for budding young Orkney poets, book reviews, Orkney culture, or lack of it, and reviews of dramatic productions. He not only reviewed such performances but wrote plays for the Stromness Dramatic Society, *Spoils of the Sea* and *The Wheel o' Fortune*. There were also two years of unattributed leader articles, from September 1945 to September 1947, in *The Orkney Herald*. These 'Opinion' pieces have a turn of phrase and range of preoccupations, for example, with Saint Magnus, typical of Brown.

Brown wrote his 'Island Diary' column from 25 September 1945 to 23 October 1956. Between 1945 and 1951 he wrote 282 of these columns. (After 1951 he wrote a further 203.) The pattern of output reveals how illness interrupted, though did not stop, his writing: for example, he wrote only thirteen columns in 1952 and ten in 1953, although in 1953 he did contribute a series of stories about a character called Mansie to *The Orkney Herald*. Even when he was ill he was still writing.

There was, about this time, a shift from journalism to creative writing. Given that he was not able to gather the news, through illness and isolation, he had more time for creative writing. The focus on Orkney persisted in this new writing: 'Mansie is no-one in particular, or anything you care to call him. Maybe he is the typical Orkneyman, or maybe he is just a peg to hang a few episodes on.'[7] This offers an interesting insight into Brown's approach to character in fiction; he wanted his characters to serve more than one aesthetic purpose and it did not seem to matter to him too much if this meant that they were not fully rounded. Similarly, his central characters often had a unifying role, holding episodes together. For readers who find his fictional characters two-dimensional, this might show them in a different light.

Brown's cultural critique was a recurring subject in his journalism: 'Orcadians were without any native culture: . . . the islanders were too keen on making money, to the shocking neglect of their eternal part.'[8] Journalism gave him not only a forum for publicising neglect of culture but also a mechanism for promoting it, by refreshing Orkney's people, places and history. For this, local news was important. Even as he was developing images of Orkney as 'sick', culturally, he was trying to reinvent it in his own terms. He saw himself as filling a gap in Orkney's culture and there were others who agreed. Brown was encouraged by other artists such as Stanley Cursiter and H. Croft Jackson, who wrote that they admired and agreed with what he said. Brown was taking Orkney apart and putting it back together again, analysing every aspect of Orkney society, even as he wrote about them all in his array of columns.

There were, of course, those who strenuously disagreed with Brown's cultural critique, as he himself reported in due course:

> These musings caused bitterness to well up in the hearts of several of my readers. But for a while they held their peace, and in the vanity of my heart I imagined that all was well, and that everyone was agreeing with me . . .
>
> Inevitably the storm broke . . . I was violently and viciously attacked by no less than three irate correspondents simultaneously . . . I pulled it through, however. I have a peculiar and perverse gift . . . of being able to sneer at people in print: a gift which I am quite innocent of in normal conversation.[9]

Brown's 'Stromness News' column did give readers a vivid impression of life, people, issues and events in the town, but, as he saw it, his 'Island Diary' and other series invested his journalism with cultural significance. Clearly, Brown saw himself as a journalist with a cultural mission, and not necessarily an easy one. His critique was, in many ways, the foundation of his subsequent serial reinvention of Orkney.

All this journalism gave Brown an opportunity to stir up heated debates, making waves in the local community, creating friction and tension among Orcadians. He had to face their reactions in their letters and to hold his side of the debate in the face of fierce criticism. Perhaps most importantly, he flushed out other people, including writers, who agreed with many of his contentious opinions and with whom he could discuss and develop his ideas.

The Orkney Grand Tour

One phase of Brown's reinvention of Orkney was conducted in a tour of key sites, involving his personal 'discovery' of Maeshowe, the islands of Rousay and Hoy and other places in 1946 and 1947. What he wrote amounts to an inventory of what have since become tourist stops for visitors to Orkney and recurring settings for his creative writing.

This Grand Tour might have been Brown's response to the criticism that he was writing about Orkney without having seen it for himself. He decided he would see it for himself and described his first impressions in four *Orkney Herald* columns over four consecutive weeks in the summer of 1946. In the first two pieces Brown drew a striking contrast between the tame summer landscape of the lush side of the island of Hoy and the dramatic desolation in the middle of the island. His enthusiasm for what he called a 'purpose-less' visit, his enjoyment of the landscape, flowers, even a dog he met, convey the attraction of this remote place. Equally clear is the attraction, for him, of writing about it.

His description of the journey to Rackwick Bay off Hoy conveys the strange appeal of the desolate valley. The next column described the beauty of Rackwick itself:

> I noticed here one of the most satisfactory things about the Orkney heritage. There were hardly any fences or material boundary lines of any kind . . . Once on a time all Orkney was like this, without the stone walls and fences, with which each man jealously encloses his land. Now only Rackwick is free of them; but probably not for long . . .
>
> The famous high cliffs that enclose the beach of Rackwick are rose-pink in colour. To the left, the beach is fine silver sand; to the right, thousands of huge, almost spherical, rose-red boulders . . .

> Where the clamorous burn went by to the sea, the grass was starred with brilliant yellow marigolds . . . Rackwick lay at our feet, absorbed and dreaming in the early evening sunlight. It was hard to believe that any shadow of trouble could touch this lovely valley and its peaceful inhabitants.[10]

This marked the origin of his idea that some places – here a specific place – should be protected, particularly places that had become imaginative havens for him. In another essay he took this idea further:

> The calm of evening lay over Rackwick. I don't know what like Rackwick will be in the midst of snow and winter, and I hope I never shall know. I want to remember it as a place of balm and consolation, like the mythical island valley of Avilion where King Arthur went to recover from his mortal wounds . . . Perhaps Rackwick is Avilion, because no one has ever known where Arthur's island valley is, and Orkney, of course, was one of the distant parts of his kingdom. King Arthur's people believed that one day in the future, when the world was wholly given over to evil, King Arthur would return from Avilion, with his terrible wound healed, and that he would restore justice and peace to the land with his mighty sword, Excalibur. That was many hundreds of years ago. Arthur, the good king, never returned. We never had such need of him as to-day.[11]

Brown's poetry was beginning to feed off, or grow out of, his experience and selective memories. More importantly, he was beginning to develop his own mythology of specific places in Orkney. In a postscript to the last of these four pivotal essays Brown conceded that they were, in many ways, a diversion from the usual subjects of his weekly column: 'Next week our "Island Diary" will proceed on its usual lines of acrimonious discussion.'

These pieces of descriptive prose can be directly linked to Brown's poetry. This is illustrated in the collection *Northern Lights* (1999), whose subtitle, *A Poet's Sources*, conveys the nature of the book: it brings together Brown's earliest descriptions of Orkney and poetry that seems to have grown directly out of the prose. For example, there are several distinct echoes of his Rackwick essays in the economical little poem that offers us a snapshot, dated 1950.

Rackwick

Let no voice idly whisper here.
Between those strong red cliffs,
Under the great mild sky
Lies Orkney's last enchantment,
The hidden valley of light.
Sweetness from the clouds pouring,
Songs from the surging sea.
Fenceless fields, fishermen with ploughs
And old heroes, endlessly sleeping
In Rackwick's compassionate hills.[12]

In this poem, before we can read the description of the place, the first line, 'Let no voice idly whisper here', shifts the tone from that of the strolling, 'sprawling' tourist to the awe and respect commanded by the place, as it works on the poet's imagination. Equally important for understanding the transformation at work here, are the extracts in *Northern Lights* from Brown's Shetland Diary, which reveal the 'reflective framework' that drove the writing and held the works together. The main features of the prose descriptions are all here: the red cliffs, the sky, the lingering heritage, the discovery of the valley, the fence-free fields, the link with King Arthur and the healing effect. This is a distillation of the prose pieces, emphasising the impression the place made on him. Three words, 'fishermen with ploughs', capture what was to be the title of a future collection of his poems.

Although Brown deliberately did this Orkney Grand Tour as part of his cultural crusade, in order to acquire first-hand experience, he had begun, at the same time, to cast what he saw in a particular way: 'the time and place do not matter, seeing that the events narrated have a timeless significance,' he wrote to Ernest Marwick on 24 October 1946. In this long letter he described his poem 'Journey to Avilion', written in 1946, at the same time as the tour. In the poem he shifted the Arthurian legend to an Orkney setting; Rackwick is a 'Tir-nan-og or "Land of the Ever Young": I have fused this fable with an account of events in a trip to Hoy and Rackwick.' It is this poem, in which the light-hearted young Stromness visitors, Brown and his friends, are transformed into troubled Arthurian knights, that he saw as his *magnum opus* of 1946:

> The whole Prose Poem, of course, is a meditation on Leadership, Defeat, lost glory etc. . . .
>
> 'Journey to Avilion' is my magnum opus so far. I got great delight from writing it. I get great depression from the certain thought that if I printed it for the delight of the Orkney people it is primarily meant for, it wouldn't mean nearly so much as a flowery article by Robert Leitch or a poem by O. R. Cadian. God help us all!

Time-shifts involving characters who respond to the same pressures across history dictate the structure of this poem. The desperately ill Arthur's progress to his destination is given a known Orkney setting: Rackwick in North Hoy. The first of three sections describes the king's journey. Part two is an extract from a letter from a lady. Classical names are given to the characters to reinforce the idea of timelessness. The narrator is a 'fanatical follower' of Arthur.

A month before he began 'Journey to Avilion', Brown was protesting his low opinion of journalism, yet some of his best pieces resulted from this excursion. That in turn prompted the prose poem, not in the sense that he consciously sat down and thought about how he could recycle the visits in different forms, but that he recreated the lives of previous inhabitants of places visited. He particularly seemed to want to recreate their world view and values. What links all these pieces is a focus on the desire for affirmation and renewal.

At this time lyrical passages were creeping into his journalism more and more frequently:

> That summer is on its last lap is only too evident these nights, when the shadows begin to 'creep in' soon after nine o'clock, and a spectral nip in the air foreshadows autumn. But the darkness has its compensations, and a low pale moon over the Orphir hills last weekend, making a shimmering pathway of broken silver on the smooth water, was one of the most enchanting sights of the late summer.[13]

Prose poems

Alongside his prodigious journalistic output, Brown continued to write poetry. His remarks on his poems give interesting insights into later works, particularly his definition of the prose poem, a genre he was to promote and practise for the next fifty years.

His two most ambitious efforts in the genre gave rise to extended commentaries in Brown's letters to Ernest Marwick. Marwick, born in the West Mainland parish of Evie, fifteen miles from Kirkwall, was a generous self-taught researcher and scholar whose interest in Brown's conversation and letters on literary topics developed into a warm, lasting friendship. Brown's letters to Marwick are an important source of information on his literary intentions and aspirations. For example, it was here that he explained, more fully than anywhere else, what he set out to do in his prose poems:

> I somehow have the feeling that a good Prose Poem exists by reason of the continuous waves of suggestion it throws out. Every word and line must, of course, have significance. I have tried to make my Prose Poems distilled short stories, with all the powers of the lyric to surprise and strike with wonder. The Prose Poem is, I assure you, a most exciting medium, and English poets have not explored it nearly enough.[14]

> I have been experimenting with a form of composition which I call 'Prose Poem' for lack of a better word. It is more akin to musical form than to poetry.[15]

Brown revealed how much he enjoyed this form of writing: 'the writing . . . one cold night last February was one of the happiest experiences of my life.'[16] This letter also reveals the depth of Brown's knowledge of poetic form. He knew how to use different genres. There is also evidence of his fascination with different periods of time and delight in formulating symbols for them within a unified structure. Six of the eighteen poems Brown sent to Marwick at this time were reprinted, with major or minor changes, in his 1977 and 1996 collections.

Although several of these long, ambitiously conceived and annotated prose poems are not comparable to Brown's later poetic work, they do illustrate characters and themes which were to figure largely throughout other poems. For example, there is a forerunner of the recurrent character of Gregory, the drowned sailor, in a poem showing the influence of T. S. Eliot, 'Swan's Way':

> Rainbow coloured fish rose from
> their sleep among the drowned sailor's ribs; and
> sea spiders crawled out of his eye sockets.

While Brown's journalism showed his ability to handle almost any subject in prose, the prose poem hybrid allowed him to change the emphasis of elements of a story. He had found a combination of freedom and form that suited him; there was a new freedom from the 'facts' and a new form to bring some shape to his ideas.

Mentors

When Brown was twenty-two years old, a further source of encouragement arrived when the published poet and critic Francis Scarfe was billeted in the Browns' house from April 1944 to June 1945, while he was a captain in the Army Education Corps. He gave Brown copies of T. S. Eliot's *Four Quartets* and introduced him to a selection of works that very few people in the country would have had at that time. He and Brown wrote and exchanged drafts of their poems, and this interaction confirmed Brown's impulse to write poetry, much of it showing the influences of Eliot and Auden. Francis Scarfe's encouragement did much to settle and encourage the young Brown, recently discharged from hospital, 'unemployed and unemployable'.[17] The vacuum created by Scarfe's departure was filled by Ernest Walker Marwick (1915–1977).

Ernest Marwick was an indefatigable reader of Brown's work over the years, offering comments, suggestions and constant encouragement. Marwick acted as his researcher. For many years he was Brown's proof-reader, adviser on lay-out, typing for him, suggesting themes, providing perceptive reviews, collaborating with Brown on literary projects and interviewing him for radio programmes in which Marwick's shrewd questioning and friendly manner brought illuminating remarks from Brown on his ideas and practice. These interviews were scripted in advance, Marwick giving Brown questions beforehand and Brown writing out his answers, suggesting that he lacked confidence to react spontaneously when speaking in public.

Brown's early letters to Marwick contained extended frank statements of his poetic interests and aspirations, illustrated profusely by texts, many of which survived into his first collection, *The Storm and Other Poems* in 1954, and even on to the last *Selected Poems* Brown sent to press in 1996. The first letter extant, with its formal address, 'Dear Mr Marwick', offered Brown's suggestions for Marwick's *Anthology of Orkney Verse* (not published till 1949), before Brown first requested his new acquaintance's opinion: 'I've raked up a few of my own Orkney poems, including some Prose Poems . . . See what you think of them. There are 18 M.SS [*sic*] altogether, ranging over nine years.'[18] There is an attractive openness about the young poet – at the age of twenty-four – flitting from suggestions for the anthology to the results of his own poetic efforts over a considerable period. Volunteering his work for Marwick to assess was to continue for thirty years in more than a hundred letters and as many meetings and phone calls. Marwick's comments were valued, although not always adopted.

Letters written between 1946 and 1951 show Brown rejecting journalism as a permanent occupation and becoming committed to creative writing: 'I have cultivated this secret vice of poetry for 9 years, since I was 15 years old, and it is my ambition some day to leave one or two really good poems behind me. At present I know I am very far from realising this ambition, but at the same time am conscious that every year finds me in a stronger position.'[19] Whether or not we take this statement at face value – it may be that Brown was still overstating the case for effect, given that he was still producing a considerable volume of journalism – it does express changing priorities.

Marwick introduced Brown to other Kirkwall writers. He responded eagerly to the stimulating new environment in which the poet Robert Rendall, short story writer, and poet Christina Costie and Marwick himself discussed their on-going work and that of established writers. An indication of how Brown's self-esteem was promoted by all this was his composing a lecture on modern poetry for the Kirkwall Arts Club. Not for the last time, he shrank from public exposure, pleading illness, and Marwick read the well-received script on his behalf.

As the years went on, Brown's letters to Marwick decreased in number and length, partly because of Brown's absence from Orkney for periods in hospital and study at Newbattle (1951–52, 1956) and Edinburgh University (1956–64), partly because the telephone replaced the need for letters and partly because he had settled into a productive way of life, writing three hours a day, six days a week.

While he was a student at Edinburgh University Brown sent Marwick two pieces he had written on the deaths of two friends (David Fox and Danny Watt), asking Marwick to help him get them published in *The Orkney Herald*. Later, he did the same with his moving account of Edwin Muir's funeral service. That the pieces were printed indicates Marwick's continuing support for Brown, even when the latter was away from Orkney. Marwick also sent Brown *The Orkney Herald*, as he was still anxious to read it every week. Marwick, himself a regular contributor, took on much of Brown's role at the newspaper and continued to be Brown's link with it.

In the course of these extended interactions with Marwick, Brown developed confidence in his own tastes and ideas, and could comment comfortably on his own early writing. His ambition was to leave one or two poems behind him, since there was no one else in Orkney who could do so:

> And there are no poets in Orkney;
> Stirred by breeze and blood and ocean
> I set the trumpet to my lips. I only.[20]

That was before contact with other writers had spurred him on, to reduce his sense that he was working alone. 'I only' may sound arrogant, but it also reveals his sense of isolation and sense of his calling before he met Scarfe and Marwick.

Magnus

Brown's journalistic career allowed him to move across multiple modes, hundreds of topics and a wide range of tones and voices, but there was one constant point of reference: the story of Magnus pre-occupied him from the very start until he died. Using the *Orkneyinga*

Saga, in translation, as a source, he made many different stories from it. So important was the story of Magnus that he used it to end his autobiography: 'I say, once a day at least, "St Magnus, pray for us."' This literary subject had become his personal liturgy.

Brown made Magnus the subject of many quite different writings in this period, in poems sent with letters to Marwick and in stories for *The Orkney Herald*, for example, 'Meditation on a Murder'. Brown went on to tell Magnus's story from different points of view and in different voices. He even turned it into a boy's story in 'Fragment of an Abandoned Novel'. He published a Magnus story in the Newbattle magazine. Two anonymous leader articles on Magnus in *The Orkney Herald* are in Brown's distinctive style. There are unpublished poems, dated between 1944 and 1946, on Magnus in the Orkney Library, showing Magnus as victim, martyr, miracle-worker, Corn King and symbol of faith and renewal, for all times:

> The life of a man but one station: in a
> pilgrimage that
> wheels on for ever.[21]

There is a string of more than a dozen writings dealing with the subject of Magnus from every conceivable viewpoint. There are even examples in these early writings of updating the narrative to modern times, a device that later featured in his novel *Magnus* (1973). This sequence of Magnus pieces shows Brown's drift away from journalism, from documenting the life of the community, and towards creative writing, in which 'the facts' were only the starting point for writing.

In 1945 Brown wrote an article criticising John Gunn's *Orkney Book* (1909) for its apparent attempt to flesh out the vague and ambiguous character of Magnus, a view which directly contradicts Brown's growing obsession with him:

> . . . enlivened here and there with stirring passages from the Sagas. Where it fails is in such passages as the following:– 'St Magnus, the isle earl, was the most peerless of men, tall of growth, manly, and lively of look, virtuous in his ways, fortunate in fight, a sage in wit, ready-tongued and lordly-minded' etc. etc.
>
> Now the truth is that the character of St Magnus can never be

certainly known. He may, for all we are aware, have been a moral coward and a hypocrite. In the above quoted passage the author, conscious that he must supply Magnus with some kind of character, brought forth all the noble, abstract epithets in his vocabulary, and cluttered up the page with them. Much better had he confessed to the general hazy ignorance which shrouds the subject.[22]

Brown's use of the abbreviations 'etc, etc' sounds dismissive and characteristically, for Brown's journalistic voice, combative. Yet for fifty years the fact that 'the character of St Magnus can never certainly be known' was exactly what stimulated Brown to write about him.

Conclusion: 'flashes of honesty in that desert'

By the end of the 1940s, as he approached thirty, Brown was widely known in Orkney through his journalism, but he found it limiting: 'To tell the truth, I cared for the "flavour" of a bit of news more than for the stark facts, and so I frequently got into trouble.'[23] As a young man he was led to commit overstatements such as his 'Orkney has no culture' slogan that, as he matured, he began to disown: 'I would certainly blush now to re-read some of these naïve effusions which, generally speaking, looked forward to a day not too far remote when Orkney would be crazy about Picasso and Bach and Ezra Pound. It was a hideous mirage, and I was a false prophet; but yet there were occasional flashes of honesty in that desert.'[24]

This period was, above all, Brown's apprenticeship in writing. The discipline of deadlines, attending three-hour Town Council meetings in order to write a report for the newspaper and working within constraints of time and space were all good practice for the developing writer: '. . . at a whist drive the prize list might be all jumbled, but the noise of the band at the subsequent dance might get through, a faint, ghostly tintinabulation [sic]'.[25]

At the same time, and in the same newspaper, he was emerging as a short story writer and 'coming out as a poet'. Personally and professionally, he had consolidated his image of himself as a writer and his identification with Orkney and with other Orkney writers.

It was time for him to go elsewhere for intellectual nourishment.

This was a watershed. It is as if he gave himself a shake and looked outwards. He responded positively to encouragement to return to formal education. Although he had been, as an adult, self-taught and self-motivated, he would soon benefit from a course of study of other writers beyond Orkney and beyond those he had come across thus far.

This was a period when Brown published little creative writing – although he was still producing a fair amount of it – and vast quantities of journalism. From this point on, the balance was to tip the other way. Although he continued to write prolifically for the Orkney newspapers, Brown's main impulse was now creative writing.

3

Closed Societies of Island, College and Hospital:
The Storm
1951–56

Introduction

> How nice to get away from Orkney sometimes . . . for many reasons I
> had to get away, towards the end of winter. The tide of the spirit was
> shrunken, ebbed far out. The great clouds of 'morbus Orcadensis'
> hung overhead, threatening engulfment. In short, it was time to make a
> break.[1]

Brown badly needed a change. His journalism was prolific and
constant up to 1951, but it was no longer satisfying. Severe health
problems were followed by his brother's death in March 1956.
The effort of deconstructing Orkney had taken its toll; as far as he
could see, his attempts to promote Orkney's culture had not been
significantly successful: 'I was bored, you know, hanging about at
home – and idle and that, and reading and drinking beer . . .'[2] Again,
'In some ways I miss Orkney, but my mode of life there was no good.
I had to get out, or I'd have gone mad.'[3]

Island, college and hospital were closed societies, havens from the
outside world, vantage points from which Brown could comment,
safely, on it. Growing up in Orkney, university years and spells in
hospital, were oases, enchanted times in protected spaces. Since he
could see nothing in Orkney for him except a destructive lifestyle of
over-indulgence in alcohol, no opportunity to make a living and
subsistence on social welfare, he had to find an alternative.

Three spells at Newbattle Abbey College and a four-year university
course, followed by two years' research at Edinburgh University, gave
him new contacts and motivation, away from the lifestyle into which
Brown had settled in Stromness. He took a positive stance towards
developing himself, instead of Orkney: 'One way of escape suggested

itself: a university course',[4] and in Edinburgh he found a niche among the literati: 'But at Edinburgh University, as at Newbattle, friendship was more rewarding than books . . . the poets and artists of Scotland fore-gathered at weekends (MacDiarmid, McCaig [*sic*], Scott, Senior, Garioch, Campbell Hay, Goodsir Smith). I was quickly welcomed among them.'[5] And of his earlier experience he wrote: 'To live at Newbattle for a spell is to add a permanent enrichment to life.'[6]

Biographical notes: 1951–56 (aged 30–35)

Alex Doloughan, Assistant Director of Education (County Council), suggested Newbattle Abbey College to Brown. It was an adult educa-tion college, and, luckily, the Warden, Edwin Muir, was both a poet and an Orcadian. With one reservation, he welcomed Brown's application in a letter of 20 April 1951:

> I feel I should not try to influence you too much, seeing that your health is so uncertain. But I can assure you that you would not be driven in this College, unless you might have the desire to drive yourself, which is rather common among the students here. They are all so conscious that they have only this one year into which they have to pack all the things they want to study. I should suggest that if you come you should not take too many subjects; actually students are at liberty to take only one.

In October 1951 Brown accepted the offer of a place at Newbattle, which he later described as the 'happiest time of my life'. It suited him in every way. He was free from pressure, had the dignity and identity of a student, the literary atmosphere, nurturing literary tal-ent, self-esteem and talks with Muir about his work: 'There was some faint air of Eden about the place then', Muir wrote to Brown on 20 December 1956. He had three stays there over a period of five years: the academic year October 1951 to June 1952, the winter term October to December 1952 and the summer term in 1956.

Brown was no longer an isolated writer. He had the respect and affection of a new group of peers. He had time to revise work in progress, or composed before his arrival, and to embark on new themes. With hindsight, it is not surprising that the poems for his first collection, *The Storm*, some of which he had been working on for up to ten years, were brought to their final form at Newbattle. The impact of Newbattle and Muir on the developing writer cannot be overstated: 'But for Edwin Muir, I would not be writing these words now. He opened the door to the marketplace for me, where I could sell the tapestries I had woven, and begin to be independent and sure of myself.'[7]

Brown must have been dejected when he had to leave Newbattle because of his illness in 1953 and return to Orkney, where he was confined to hospital and his mother's house in Stromness for over a year. Dejection, and possibly depression, can be read into his writing of this period:

The Stoic

> The wind has fallen, the rain keeps on.
> My torn feet on the road
> Go quietly, doggedly onward
> To emptiness, or God.[8]

Brown wrote a very depressed letter to Ernest Marwick on 19 October 1953, which Marwick commented on to Muir: 'I had a very pathetic letter from G. this morning. He is at a hospital in Aberdeen, which he describes as a "charnel-house", and he is manifestly afraid of the methods of surgical investigation, and finally, of operation, practised there.'[9]

In spite of these bouts of serious illness, Brown edited both Newbattle's student magazine, *The Sun*, and the Eastbank Hospital magazine, *Saga*.

The Sun

Brown published, in *The Sun*, old works, others that he had been working on for some time, and new pieces, with new subjects and forms, some influenced by his reading of contemporary poets. He deliberately changed voice, theme and form, looking for new effects. These are exercises in formal control, as much as anything else, and not all of the experiments are successful. Taken together, the old and new works show Brown looking beyond his favourite themes and forms, without leaving them behind. Between breaks in his attendance, *The Sun* was edited by other students, but he still had contributions in it, solicited by Muir.

Muir wrote a Foreword to the first issue of *The Sun* in Winter Term 1951: 'Coming from a college which has been open little more than a year, and numbers at present only twenty students, I think the magazine shows striking originality and imagination.'

Brown wrote twenty-one signed pieces for seven issues of *The Sun*, a total of thirty-seven pages. 'The Viking Cruise (An incident from a long story)', published in the opening issue, is a familiar subject, with modifications to the short story form, providing only 'an incident': 'In the morning we sailed south again, and now the wind had moderated, and the sea glittered in warm sunlight. It seemed the rhythmical oars, when they lifted from the water, dripped living silver. And the men, in spite of their pinched bellies, sang as they drove the ship along southwards, under the mountains.'

By contrast, he also wrote short poems, developing fine, fully realised imagery:

Dawn

The lark, a tangled
skein of song,
awakens the dawn.

Slowly the woman of dawn
raises her head,
spreading her bright hair
over the sea,
over the bitter sea.

In the Spring Term 1953 issue Brown translated a Newbattle legend into poetry, in the form of a dialogue in which the dramatic narrative form combines well with Brown's spare style. The original story concerned a secret affair between a monk and a woman who were found out and burned alive in the monk's house. It is one of the best early examples of Brown's skill at combining poignant narrative and character with a pared down, yet patterned, style:

Death by Fire/The Monk and the Woman

WOMAN

A long time ago I saw it, a bud of flame
That shook out petals and was a delicate flower.
Then they were everywhere, those crimson blossoms
Spreading on wall and floor a riotous garden.
Heat pierces me like swords. I cannot hear
His voice in the fire's clamour.

MONK

This is the end now,
The tongues reach out to scarf her, like my lust.
Strange loveliness is cast upon the room.
Gently she breathes, as if it were a dream
Swinging across her brain from time far back.
What of the night outside? Her father waits
With a dying torch in his hand. The country folk
Redden their faces gaping on this doom,
Tangled in wind and stars and curiosity
But we must die.

These first two stanzas cleverly convey the mingled emotions of the woman and the monk as the burners approach the house; fear, anxiety and guilt do not quite extinguish the feelings they share. Their poignant realisation that they are about to lose each other is foregrounded here, 'I cannot hear/His voice', while the reality of the burning is brought home in the final two stanzas:

WOMAN

When I was a girl
Fevers I felt on my bed, and twisted and tossed
Hungry for morning. But this ardour rages
Through flesh and blood and bones, and will not end
Till the heart melts. Morning will never break
For me, sky-silver and merry cockcrow.
A world apart, he suffers and smiles alone.
And now I see a snake slide through the garden.

MONK

And now I see a snake slide through our garden
Of tossing flames. He pokes with his club face

At her shimmering foot, and rears: and then withdraws
Troubled at her innocence. A red rain bursts about her.
Her hair is a glory about her quiet throat.

Brown reconstructed this story from fragments he heard, adding convincing voices and recreating the characters. The image of the snake in the garden is a startling echo of biblical imagery, but it also suggests the first snaking burst of flames. The monk's reference to 'our garden', rather than the obvious 'the garden', conveys the touching closeness between the two in this moment of their death.

One of the best of Brown's poems in this period is 'The Shining Ones'. The dedication to the version that appeared in *The Sun*, subsequently dropped from later versions, gives us a new reading of one of Brown's most interesting poems: 'For H.B.', revealing that this was an elegy for his brother Hugh:

The Shining Ones
(For H.B. 1912–1956)

They locked their crystal wings, and gravely eyed
The man coming in, cold and remote and silent.
His foot on the last step, he turned again
And threw one wild look backward. But the night
Was a funnel of darkness, roaring with stars. Beyond
Ranged the great beasts of time.

                                 The watchers stood,
And still his feet came on.
                                  He could not tell
If they were angels or demons, or if the road
That drove him through his death now swung him sheer
Into eternity (a flower pressed dry
By poets, preachers, all the literate humbugs),
Or was the bitter cobbles of a dream
Where he must walk till morning shook the clouds
From his blunt brow, and storied Legion ale
Gushed from the lever pressed to his tired heart.

'This is the house of death', he prayed, and grief
Salted his eyes.

The Storm

They watched.
There as he faltered
Into the cruel dawn, twin blessings fell
From that hard cry; its echoes Bread and Breath
Had in his father's house with enormous love
Shored his first steps, and now they blazed into
The immortal cornstalk.

The birds of Dread and Dearth
That all the dolorous way clung to his wrist
Shrieked down their homing gale.

A new wind rose
And stripped the rags of anguish from his shoulder
Supple as tulips, brighter than the hour
He fought Young Kelly in the Lammas booth
(The surgeon's scar still vivid on his side)
And thrashed his man, and won his thirty bob,
And sent that profit raging down his throat.

The sky grew tall as lupins. Far below
Wave and boat swayed like familiar dancers.
That sea must hold him now. It swung him over
To the purgatorial hill.

The silent watchers
Out of the dawn lifted their swords. They blazed.[10]

This is an allegorical version of his brother's life, but Brown still captured the individual's character in vivid concrete images. For example, the cosmic background of the first stanza's 'crystal wings' contrasts with the image of 'a funnel of darkness'. Hugh Brown was a bar steward in the Stromness Royal British Legion, which throws light on the lines, 'From his blunt brow, and storied Legion ale/Gushed from the lever pressed to his tired heart.' In the 1959 version of the fifth stanza his brother is 'a legend' but still his drinking is vividly described in 'sent that profit raging down his throat'. There are these contrasts throughout the poem. It is interesting that this image, full of life and gesture, should come so close to the end of a poem which in many ways strips the humanity from its subject in order to capture both his essence and his departure. The poem ends with his brother being absorbed into an unspecified Heaven. Again, it is interesting that this place is described as if it were a local landscape: 'sky . . . wave . . . sea . . . hill'. The scene is at once a spiritual and a familiar Orkney place. The final tone is reassuring for reader, brother and, above all, writer, with Bunyan's influence evident.

Without the link to his brother, the poem is an apocalyptic vision. With the link, it is an intriguing counterpoint to Brown's representations of the domestic bliss of his childhood. Brown presented his brother as a man with several social roles, popular for his exploits and personality. The poem is dated May 1956, around the same time as Brown's own bouts of serious ill-health.

Many of the poems that appeared in *The Sun* evoke spiritual journeys or ordeals. Brown's raging and ranting against society was transformed into a quest to find meaning and salvation through writing.

Saga

While *The Sun* documented – and maintained a link with – a creative, contented spell at Newbattle, *Saga*, the Eastbank Hospital magazine, had a grimmer setting and an apparently more serious purpose. Yet, in spite of the hospital environment, much of the writing in *Saga* is bright and light, finding affirmation and humour in ill-health. In the five issues that appeared between Summer 1953 and Summer 1954, Brown wrote twenty-three of the fifty-six pieces, a total of about thirty-five pages, including editorials, prose, poems, a descriptive essay and a parody of the crime genre.

In issue number two (Autumn 1953) he had a poem, 'Eastbank Blues', under the pseudonym 'The Horizontal Bard' and an essay 'Summer Night', signed 'George M. Brown', which give insights into his life and thoughts and show him using his vantage point from the sanatorium, literally, as a stimulus for his writing. Two vignettes illustrate his vivid descriptions of the scene in his room and outside his window. The bright original language and imagery, which some would associate with the illness itself, show him persevering with his craft and seeking out new and familiar scenes and symbols:

Moths

It grew darker. A nurse, passing along the corridor, opened my ward door slightly to switch on the light, for now I could only read with difficulty, and a furrowing of the brows. For ten minutes or so nothing happened. I watched the lights springing up, one by one, in the houses in Kirkwall . . . Then something spurted out of the darkness, and hit the electric light bulb with a venomous thwack. It was a moth, the first of many that terrified me that night . . .

Moon

. . . After half an hour of wrestling and tossing, I opened my eyes and looked out. The night was glorious and transfigured, like a Chinese palace, all magic and crystal. The moon was out and abroad; not the slim silver virgin of November, nor the wandering minstrel of March, cloud buffeted, but the broad-faced russet moon of harvest. Benign and tranquil, he hung over the hedge like an old farmer who now sees the fruit of his labour ready for gathering and storing. Quiet under him lay patch-work islands and glittering sounds; ripe fields of oats and bere; recumbent sheep and horses in their pastures; lovers on the hillside and fishermen waiting for dawn.

He provided glimpses of the less than idyllic life of the sanatorium and of the treatments for tuberculosis, in the story 'Mansie at Eastbank':

Gentle and probing, the stethoscope went here and there about his apathetic torso. The knocking fingers lured echoes out of the branching cave of his ribs. Finally, looking very thoughtful, the doctor left a little bottle for Mansie to spit in and drove away . . .

The second morning he was in, Nurse Fox gave him, along with his breakfast porridge, a little cardboard tub half-full of big red pellets. He was told he had to swallow all thirty of them before nightfall. These were the famous PAS tablets. With a heroic effort Mansie disposed of them all.

The next morning the little tub with the thirty tablets was there again.[11]

Discomfort and uncertainty are not disguised. This is the public face of the Eastbank patient; private fear and pain are not disclosed. The specifics of treatment do not betray his feelings about this time. Nor is Brown attempting to make 'art' out of this experience; it is almost documentary.

The private face is revealed in as yet unpublished writings. A piece of descriptive writing from this period shows a change of tone from the enjoyment of the sanatorium's tranquillity and the reassuring stimulus of the new perspective, to the difficulties, mental and physical, of his daily routine. Brown's notebook shows him using his daily routine as a subject for regular writing in 'A Day in the Life of a Literary Hack', dated 23 June 1954:

> He woke with a faint unease in the small of his back, which meant that he was not in the best physical condition. He lay, thinking of stale bitter things. In a daze he felt his temperature and pulse being taken, then he lurched up in a sitting posture and began to cough. He shaved each alternate morning, and this was a shaving morning. He took his toilet bag, his razor, his towel, and the mug in which his upper dentures reposed seething quietly, got into brown slippers and brown dressing gown, and walked to the bathroom.
>
> For breakfast he delivered at the kitchen an egg to be boiled, marked thus [GMB 3½] which meant that it belonged to him and was to be boiled for threeandahalf [*sic*] minutes. The porridge was thick and stodgy, the tea not good, the marmalade stung the inside of his mouth, the egg had been boiled for at least five minutes . . . Dinner is soup and mince and mashed potatoes and rice and milk: not appetising, but he stows it mechanically down his throat . . .
>
> . . . Occassionally [*sic*] the dampness in the air condenses into a drop that falls, light and cool, on the back of his hand or the side of his nose. He begins to sweat, and he thinks, 'Fourteen months of this sanatorium, and I am as bad as ever I was.'

Passive attitude, third person narration and the unflinching focus on the mundane and mechanical capture the scene well, but what is even more striking is the contrast between these two pieces, written around the same time; there is none of the vivid imagery that featured in the previous piece. Neither can be taken as Brown's 'reality'; taken together, they show him drawing on his experiences in his writing, though only the first piece was offered for public view. The darker one was never published.

The experience of illness is more clinically described in three unpublished essays, 'A Seat by my Bed' (1957), 'Sanatorium, 1941' (1980) and 'The Cleansing of the Eye' (1988) and mentioned memorably in the poem 'Snow: From a Hospital' (*Northern Lights*, 1999). Although written later, they describe Brown's experience in a period of ill-health. They reveal how he was thinking about his illnesses, a complex mixture of refusal to feel self-pity, onset of what appears to be depression and using these experiences as raw material for writing. There is ambiguity in what he calls 'the will to be ill', perhaps recognising the appeal of the hospital environment.

'Closed societies'

Having had a taste of the writer's life at Newbattle, where he could, he said, have stayed for ever, Brown found that Orkney life presented a violent contrast, seeming squalid, narrow and closed by comparison, in the sense of shutting out the stimulus and self-esteem that he needed to write. Several unpublished pieces written between 1950 and 1954 present an acerbic Brown whose image of Orkney is startlingly at odds with the idealised and patterned representations in his other works of this time and in later works which are often seen as typical of him. It is as if his dissatisfaction with the life available to him in Orkney, expressed in his journalism, had become unbearable. There is nothing about aesthetics and culture here. His distaste was directed at individual Orcadians, rather than Orkney in the abstract. It is just as well these pieces were not published then or since, as they are about real, named, local people.

Perhaps Brown was trying in these pieces to avoid romanticising, bringing balance to his representation of Orkney. Perhaps he was trying to be more comprehensive and inclusive. Many of the people he wrote about in these pieces were eccentrics; that is, he chose those who stood out for some quality or other. These portraits are anything but sweetness and light.

> When I first knew him, he was drinking methylated spirits, quite openly and unashamedly. He would decant a generous measure of the thunder-blue stuff into his smoking tea, and quaff it with relish. Then he would lick his writhen lips and say: 'That cheers the he'rt and waarms the blood'.
>
> One final picture of him. He is sitting, on a winter's evening, amid his stink and dirt, beside a glowing fire. The paraffin lamp on the

mantel piece throws a feeble light on his soiled face and twinkling blue eyes. He lifts a sputtering rasher of steak from the frying pan on to his plate, fills his half-pint mug with strong tea, and spreads his bannock thickly with Stork margarine. As he eats his jaw drives up and down, up and down, as if driven by clockwork. He has no teeth to chew the meat thoroughly; after he has champed most of the succulence out of it, he takes the bleached pulp from his mouth and puts it under the table, where the cat devours it. It is a good substantial meal, and [he] enjoys it, for hard living has not impaired his robust digestion. When he has finished, he leans back with a sigh of pure contentment, and fills his pipe with bogey roll. Then he carefully opens his favourite book, Jack London's *People of the Abyss*, and begins to read.

Taken together, these unpublished essays represent a form of 'Parish Register', working through the inhabitants one by one. Taken individually, they give us a bleak, uncompromising look at notable characters of the town. This 'warts and all' treatment certainly gives us a more rounded view of Brown's perspective and of his descriptive skills than we would have from the published writings alone.

It is a body of writing far removed from the journalism, which could be quite critical too, but was generally not personalised in the way these essays are. One wonders also how much they are an expression of, not only Brown's move away from the more neutral, journalistic voice, but also his distancing from Orkney itself. His sense of the necessity of leaving Orkney – in order to become a writer – was at its most acute at this time, when he had been forced to return. It may be that it was coming through in his writing, shaping his treatment of these subjects. It may be that serious ill-health, and the continuing threat of death, intensified his desire to speak his mind. We can easily surmise why Brown decided not to publish these works; but we can only guess at what compelled him to write them.

That Brown felt like an outsider in Orkney was partly about his writing and partly associated, for him, with his illness. His description of the journey to the sanatorium shows how he felt excluded from the world of the well: he refers to himself as 'like a man going to prison . . . an explorer . . . a soldier . . . an exile' and to the patients as 'tinkers

. . . outcasts'.[12] Finding himself on the margins of Orkney society, yet again, he was advised that he would have to stay there:

> DOCTOR. You must live quietly, like the dream of some 18th century poet, 'content to breathe your native air/In your own ground . . .' You must never tire yourself overmuch. You must eat good food, and get your fill of sleep every night, and avoid occasions of riotous living. We've built a house of good habits round you: outside is the storm, and you venture into it at your peril.[13]

This reference to the 'storm' points to a new tension for Brown, between the pursuit of perfection in poetry and the internal struggle to be well, between the idea of 'silence' and the raging storm 'outside'. *The Storm* was the title he gave his first collection of poems; it was appropriate, defining his mood and the way he had decided to face up to life.

The Storm and Other Poems, 1954

Published at his own expense, this collection made an immediate impact. Taken together, the poems have a collective force; a core of images, ideas and themes binds them together. That putting the volume together was more than just a shuffling together of separate pages, is illustrated by a letter Brown wrote to Marwick on 15 December 1953:

> I have been working steadily on my poems, and have made a lot of alterations, and I am sure it is as good now as I can possibly make it meantime. I have lost much sleep and sweat over it, and am happy to have got it off my hands. They will not be popular poems and I am sorry about that, for now I increasingly see that poetry is not much good unless men in public houses can repeat it over their beer and even bairns chant it when they're catching sillocks or flying kites.

Brown was concerned about the reception of this collection – both inside and outside Orkney – and on 7 August 1954 carefully summarised a fascinating array of critical responses in his notebook:

> Reactions to '*The Storm*'. A little piddling review in *The Glasgow Herald*. A friendly but meaningless comment in *The Scotsman*. In Arts Review

(BBC) Alexander Scott echoing Edwin Muir, only more faintly. Bob Johnston in *The Orkney Herald* emptily flattering. Intelligent praise from Archie Bevan in *The Orcadian*. Eric Linklater – 'beauty and accomplishment'. Joseph MacLeod – 'very impressed'. E. M. Forster – 'they celebrate the love that endures beyond time'. Neil Gunn – 'I like their instancy . . . magic is active'. Bill Drysdale – 'bourgeois decadence'. Jim Stockan – 'nonsense, a true mirror of the man'.

The edition of three hundred copies sold out in two weeks.

The Storm showed that Brown had something to show for his years at college; several of the poems assumed final form at Newbattle. Some were written much earlier, some were revised many times, some had appeared in the Newbattle magazine, *The Sun*. All except two had been published: 'The Tramp' and 'Orcadians: Seven Impromptus'. The title poem had been a work-in-progress for at least five years and possibly more, as there is a version of the poem, probably the first, dated August 1947. We know from his letters that Brown offered it to Marwick for his Orkney *Anthology* which appeared in 1949. It was finally published in March–April 1950 (No. 22, p. 30) in *The New Shetlander*, which published many of his early poems including a number that never appeared in print again.

His fascination with Orkney characters continued in *The Storm*: 'I am trying to write a series of short poems, rather Chinese in manner, about imaginary Orkney folk. They have the same end in view as Joyce's "Dubliners", to give a picture of the community. To date I have written six, but hope to have a dozen or twenty in the complete series. They are very short, and in free verse.'[14]

On 18 July that same year Brown sent Marwick sixteen of these 'impromptus', some based on real people, suggesting that he progressed with his plan quickly. Seven of the characters appear as 'Orcadians: Seven Impromptus', dedicated to Edwin Muir, in the last section of *The Storm*: 'Lifeboatman', 'Fisherman', 'Chicken', 'Crofter', 'Doctor', 'Saint' and 'Them at Isbister'. Apart from marking a significant literary influence – James Joyce – these poems had a particular purpose for Brown, to lighten up the collection: 'This cycle pleases me more because it balances the serious qualities of the early poems than because of any intrinsic merit.'[15] These words may mark a turning point, as Brown advanced his techniques for balancing the light and dark elements in his writing. He seems to have had an acute awareness of his own development as a writer, both in terms of his preferences and his limited, but growing, technical repertoire.

Joyce provided a literary model for making the real, or caricatured, into the archetypal and Brown's urge to lighten the serious tone, or perhaps to avoid having the book condemned for non-literary reasons, may have been the impulse for editing out a stanza of the first poem, 'Prologue', which can be read as a kind of 'credo' for his work:

Prologue

For the islands I sing
    and for a few friends;
not to foster means
    or be midwife to ends.

Not for old Marx
    and his moon-cold logic –
anthill dialectics,
    neither gay nor tragic.

Not that extravagance
    Lawrence understood –
golden phoenix
    flowering from blood.

For Scotland I sing,
    the Knox-ruined nation,
that poet and saint
    must rebuild with their passion.

For workers in field
    and mill and mine
who break earth's bread
    and crush her wine.

Go, good my songs,
    be as gay as you can.
Weep, if you have to,
    the old tears of man.

Praise tinker and saint,
     and the rose that takes
its fill of sunlight
     though a world breaks.

Although this poem did not appear in later collections it can be taken as an important statement of what Brown set out to do at that time: to rehabilitate his country through the impression his writing had on 'workers in field'. The stanza that he cut would change the tone:

(But, as Our Lord said,
     the rich doing well
out of their usury
     may roister in hell.)

This change can be seen as part of Brown's shift away from courting and creating controversy, so much a feature of his journalism. It may be that he was acting on the advice of Marwick or Robert Rendall. Whether or not he was advised to drop this or decided to drop it himself, the main point is that he saw the sense of doing so, in order to shift the emphasis from those he was ranting against to those he was 'singing' for. Similar reasoning accounted for his replacement of actual names by fictitious ones in several of the 'Impromptus'.

In 'Fisherman' Brown explores stark contrasts of the fisherman's life: the beauty and danger of the sea, in 'The great ocean/Makes the gentlest of motions about the turning world', labour and tranquillity of the work in 'The creels lie still on their weeded ledges' and sudden death disrupting this contemplative moment:

Three days ago a storm blazed here, and drowned
Jock Halcrow among his lobsters.

The fisherman's setting is 'Peaceful the air, the sea / A quiet scattering of stars', while the Doctor inhabits a place drenched in its past, from which he stands, 'sneering', very much apart:

He should be whetting his brain on the stone of some city,
Not on these gentle hills
Scattering barren wit.

The Storm was an assertion of Brown's artistic impulse, evidence that he could write. It was, finally, a realisation of his newly heightened expectations of himself as a writer. His Prologue, 'For the Islands I Sing', echoing Walt Whitman, asserts his artistic agenda. He gave his own assessment of it in a letter to Marwick on 12 January 1954:

> I am not complacent about the volume. I am not satisfied with the kind of verse in it, nor do I expect the public of Orkney to take kindly to it. If I manage to write enough poems for a second book, they will be simple and forthright and such as a crofter or a fisherman would read and remember with pleasure. Or rather that is the light towards which I'll strive.

So Brown was not, if we take these words at face value, completely satisfied with his work and although he was dedicating it to Orkney – 'For the islands I sing' – there was a tension between writing for Orkney and recognising that Orkney, and Orcadians, did not see him as writing for them.

Conclusion

'Closed societies' – hospital, college and university – would continue to provide safe havens from the pains and distractions of life. It was not Orkney that was a closed society; paradoxically, it provided few if any of the features of these other environments for him. What he needed most, at this stage, was to develop a sense that his writing was valued and important. He needed the silence that these closed societies provided, away from the noise of other responsibilities and motives. He withdrew psychologically and physically – through illness – from Orkney life, from any life. Orkney was unhealthy for him, and he had come to see it as repugnant.

Yet Brown wrote the text for three guide books to Orkney – another expression of his desire to refashion Orkney: *Let's See the Orkney Islands* (1948), *Stromness, The Orkney Islands: the Official Guide* (1955) and *Stromness, In the Orkney Islands: Official Guide* (1963). In the last he wrote: 'Edwin Muir has said that "in Orkney the lives of living men turn into legend" . . . The visitor to Stromness should always remember that he is not simply in a place; he is, for a short time, part of an old and still unfinished ballad.'

These guides show Brown's characteristically competent journalistic approach, using the language of the guide book, conveying necessary facts, but also revealing his artistic vision, not just in the imagery he used, but in the reshaping of the physical landscape. He unpeeled layers of myth, legend, history, religion and the present time and people of Orkney. What was new was the unity of description; instead of isolated descriptions of places, there was a blending together of all elements. As he said in a later note on Muir's expression in the above quotation about the lives of men turning into legend: 'What he meant probably was that in a small community, enclosed by sea and sky and fields, it is possible to see a man's life as a whole. It has a clear outline. It becomes elemental and larger than life.'[16] Brown had begun to move freely from myth to history to legend to contemporary issues, to his own poetic ideals. This gave him freedom to create and express his own vision in Orkney.

In other ways too, he had begun to move away from – and ultimately remove – the personal element. His own life and his own perspective on Orkney had faded into the background. It is as if he wrote himself out in order more fully to escape from his own life in his writing.

Like Scott, Wordsworth and Burns, Brown created an industry of visitors to the places he described imaginatively; tourists have been drawn by the descriptions of a creative writer, rather than the guide book. It is the creative writing, with its full imaginative response, that takes them to the Trossachs, the Lake District, Ayr or Orkney.

After this period we hear fewer and fewer influences and echoes of other authors in Brown's poetry and prose; we hear more and more of his own voice. Yet the security of this spell would not make up for the loss of the company of other writers and kindred spirits. He would have to work harder to find enough in Orkney to sustain him, both financially and inspirationally. The clouds were gathering again and some of his best work was to emerge from his darkest days.

STROMNESS
1954

The population of Stromness nowadays is about 1500, ~~but you'd better not call it a village in the hearing of any of the inhabitants.~~ It is what is called in Scotland a burgh of Barony, with magistrates, councillors, a provost, a town clerk, and a burgh chamberlain. ~~He will be quite satisfied if you call it a town.~~

Walk with me, stranger, from the North End to the South End, along the one long ~~undulating~~ street, Stromness being one-dimensional. And walk with me now, at once, for Stromness is changing. Month by month, year by year, it is deteriorating, losing character. It doesn't take long to rip up one of those fine blue barston flagstones and replace it with a uniform corpse-coloured concrete flagstone.

'Stromness 1954'. The start of a long essay which became a guide book to Stromness (1955) after considerable revision, 1954.

4

'A swarm of symbols':
Loaves and Fishes
1957–60

. . . this masquerade
Was a pure seeking past a swarm of symbols,
The millwheel, sun, and scythe, and ox, and harrow,
Station by station to that simple act
Of terror or love, that broke the hill apart.[1]

Brown's next collection of poems was a new departure in which he developed a kind of consecration of the everyday, a transformation of the commonplace, overrun by a variety of verse forms, and a 'swarm of symbols', fanning out from his chosen locus of Orkney.

Brown attempted to capture the variety of Orkney lives. Poems with a personal dimension, each with its individual notes, were given a new direction; everyday life, with its predictable repetitive pattern, was transformed into meaningful ritual; and there was a new note of hope – 'a pure seeking'. This was another form of Brown's idea of silence, the ideal that, he imagined, lay not in his words, but beyond them. Behind his symbols there was some form of 'simple act', that bound the 'swarm' together.

Brown was not as interested, in this phase of his writing, in the range and variety of experience and character for their own sake. Nor was he any longer absorbed by the patterns of seasons and cycles in themselves. In fact, 'swarm' suggests that he felt he was in danger of being overwhelmed. Instead, he became absorbed by what he saw as the overarching blend of faith, habit, personality and economy that compels people to act, endure and create.

This period shows Brown's developing range of techniques and subjects, and these are explored in commentaries on selected poems. More importantly, Brown's revision of a key poem is analysed in some detail, as it shows how he engaged with tensions between the personal and the archetypal in his writing.

Biographical notes: 1956–60 (aged 35–39)

Brown attended Edinburgh University from 1956. He graduated in 1960, with a second-class MA in English, having won second prize in his first year. His course included Old English, and in his copy of C. L. Wrenn's edition of *Beowulf* he listed stylistic devices, such as the condensed metaphors known as kennings that were to feature so frequently in his poetry. He was well versed in the Old Norse sagas in translation.

He attended teacher training college, at Moray House in Edinburgh, though it was immediately clear to him – and to everyone else, including Peter McNaught, his tutor – that he was not suited to teaching. A spell of illness got him out of it. He wrote to Ernest Marwick that he was thinking of applying to the School of Scottish Studies at Edinburgh University for a position with the School's Customs and Belief Section, hoping not to have to return to Orkney unemployed, but nothing came of this.

In Edinburgh, his social life was focused on the Rose Street crowd who drank in Milne's Bar and the Abbotsford. He spent much of his time in the company of other writers, his peer group for writing, recognition and self-esteem. Although this was not in every way, for him, a healthy lifestyle, he credited the pub scene with not only his own but other poets' progress: 'Some of the happiest hours of my life have been spent in these two poets' pubs . . . Never did the bird of poetry sing so sweet and true!'[2]

Redeeming cycles: *Loaves and Fishes* (1959)

While his previous collection, *The Storm* (1954), was not one in which Brown worked at overall unity, in *Loaves and Fishes* he did, drawing on characters invented and remembered, using local people and events to bring out their significance in eternity, so that they were more than locally memorable and significant. The title *Loaves and Fishes* brings together land and sea, shown as the two great providers for Orcadians. It suited Brown, at that time, to bring such contrasting landscapes together and to echo a religious miracle in his search for archetypes.

What made this volume a new departure was not only the variety of form and theme but also the technical development. There was a shift away from the particular treatment of Orkney places in his previous writing: 'States of mind, or "inscapes", inspire me more than people or places',[3] 'inscapes' being a word, and poetic device, Brown borrowed from Gerard Manley Hopkins.

Twenty-five poems are arranged in three parts: 'The Drowning Wave', 'Crofts Along the Shore' and 'The Redeeming Wave'. It is a redemptive cycle: 'The Drowning Wave' is about the threat of the sea and death at sea; 'Crofts Along the Shore' is about life on land; and 'The Redeeming Wave' is about redemption, not simply in terms of Christian and natural cycles, but redemptive in any sense.

There are two sets of characters, with very different lives: those associated with the sea and those tied to the land. The theme seems to be that no matter what their occupation, everyone was to be included. Readers of this collection are faced with the question of whether or not Brown manages to sustain this weight of symbol. Some would argue that the characters are reduced to symbols; others would maintain that telling details capture the individuality of the farmers and fishermen.

A 'swarm' of forms

Brown believed that poets should be acquainted with all the poetic forms and we can see his interest in using a wide range of forms in this collection: there are sonnets, 'Port of Venus', 'The Death of Peter Esson' and 'The Old Women'; narrative poem, 'Hamnavoe'; symbolic narrative, 'That Night in Troy'; masque, 'The Masque of Bread'; lyric, 'December Day, Hoy Sound'; elegy, 'Gregory Hero'; allegory, 'The Stranger'; nursery rhyme, 'Childsong'; and ballad, 'The Heavenly Stones'. There is also a range of treatments, including monologues, epiphanies, visionary and apocalyptic perspectives. The variety is not contrived – Brown was not deliberately working through each form in turn – but stimulating, for readers making their way through the whole collection, and refreshing, given that some of these poetic forms, not widely used at the time, are given new life here. The core images of the sea and the land, side by side, and the people who have to be both fishermen and farmers, are neither obvious nor oppressive. This is an impressive display of poetic skill and vision, quite advanced for a second collection.

Consecration of the everyday

There is a strong religious theme in *Loaves and Fishes*. Brown deals with this way of life, not just in terms of how the people earn their living, but also relating it to religious rituals and stories: for example, there is the ploughman who, in springtime ploughing, is shown conducting the 'liturgy of April'. The farmer, like the clergyman, has his own rituals, echoing religious ceremonies. The effect is to give religious significance to routine agricultural and fishing activities.

Contrasting with these hallowed figures are the tinkers, represented as free spirits, beholden to no one. Brown's father had particularly liked tinkers because they lived on the margins of society. They were, in some ways, separate, not tied to the land or the fishing boat. They are shown as opportunistic; while they steal, Brown credits them with integrity.

'Hamnavoe'

'Hamnavoe' is one of Brown's most anthologised poems. It started out, in an earlier form, as 'Summer Day' (1947). Brown wrote to Ernest Marwick about the poem's purpose:

> In 'Summer Day' which I don't think is quite so successful, an anchorite withdrawn from the world meditates on the petty vanities which, even in the life of a small place, obscure the divine glory. The syllabic structure here, though as strict from stanza to stanza, is much freer. The final stanza breaks the bonds, which I have not yet decided is a help or a hindrance.

Interrogation of Silence

Summer Day

Anchorite of God, I raised eyes
One golden summer morning from my script
     And saw beneath me
     The small town's heart pulse

The sunlit hours away. Fishing boats
Raised anchor, offering red sails
     To the west wind, drifting
     In the tidedark Sound

Under the dark eagle capped pillars of Hoy.
The coach with sweating horses
     From Kirkwall, drew up
     At the white Custom house,

And towards noon the wealthier merchants
Strolled in blackcloth across the square
     Consulting watches, talking
     In deep grave tones.

The town lay all afternoon, tranced
With sapphire. Dogs sought the shadowed doors.
     A child's bare feet
     Fluttered across the cobbles.

At evening the dark sails returned. The harbour
Spun with life. Gaelic fisher girls
     Made melancholy croon
     Over stinking stalls,

And ragged boys ran home, with bunches
Of burnished herring. From the dance loft
     Cups rattling, the screech
     Of a cracked violin.

Hoy gloomed the Sound. One lyrical star
Prologued night's pageantry. The shawled harlot
     Crossed the wet field to
     The bailie's granite house.

Vanity of vanities! By taper light
I read how, thralled in Time, men walk blind

The cloud-dappled alleys of
God's eternal city.

'Hamnavoe' shows the development of his own frame of reference, particular to Orkney. The technical aspects of this version, such as the patterning of rhythms, show that Brown was paying close attention to technique. He represented the onlooker, from the point of view of someone who has withdrawn from society and comments on it, from a specific, distant point of view. While 'Summer Day' described Stromness from the point of view of a monk, 'Hamnavoe' describes Brown's father's daily journey through Stromness, in his role as postman, in a form of celebration. The title, the old name for Stromness, becomes appropriate, rather than anachronistic, given the new setting of his father's life:

Hamnavoe

My father passed with his penny letters
Through closes opening and shutting like legends
      When barbarous with gulls
      Hamnavoe's morning broke

On the salt and tar steps. Herring boats,
Puffing red sails, the tillers
      Of cold horizons, leaned
      Down the gull-gaunt tide

And threw dark nets on sudden silver harvests.
A stallion at the sweet fountain
      Dredged water, and touched
      Fire from steel-kissed cobbles.

Hard on noon four bearded merchants
Past the pipe-spitting pier-head strolled,
      Holy with greed, chanting
      Their slow grave jargon.

A tinker keened like a tartan gull
At cuithe-hung doors. A crofter lass
      Trudged through the lavish dung
      In a dream of cornstalks and milk.

Interrogation of Silence

Blessings and soup plates circled. Euclidian light
Ruled the town in segments blue and gray.
        The school bell yawned and lisped
        Down ignorant closes.

In 'The Arctic Whaler' three blue elbows fell,
Regular as waves, from beards spumy with porter,
        Till the amber day ebbed out
        To its black dregs.

The boats drove furrows homeward, like ploughmen
In blizzards of gulls. Gaelic fisher girls
        Flashed knife and dirge
        Over drifts of herring,

And boys with penny wands lured gleams
From the tangled veins of the flood. Houses went blind
        Up one steep close, for a
        Grief by the shrouded nets.

The kirk, in a gale of psalms, went heaving through
A tumult of roofs, freighted for heaven. And lovers
        Unblessed by steeples, lay under
        The buttered bannock of the moon.

He quenched his lantern, leaving the last door.
Because of his gay poverty that kept
        My seapink innocence
        From the worm and black wind;

And because, under equality's sun,
All things wear now to a common soiling,
        In the fire of images
        Gladly I put my hand
        To save that day for him.

In the process of revision this poem has changed significantly: the first version, 'Summer Day', survives as a typescript, dated August 1947, in the Archive of the Orkney Library, Kirkwall. The second was published in *The New Shetlander* (March/April 1950), with the subtitle 'Brother Jon Meditates on the Vanities of Existence' and a note at the end, 'A picture of Stromness in the herring fishing boom of the

1890s'. The third version, substantially altered, survives as a typescript in the Orkney Library (undated) with an added subtitle 'In Memoriam J. B. 1875–1940' (referring to Brown's father). The fourth and best version, printed here, was published in 1959 in *Loaves and Fishes*. A fifth, published in *Poems New and Selected*, 1971, was identical, except for the omission of stanza six and the subtitle. A sixth appeared in 1991 in *Selected Poems*, 1954–83, with several new changes which dilute the impact, as Brown removed references to sex and social comment, leaving the scene ambiguous and tame:

> And lovers
> Unblessed by steeples, lay under
> The buttered bannock of the moon.

becomes

> Ploughboy
> And milklass tarried under the buttered bannock of the moon.

As he changed 'Holy with greed' to 'Rosy with greed' and 'A stallion' to 'A cart-horse' he seems to have had a new sense of the risk of offending those with religious beliefs.

The poem describes a day in the life of 'Hamnavoe'. Stanza one describes Brown's father setting off first thing in the morning, before the town is awake, on his postman's round, the title having located the poem in Stromness: 'legends' conveys the fact that families have lived there for generations. Each house has its own identity and associations, its own 'legends', surviving to the present day and known to all. Since the closes did not have doors, the 'opening and shutting' represents the postman's point of view; that is, as he passes the opening and/or passes through it, the passageways – permanently open – appear to him one by one, and are closed, disappearing, as he passes on.

The view beyond the street features in the second stanza, as we are shown what the postman sees at the end of the close – herring boats in the harbour, bringing us into the town as it is in the present. The silence of the harbour is conveyed by the contrast with 'barbarous . . . gulls', the birds screaming. In stanza three the fishermen head out of the harbour, and the focus shifts back to work on land, both overlapping in two stanzas. In stanza four it is noon, and the merchants appear on cue, 'Holy with greed', contrasting with the idling, pipe-smoking fraternity at the pierhead. In stanza five the postman moves out of the town and into the countryside, showing the extent of his round, delivering to the farms and their workers. Then it is lunchtime and he turns back to the town, while the children go home for their meal.

As the shadows lengthen, with the sunlight casting geometrical shapes through the 'ruled' streets, drinkers pass the afternoon in the pub. The fishing boats return. The gulls resume their screaming, this time in a frenzy round full boats. The fishwives process the catch. The children come out to play at fishing. Blinds are drawn in one house to mark a death by drowning. Some seek comfort in the church; others use moonlight to court in the countryside, as the postman finally finishes his round in darkness.

The last two stanzas shift from narrative to reflection on Brown's father: he protected Brown from poverty, death and depression – 'black wind', an image conveying illness that is, like the wind, invisible. Finally, Brown's gratitude is expressed: he makes his own sacrifice by confronting the 'fire of images'. This poem is therefore a statement of the role his father played in his life, together with his acceptance of the challenge, and suffering, of the writing life. This suggests that Brown might have found motivation – in this poem and elsewhere – as a writer in paying back his parents, enduring purgatory for those who made sacrifices for him. There is, perhaps, an implication of guilt here; Brown never had to do such physical labour as the farmers, the fishermen or his father.

The remodelling of this poem shifts it from a general theme to a highly personal perspective, in time setting, from 1890s to 1930s; in theme and tone, from condemnation to affirmation and gratitude; from a perspective set apart from the community to integration with the community, in terms of social role and family unity; from the triviality of men's actions in the context of one belief system to an affirmation of the contribution one generation has made in nurturing the next; and from an interlude in one person's day, the monk's, to an overview of everyone's day in the town.

Many changes sharpen the focus; unity is established by references throughout to the various stops the postman makes on his route. Contrasts between morning and evening are clearly drawn. Brown used snippets of local news to illustrate the view of the town bellman, using the actual titles of newspaper articles in the thirties: 'The brass/Tongue of the bellman fore-tolled/ "Coon concert" . . . "Cargo of English Coal!".'

Brown's habit of 'consecrating' the everyday was in this instance part of an argument against the public performance of religion. In the earlier version, this seemed to originate from the monk's perspective on the inhabitants' shortcomings. However, in the later version, it is less clearly associated with one viewpoint. It is tempting, therefore, for readers who only know the later version to see this as Brown's preferred view, but the personal dimension in the last two stanzas creates another kind of context: the elevation of the everyday, and the reduction of the elevated, is part of his celebration of his father. His father emerges as a community and family hero, as does Brown, for courage in writing.

As an elegy, this poem conveys a disturbing aspect of Brown's childhood and imaginative development, terror brought on by his father's depression. It shows his father's stoicism, which enabled Brown to remain innocent at the time, though he later suffered from depression himself. The expression 'the worm and black wind' in this context works to convey not only depression but also tuberculosis. In some ways the poem is idealised, but there are darker notes, a typical combination in Brown's poetry.

'The Masque of Bread'

'The Masque of Bread' is not, at first sight, an inviting poem, being more abstract and obscure, and certainly less personal than 'Hamnavoe'. However, it is interesting for its display of Brown's themes:

The Masque of Bread

What answer would he give, now he had reached
The Inquisitor's door, down seventy hungry streets,
Each poorer than the last, the last a slum
Rambling like nightmare round his winter feet?

The Inquisitor's door? The walls were all blank there,
But a white bakehouse with a little arch
And a creaking sign . . . Against the fragrant doorpost
He clung, like drifted snow, while the shuttered oven
Opened on hills of harvest sun and corn.

The loaf the bakers laid on the long shelf
Was bearded, thewed, goldcrusted like a god.
Each drew a mask over his gentle eyes
– Masks of the wolf, the boar, the hawk, the reaper –
And in mock passion clawed the bread.
                                        But he
Who stood between the cold Plough and the embers
In the door of death, knew that this masquerade
Was a pure seeking past a swarm of symbols,
The millwheel, sun, and scythe, and ox, and harrow,
Station by station to that simple act
Of terror or love, that broke the hill apart.
But what stood there – an Angel with a sword
Or Grinning Rags – astride the kindled seed?

He knelt in the doorway. Still no question came
And still he knew no answer.

                            The bread lay broken,
Fragmented light and song.

                            When the first steeple
Shook out petals of morning, long bright robes
Circled in order round the man that died.

Technically, a masque is an entertainment or spectacle, perhaps royal or classical, a sequence of highly imaginative actions, idealised and ornate, with a fragmented structure but dramatic unity in a single concentrated scene. Brown's masque has most of the conventional features, moving towards order through Christian elements and farming and baking rituals. It demonstrated his willingness to use a new poetic form for its own sake. It also showed that he was not afraid to use forms that had fallen out of fashion.

Yet this poem shows how his writing could become too patterned and his expression frozen. His use of symbolic figures did not always work; baking becomes a symbol of martyrdom, ploughing of resurrection. We begin to anticipate that a fisherman will become *the* fisherman, a word will become *the* word. His later use of incantations and lists showed him leaning too much on formal elements. What is interesting here is his use of ambiguity: there are underlying notes of menace and violence in this 'mock passion'.

The poem may be an account of the sacrificial death of Jesus Christ, indicating Brown's growing interest in religion, ending with the 'order' that Christ's death and resurrection are believed to have brought. Yet, there may be more than a little irony in this ending; the language of the last three lines breaks free from the poem's symbolism, as if unravelling it.

The two most important words in this poem may well be 'in order'; this was a period in which Brown was finding – some would say forcing – order in his gathering stock of ideas and forms. 'The Masque of Bread' is a model of that process, as Brown follows through a clear, complete structure and brings it all to a neat end.

'Dream of Winter'

In a letter to Marwick, Brown said that this poem was founded on personal experience – clearly, his illness and recovery. It was published in Ernest Marwick's anthology of Orkney verse in 1949, in *The Storm and Other Poems* in 1954, then in *Loaves and Fishes*, with minor changes. Through his revisions, Brown again, as in his changes to 'Hamnavoe', removed the personal element, replacing the 'ten pen-grooved fingers' with more general emblems of regeneration: 'Spring on the hill/With lamb and tractor, lovers and burning heather.' Where the earlier version seemed to represent a personal perspective, in the later version 'he' could be anyone.

The poem conveys a foreboding scene, with a 'swarm of images', bleak and ceremonial, timeless and elemental. There is a fatalistic denial of movement in the first stanza, with images of sterility suggesting not just winter but evil and misery:

> These were the sounds that dinned upon his ear –
> The spider's fatal purring, and the gray

Trumpeting of old mammoths locked in ice.
No human sound there was: only the evil
Shriek of the violin sang of human woe
And conquest and defeat, and the round drums
Sobbed as they beat.

There is a sense of necessity, that this is an event that was planned for, part of or in tune with natural cycles, with the sacrifice and resurrection; the killing of a man in order to ensure renewed life, so that the harvest will prosper and support the community. The ritual is a narrative, with symbolic actors and agents. Again, there are explicit echoes of Christ's death, 'the victim nailed against the night . . . merry with curl and thorn', as Brown blended pagan and Christian myths.

A prayer is answered, in stanza three, with the actual manifestations of spring, but less of the Christian myth. (These are taken up in the poem which follows 'Dream of Winter', 'Saint Magnus in Egilsay', a story of Christian regeneration.) While the winter descriptions were ritualised, the spring ones are not. Nature appears to fill the void; it is the agency of the cycles. Both Christian and pagan frames of reference are set aside in this final stanza, although the last line has echoes of sacrifice and rescue from winter: 'The wind's blue fingers laid / A migrant on the rock.' 'Migrant' emphasises the cyclical nature of the process; the bird has its own compulsion to migrate and return and migrate again, keeping the cycle going. Echoes of sacrifice and rescue hint at the migration that will follow this cycle of return.

In this poem 'human woe' is followed by visions and versions of rejuvenation, and these, in turn, are followed by the natural seasons coming around. This perhaps reflects the removal of the threat of Brown's own death, from tuberculosis, and his delight at a temporary respite from the disease.

Conclusion

Brown used to say that he wrote almost nothing during his Edinburgh years, but new poems, articles and a fine play make up a substantial body of work from that period. Perhaps the quantity of writing he had been producing when he was writing for *The Orkney Herald* made it seem, to him, as if he had written hardly anything. The transition from journalism to poetry had not been easy, particularly as he was writing for university courses at the same time, but he had managed it. He had moved on, abandoning the prose poem, a form to which he had been so attached in his earlier years.

Although the two volumes had many subjects in common, in some ways *Loaves and Fishes* was a major advance on *The Storm*; in other respects, with its tight narrative structure, there was a risk that *Loaves and Fishes* would prove more challenging for readers.

Brown's growing unease at the march of progress and materialistic values led him to take up a clear position against wealth and power. He valued the everyday, the commonplace. He redefined who the 'important' ones were: for him, it was not those who held material wealth, 'holy with greed', an image that also manages to strike a blow at religious authority, but those who were prepared to provide and make sacrifices for others.

The religious imagery of, for example, Stations of the Cross in 'The Masque of Bread' signified Brown's growing interest in organised religion:

> . . . this masquerade
> Was a pure seeking past a swarm of symbols,
> The millwheel, sun, and scythe, and ox, and harrow,
> Station by station to that simple act
> Of terror or love, that broke the hill apart.

This interest moved him towards the Roman Catholic religion in the next phase of his life. His faith and his ideas would continue to be interwoven; his ideas about religion were bound up with his ideas about his writing. That this connection was important to Brown is suggested by his regular use, from time to time, for the rest of his writing career, of ritual and religious ceremony in stronger, more explicit forms. Even then, this was not simply a statement of faith in a Christian religion; instead, it was driven by his belief in redemptive cycles of many kinds.

His 'true task' was to transform his, and others', 'swarm of symbols' into some type of redemptive process. There was to be a terrible tension in some of his subsequent work, as he tried to achieve unity without insularity. This must have been one of the reasons for his regular use of time-shifts, since they would liberate his imagination, and his readers', from any one frame of reference or any one belief system or creed.

That poetry had become Brown's 'true task' is clear from his achievements: as he was sitting his final undergraduate examinations he had two volumes of poetry already in print and had consolidated his central artistic themes. But he had to face up to some serious questions: what next? How – and where – would he make a living as a full-time writer?

The first four chapters of this book have described how Brown came to face these questions. During this period there was much interplay between the life and the work. This would not be so much in evidence from now on, as he produced a steadily increasing stream of publications and as his life began to centre on writing. Consequently, there is more focus on the writing from Chapter Five on.

PART TWO: 1961–1974

From Journalism to Literature

5

'The Way of Literature':
The Year of the Whale
1961–65

Introduction

Part Two of this book shows the focusing of Brown's vision of religion, life and writing in his work, as he combined religious and natural cycles. A key element was his exploration of Gerard Manley Hopkins' poetry, which brought religion and poetry together.

The title of this chapter is taken from an essay Brown wrote about his conversion, which he linked explicitly with his writing, in which he revealed the standards of writing he was aiming for, naming his literary models and key themes: love, peace, caring and intellectual and moral rigour. It may strike some readers as a dry, academic piece, yet it does show him developing his own routes on the journey towards life as a writer. These were the touchstones of his efforts in writing. That this was an important essay was indicated by its inclusion in his autobiography.

'The Way of Literature' could mean two things: a method of writing to be adopted or the *via crucis*, a route to salvation through writing, the Way of the Cross being a recurring theme and form in Brown's work from this point on. It became a poetic exercise, giving security, familiarity and meaning, but could also appear constrained. Having established a strong vision, with a set of forms and themes, the challenge for Brown was now to avoid formulaic writing. In fact, there was an immediacy about his work at this time, a fresh response to old themes.

Biographical notes: 1961–65 (aged 40–44)

The Orkney Herald closed in January 1961, ruling out a return to professional journalism. Moreover, Ernest Marwick had moved from that newspaper to write for *The Orcadian*. Even if Brown had wanted to return to journalism, there was no opening for him. Brown realised that he was not going to find a conventional career; in fact, he had said earlier that he did not want a 'respectable' job. An academic career was unlikely, since he had not gained a research degree. School teaching was not for him. This narrowing of his range of options focused his thinking all the more sharply on his writing, which he had continued throughout his undergraduate and postgraduate courses: 'I'm looking forward to exploring Hopkins. The great thing is I'll be left almost entirely to my own devices – no lectures, tutorials, etc.; just an occasional chat with my supervisor. So I expect to be able to do a good lot of my own writing.'[1] Again: 'I suppose it's possible to get bored in these places, but I keep myself occupied doing a little daily darg on G. M. Hopkins and also some writing of my own.'[2]

Although the threat of ill-health remained, complicating his sense of choice and threatening further disruption, his letters from this time show a growing commitment to the writing life; time in postgraduate study and in hospital became time to focus on his writing: 'The question now arises as to some other occupation – I think I'll settle down in Orkney and try to do a bit of gainful writing . . . and that doesn't mean poetry, unfortunately.'[3] At the same time he put his position, literally, on record for 'The Poet Speaks': 'I don't think poetry's a mission either. It's just the only thing that I *can* do you see, I have a sort of *gift with words* and I indulge this gift. Whether it's a "mission" or not I wouldn't claim. I just try to do what I can with them. This is something that troubles me all the time and I've *had* to do it – so long as I'm the way I am.'[4]

In terms of actual written output, he looked through what he had written and began to gather it into a volume of poetry, so that not long after his two years of research he had enough for a third volume. He had not abandoned prose, but the focus for the moment was on his next volume of poems, *The Year of the Whale*.

'Skatehorn the Tramp': Manuscript of a poem published in
Lines Review, 1962.

The Year of the Whale

> Thorfinn, you will learn more in Orkney
> Than Mansie did
> Who made seven salt circles of the globe.[5]

Orkney became a microcosm. There was the domestic Orkney, with its contemporary people and activities, along with those of their predecessors and the recorded tradition and the imagined life of archetypes. Brown fleshed out well known characters, myths, legends and superstitions, some drawn from books, others transmitted orally. There was a clear link between his early journalistic treatments of Orkney and his imaginative ones. As he worked hard to blend religious, pagan and natural cycles, the story of Magnus moved to the centre of his writing.

Brown told Marwick that *The Year of the Whale* was an attack on progress: 'the whole book is an implicit criticism of us & our time – dry faith, thin language, the growing lust for machines & possessions – awful!'[6] In this letter, with an apparently dark view of the contemporary world, Brown's growing commitment to the writing life was expressed in one of his most characteristic statements:

> The main business of any poet is to keep the roots & sources clear. He starts with language, since that's the material he works in – 'purify the dialect of the tribe' – restore images, use words sparingly & accurately. For if the language gets fouled, then all values go – people think wrong, or sloppily, then all proportion & value are lost, life becomes meaningless or a nightmare. Under the present-day prosperity of Orkney, and indeed the western world, terrible negative forces are at work. I have tried to open a few of the old springs that have become choked and neglected, in the hope that one or two folk, here and there, might taste and think again.

However, there was for Brown at this time another side of the coin: 'That's the serious side of the coin; but of course poetry is primarily gay; and so I hope the book might start some dancing somewhere.'[7]

The characters in *The Year of the Whale* are there to embody the negation of what Brown saw as destructive modern values. The title poem tells the story of the killing of a school of whales which occurred at a point when the local community was having a lean spell. The first stanza describes the potential death of this story itself, the second describes the community and the third describes the event. In fact, the purpose of the poem is explicitly to preserve this story, to capture it before those who remembered it and kept it alive in pub conversations, were dead:

> Only myself and Yule
> In the ale-house now, speak of the great whale year.

The poem can be read as 'an implicit criticism' of modern times, of that version of modern times which over-emphasises individuality at the expense of communal activities. There is also a critique of materialism, since no one in the community wants to profit from the windfall. The immediacy of the community's response also suggests that communal values or loyalties are still in place. Nor is the community's action dependent on any individual or hero. The poem seems to be about the community more than the whales, with two stanzas for the community and only one for the creatures. Not that this particular whale hunt necessarily occurred, though many like it are documented in Orkney newspapers and elsewhere; Brown did not set out to record a historical moment in this poem, but to explore how the detail, atmosphere and effects of such events may be recorded or lost.

Although religious language is used, there is no religious cycle, as in other Brown poems; instead, devotional imagery is used to define the world view of one of the characters: 'Resurrected . . . stations of bread . . . sacred lamps'. The last of these suggests the 'dry faith' that Brown said, in his 1965 letter, he was trying to write against in this collection.

His aim here seemed, indeed, to be to 'open a few old springs', attempting to make them seem fresh. There is nothing in this poem of the extremes of 'nightmare' alluded to in his letter about this collection. There is no confrontation with 'meaninglessness' as yet, although the possibility of the death of the community's story is there from the first line: 'The old go, one by one, like guttered flames.'

THE YEAR OF THE WHALE

The old go, one by one, like guttered flames.

This past ~~winter~~ *ewe-shiver* [margin: *ewe-shiver*]

Tammag the bee-man has taken his ~~cold~~ blank mask

To the honeycomb under the hill,

Corston who ploughed out the moor

Unyoked and gone; and I ask,

Is Heddle lame, that in youth ~~could dance~~ and saunter

~~A way to the chastest bed?~~

[margin: Is Heddle lame, that famous dancer, wherever Bow to strings was laid?]

[interlinear: that famous dancer wherever leap and wheel / Wherever fiddle was played Bow to ...]

The kirkyard is full of their names

Chiselled in stone. Only myself and Yule

In the ale-house now, speak of the great whale year.

This one and that provoked the ~~taurine~~ waves *bull-belling*

With ~~an arrogant~~ pass, *a careless*

[margin: bull-belling / a careless]

Or probing deep through the snow-burdened hill

Resurrected his flock,

Or passed from fiddles to ditch

By way of the quart and the gill,

All night lay tranced with corn, but stirred to face

The brutal stations of bread;

While those who tended their lives

Like sacred lamps, chary of oil and wick,

Died in the fury of one careless match.

'The Year of the Whale'. Corrected typescript of stanzas 1 and 2, 1965 (1990).

The title suggests another cycle of some kind, something symbolic, perhaps because of the use of the definite article, '*The* Year of *the* Whale'. However, the event is a one-off, a milestone in the community's history, a dramatic event unrelated to any others, breaking through the monotony and deprivation, bringing all the characters, previously described as pursuing their separate occupations, together in a common effort.

The 'implicit criticism' of the 'thin language' of modern times is perhaps a target of heightened language in the second stanza's description of the community:

> This one and that provoked the taurine waves
> With an arrogant pass,
> Or probing deep through the snow-burdened hill
> Resurrected his flock.

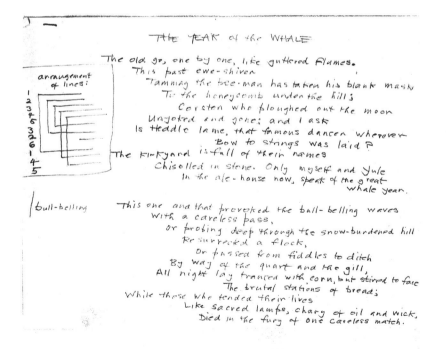

'The Year of the Whale'. Fair copy with revisions to the 1965 version, worked over in 1990.

This does not deify the characters; it is not the characters who are 'heightened'. The drama of the whale hunt itself, in the third stanza, dominates the poem. It is collective community action that is emphasised:

> Everything that could float
> Circled the school. Ploughs
> Wounded those wallowing lumps of thunder and night.
> The women crouched and prayed.

An abrupt change of subject, unusual for Brown's collections, showed that he was not only interested in preserving old stories: he chose the death of John F. Kennedy for the subject of the last poem in this collection, 'The Seven Houses: In Memory of John F. Kennedy'. While this is about a modern figure it could also be seen as a Saint Magnus poem in contemporary clothing. In fact, were it not for the dedication in the title, it would not be obvious that Kennedy is the subject. Only the sixth and seventh stanzas provide tenuous allusions to Kennedy's life and death.

This poem is a formally structured elegy, setting out seven 'houses', one in each stanza, in Brown's version of the seven ages of man: 'Womb . . . Birth . . . Man . . . Corn and Grape . . . Love . . . Policy . . . History'. Kennedy does not emerge from this poem as a recognisable person. Capitalised 'Man' and 'Woman' create an abstract account of life and death. The chronicler has a role again in the 'House of History' and the anti-machine age case is made in 'arrogance of atom and planet'. The 'thin language' brigade, finally, is given a particular identity:

> The enemies laid aside their masks,
> And later resumed them
> For epitaph, platitude, anger.
> What they say is of small importance.

But the language used in this poem does not really come to life. Not only does the character of Kennedy remain shadowy, but the ideas remain vague:

> May the lamp still burn
> And bread be broken at the tables of poor men

(The heads bowed
And the sweet shape of the dove at the door.)
This is the House of History.

The poem concludes with this ambiguous aspiration – neither pious nor assured in tone, but with elements of both – a sequence of clichés, which is far from confident or convincing.

While Kennedy is presented here as a martyr, the poem does not convince us that the outcome of this death will be peace. In fact, the ending seems bitter, uncertain, acknowledging the disruption of certainty. Those who argued that Brown was too dependent on verse patterns, with his collections of seven stanzas, patterned rituals and capital letters, were not doing justice to the ambiguities of these last lines. Perhaps it is to be read ironically. Ultimately, the poem, read in the context of the collection, is less about Kennedy the individual than about survival – or not – of communities, nations and human values.

The story of a very different person, yet one who played a similar role in the development of Brown's idea, is the subject of 'The Funeral of Ally Flett'. Here too there was an attempt to preserve the memory of a man after his death, this time a local person. These seven stanzas have narrative and dramatic elements, with ritualistic blending of natural cycles and domestic routines, making them seem almost sacramental, while the personality of Flett still emerges. Brown cleverly shaped the whole story so that it could be connected with community identity and values. Carefully avoiding sentimentality, the last stanza shows that Flett would not be forgotten.

A similar concern informs 'Culloden: The Last Battle', covering a well-known episode from Scottish history from the perspective of a survivor. There are lyrical elements, biblical echoes and a dramatic section. This is not an account of the picturesque heroism of the Prince Charlie episode, but the reality of participants, giving insights into their motivations.

In this collection Brown seemed to be saying, 'This is what we could lose'; someone had to record these events. The people who took part were, for various reasons, not likely to record them. Someone had to take responsibility for preserving them, for translating oral anecdote into written record. Brown deliberately took on this responsibility, conscious of his inheritance of story, history and myth and of his duty as an artist capable of articulating them or bound to try.

In later works his attacks on 'getting and spending', on 'progress' and other specific forms of materialism were to become more explicit. For these views he was seen as obsessive and narrow in his representation of past and present, but in this collection the critique is more subtle and, in some of the poems here, more colourful.

Conversion: the *Tablet* article

There were references to the possibility of Brown converting to Catholicism as early as the 1940s and 50s, in his letters to Ernest Marwick, and there was his growing discontent with Presbyterianism and Calvinism, which he saw as life-denying, with none of the affirmation he saw in the Roman Catholic religion. He had been going to Mass occasionally when he was a student and he had been 'receiving instruction'. This meant that he had stated a definite interest in joining the Roman Catholic Church and attended regular formal meetings, where a priest explained the tenets and ceremonies of the Roman Catholic religion. It was not possible to join the Roman Catholic Church without going through this process. He was baptised in 1961.

Conversion was gradual. He sent away for information, frequently via a friend. After his initial interest, he delayed doing anything about it. In 1982 Brown published an article in the Catholic periodical, *The Tablet*, that provided fascinating insights into both his conversion and his writing: 'Here, for the first time, [Brown] tells how he came to the Catholic Church.'[8] In a separate section of his article Brown at last stated that the key to his conversion, the actual spur to act, was literature, as the title of this piece, 'The way of literature: An apologia', suggests: 'In the end it was literature that broke down my last defences. There are many ways of entering a fold; it was the beauty of words that opened the door to me . . . The beauty of Christ's parables were [*sic*] irresistible. How could they fail to be, when so many of them concern ploughing and seedtime and harvest, and his listeners were most of them fishermen?'

Brown's *Tablet* article answers the question of how relevant his conversion was to his writing; he drew clear connections between his reading and writing and his new faith. In less than two pages he plotted his route to conversion, rooted in his responses to other writers, such as Lytton Strachey: 'the whole pageant that Strachey unfolded before me – intended to make every reader chuckle scornfully – gave me one of the great thrills I have got out of literature.'

Brown seemed to have responded to the images of human frailty – rather than those of certainty – that he found in the Catholic Church and in literature, and in other writings with connections to that Church. On Lytton Strachey he continued: 'What could any average rational being make of such a morass of error and human frailty and pretension?' He wrote of Newman: 'those passages, all exquisite and soaring as violin music, that rise clear above his own dilemmas and difficulties'; and of Graham Greene: his 'was a hunted and driven priest, and in many ways a worthless one, who nevertheless kept faith to the end.'

The endurance of this Church, over time, appealed to him: 'That such an institution as the Church of Rome – with all its human faults – had lasted for nearly 2,000 years, while parties and factions and kingdoms had had their day and withered, seemed to me to be utterly wonderful.'

Another influence was the *Orkneyinga Saga*, at first sight an unlikely stimulus to join the Catholic Church, given the violence of some of its action and values: 'I read the . . . Orkneyinga Saga, an anthology of deeds of heroism and vaunt and "derring-do"; out of the waste-land of fire and revenge, the story of the martyrdom of Earl Magnus shines like a precious stone.'

The *Tablet* article included a relatively long quotation from the saga to make the point, while Brown acknowledged that contemporary Orcadians would have a different response to the story, if they had any response at all. He felt pretty sure that they would find that the values and characters of this saga story 'have no real place in our enlightened progressive society'. His was a completely different response, however, particularly when he came to the character of Magnus: 'For me, Magnus was at once a solid convincing flesh-and-blood man, from whom pure spirit flashed from time to time and never more brightly than at the hour of his death.'

It is worth noting how Brown made his case: polarising his Orcadians' views. In 1937 and in the 1940s and 50s, he was already including Magnus in his poetry and in other genres, which, since the *Tablet* article was published in 1982, conveys the impact of this story.

Brown's discovery of his taste for religious ritual and language would have paralleled his decision to 'enter the fold'. Although we must remember that Brown was in this article, to some extent, reconstructing events in a way that would make his 'conversion' coherent, it is clear that the literary sources and religious texts helped him to formulate his theory and values. The *Tablet* article ends with an expression of his new fascination with the 'ordinary':

> The elements of earth and sea, that we thought so dull and ordinary, held a bounteousness and a mystery not of this world. Indeed, in my youth, the work of croft and fishing-boat was rather looked down on by those who sat at office-desks or stood behind counters. Now I looked with another eye at those providers of our bread and fish; and when I came at last to work as a writer, it was those heroic and primeval occupations that provided the richest imagery, the most exciting symbolism.

His conversion experience seems to have included an acute response to what he saw as the beauty of literature, causing him to reflect on reading he had done in the past and to make an explicit connection between literature and religious beliefs: 'Can it be that those beauties of literature and all the arts are a striving to return to that immaculate beginning? – the word lost in The Word.' Later, in his autobiography, Brown reinstated a selection of texts that he felt illustrated these qualities, which the editor of *The Tablet* had cut for reasons of space. These quotations make an even closer connection between literature and religion:

> The corn was orient and immortal wheat . . .
> (Traherne, *Centuries of Meditation*)

> And I must enter again the round
> Zion of the water-bead
> And the synagogue of the ear of corn
> (Thomas, 'A Refusal to Mourn')

I want . . .
a black boy to announce to the gold-minded whites
the arrival of the reign of the ear of corn
                    (Lorca, 'Ode to Walt Whitman')

Thou mastering me,
God! giver of breath and bread;
World's strand, sway of the sea;
Lord of living and dead . . .
            (Hopkins, 'The Wreck of the *Deutschland*')

This is a catalogue of Brown's favourite images, working like touchstones; some were already established in his own writing. The link he made between 'the word', his writing, and 'The Word' of God, showed his new faith in the meaning of writing, writing with a more spiritual meaning, perhaps with a new purpose, new commitment to writing itself. His passionate identification with the Magnus story also hints at the self-sacrificing poet's 'interrogation of silence'.

In *The Year of the Whale* five out of twenty-five poems dealt with religious subjects and there were religious allusions in more than twenty. Furthermore, after that volume certain religious ideas and ceremonies dominated Brown's writing. In a broadcast on 25 October 1972 he revealed that he had a plan to write fifty Stations of the Cross poems; at that time he said he had already composed about a dozen. Whether this indicates an obsession, profound faith or a clever use of 'good scaffolding' (a remark he once made in conversation about his use of sevens in describing a community) is for readers and critics to debate. Following the form of the Stations of the Cross – making it fit a variety of events and characters – was no mean feat; it was a challenging technical exercise.

In the same broadcast Brown revealed more of the role of religious faith and form in his work; if the terrible events of Christ's crucifixion were true, he said, no event was too trivial for inclusion in 'The Way', that is, the Way of the Cross. In 'Mrs Ballantyne', Brown illustrated his point with incidents from people's lives, recounted by a woman gossiping across a garden fence: in fourteen stanzas she describes a number of local misfortunes, giving her view that 'If a person's down, they love to kick them'. This is one of the methods Brown used to attach nobility and importance to the lives of ordinary people. He related these events to Christ's Way of the Cross quite explicitly, giving another explication of his glorification of the commonplace, or, rather, making strong connections between Christ's story and everyone's story. It was part of his imaginative process to use religious ceremonies and beliefs as sources of subjects and forms.

More than that, he was making what he saw as legitimate connections between the life of Christ and the life of contemporary people, which some will consider sacrilegious. The leap across great sweeps of time, and great value shifts, was something that was to be a feature and fascination of a great deal of his work. This was not just a matter of throwing two disparate elements or different time-frames together; what he achieved was to set up a resonance between the two.

Where the religious scaffolding does not work well it seems to be a dutiful exercise; where it does work, it is startling, powerfully convincing and fresh. The crofter's work *is* given meaning and beauty by elevation to the sacramental so that the reader's assumptions and beliefs about the past and its patterns are challenged. In addition, the pagan elements are still there, alongside the religious themes.

Although Brown's *Tablet* article was well written and fascinating for these insights, it was in some ways unlike Brown in its academic approach to justifying his conversion. Perhaps he was attracted by the prospect of virtually guaranteed publication. Perhaps this too was a form of dutiful exercise. Was his argument that his conversion was caused by his reading of certain literary works ultimately convincing? Where is the change of beliefs that we might expect to accompany this? There were references to Catholicism in his earlier writings, so it did not come completely out of the blue. But was Brown drawn by the trappings and rituals rather than the Church's tenets?

Many readers see him as a 'Catholic writer', as much as an 'Orkney writer'. He appeared to see the parables re-enacted around him in Orkney; he saw something sacramental in certain occupations. He sanctified certain roles, but he had been doing that for some time, since well before his conversion, with, for example, his poem about his father. Perhaps the most powerful effect of Brown's joining the Catholic Church was that it ensured a kind of 'outsider' status, and a kind of privacy. There was no Catholic church in Stromness; he had to travel to Kirkwall. There were very few Catholics in Orkney at that time, and his conversion came as a shock to some. There are some who still have not accepted it. Was it, consciously or otherwise, a device, a way of separating himself, of making sense of his alienation?

Paradoxically, membership of this Church brought him social and spiritual security, within a social minority, which gave him few kindred spirits. It was another form of 'closed society', giving him the isolation he seemed to need. His identification with Orkney's past, his time in a hospital isolation ward, his unstable identity in Orkney – early recognition for his writing came from outside Orkney – were all influences on his developing beliefs.

The Catholic message would have had little meaning to Orcadians at that time; the story of Magnus would be equally alien or irrelevant. Brown worked to find a place for himself and his imagination in Orkney, constructing his own vision of it. In rejecting the present, with its obsessions with progress, he looked back to the past and inward to his own imagination. The result was at times a surreal picture of Orkney, the clashing of different realities.

Ironically, given the popular image of Brown as rooted in Orkney, his experience made him feel very much apart from contemporary Orkney. Although he socialised with contemporaries, he preferred the company of older people. A few years later Brown wrote of himself at this time: 'Without literature I would have become a kind of scarecrow in the community.'[9] Apart from providing comfort and security, and an identity for himself as a certain type of writer, Catholicism also provided a stimulus to his writing, and growing confidence in it.

Conclusion

If we want to measure the distance Brown travelled in his writing during this period, we have only to compare the John F. Kennedy poem and a few sentences from Brown's *Tablet* article: where the Kennedy poem was ambiguous in its evocation of hope and a vista of peace, the *Tablet* article was persuasive, conveying his personal hope and commitment.

Brown's growing stature, for his poetry particularly, is indicated in a letter Ted Hughes wrote to him about the Kennedy poem (18 January 1985), in reply to a letter Brown wrote to congratulate Hughes on his appointment as Poet Laureate:

> It has to be said, George – how marvellously you would produce exactly the right poems for this job. Roll up the whole historic pageant into a beautiful, dignified, private moment. Your poem on Kennedy's death is to me the model public poem – visionary, stately, inevitable, universal, full of the moment, & thoroughly your own.

Hughes certainly captured what Brown said he set out to do in his work.

As he moved on in his writing, Brown carried with him many of his now established subjects and strategies: even as he adopted religious imagery and values, the pagan ones were still there; even as he developed scaffolded structures, there was still a dramatic element to the poetry; and even as he performed his 'true task' in poetry, he was moving towards prose. For example, 'Places to Visit', a section of the poem 'Fisherman and Boy', recalls Brown's early journalism, as it gives a tour of Orkney in poetic form:

> In Birsay they move in their furrows, bread is broken
> Half way to sacrament . . .
> Hoy guards with its blue huddle of shoulders
> An offering hand . . .
> Egilsay keeps its broken kirk;
> There one April were ploughs, nets, shawled women
> And the rose of martyrdom.
> Visit the circle of stones in Stenness;
> Know then what a dark phallic sun
> The martyrless Pict
> Compelled upon his beasts and tillage.[10]

Brown's next phase of writing took him into new territory, as he moved to a new form, the short story, in which he was to produce some of his best writing.

6

'The Orkney gift of narrative' 1965–69

Introduction

> You can't write poetry every day. Even if you could, you might have to beg for crust and cup of tea. I found, to my great relief, that I had inherited something of the Orkney gift of narrative. (It was very valuable to me, being brought up in a place of salt-tongued sailors and loam-tongued glebe-men.) It was possible to write a short story in the intervals between those surgings of the wind of the spirit that are poems.[1]

Brown was looking for a focus and an outlet. He was ill again; another cycle of pills, hospital and isolation. Yet, illness was a refuge and an inspiration, a means of breaking away, like going to Newbattle Abbey College. There was an emerging pattern of withdrawal, from the Orkney in which he lived to 'An Orkney of the imagination' in which he wrote.

He began to publish some very good short stories around this time. Although he had been writing short stories since the late 1940s, for example a series of competent ephemeral pieces on a character called 'Mansie' in *The Orkney Herald* and several 'fragments of a novel' on Magnus, the two collections published in this period were much stronger. Brown's subjects were still Orkney's history, both ancient and recent, including contemporary subjects. Read together, these stories create a dizzying sweep through thousands of years. They offer a rich picture of event and character and many have Brown's characteristic patterning: the calendar of months, the intersection of different perspectives and the catalogue of characters' reactions.

For Brown the art of narrative was related to the art of poetry:

> What the story-teller must have is a feeling for rhythm and a sense of form or pattern. These are mysteries that lie at the heart of every art,

music, dance, painting, sculpture, architecture, story-telling and poetry.

Without rhythm and pattern, nothing can be well made. Art – and by implication history and life itself – has, lacking them, no real meaning.[2]

Whether or not we agree with Brown that narrative is an *Orkney* trait or 'gift', and we could surely find Orcadians and others who would disagree, we can see that he believed he had a gift.

As he began to write prose fiction regularly – and as he continued to write about writing it – we can see Brown's emerging 'theory of fiction'. If we collect his statements, written over an extended period of time, we can reconstruct his aims and perspectives. What it amounts to is a 'difficult and delightful art', not so much 'gift', in fact, as technical discipline:

Many Orcadians are still, in spite of television and newspapers, first-rate spinners of yarns.

But the literary short story is quite another thing: a complex web of character and atmosphere and motivation and ultimate issues has to be constructed, and the whole thing must be strong enough not to break apart at the merest fret or flaw. . . .

That I am particularly addicted to the [short story] myself I attribute to quirks of character – impatience to finish a piece once it is begun; an urge on the one hand to compress, and on the other to make elaborate 'kennings' out of ordinary matters.[3]

Brown's statements about his artistic intentions were often over-simplified; they can even seem naïve. Yet, some pieces, particularly his forewords to his books, read like literary 'inventions' in their own right, more like short stories than theoretical accounts. These writings indicate a tension between his desire to make writing – not just his own – socially relevant and his enjoyment of writing for its own sake. Writing had, for him, inherent meaning and value; occasionally he perhaps protested too much in striving to find a place for art in the modern world which he feared was in danger of abandoning it.

Brown's short stories are technically brilliant, and each collection is full of variation, the form allowing him to develop character and event in new ways. His first collection of short stories was published in 1967. He had, therefore, been writing both poetry and prose simultaneously for a number of years. Though his publications gave an impression that prose supplanted the poetry, in fact, he maintained a diverse output. From this point on, he was to publish collections of stories on a regular basis. There was no limit to the forms of writing he produced from now on. At the same time, he had become a recognised member of the contemporary flourishing of writing in Scotland, the Scottish Literary Renaissance.

Biographical notes: 1965–69 (aged 44–48)

With further illness, Brown was 'the horizontal bard' again. Return to journalism was still not an option; others had filled the gap he had left in the Orkney newspaper. Nor was he ready for the intensity of the day-to-day output of earlier years. He carried on with occasional essays, both topical and reminiscent, and reviews of books he was most interested in.

He stopped writing for *The Orkney Herald* just before it closed, shortly after its centenary issue in 1961. His essay 'This scarf became a symbol', published on 19 April 1960, described his experience of writing for this paper. He was not subsequently taken on by *The Orcadian* newspaper, except for the occasional review or essay and a short weekly article, because they did not need new staff, and they already had Ernest Marwick to cover literary subjects.

Brown was moving on, seeing his earlier views on Orkney's need for 'culture' – in terms of Picasso, Braque, Bach, T. S. Eliot and Ezra Pound – as a 'hideous mirage'. He also noted a change in his temperament: 'I had the gift (nowadays considerably damped down) of cutting people to the quick.' The mildly elegiac tone of this piece suggests Brown was comfortable leaving his journalism years far behind. Lack of income, as yet, from his writing meant that he relied on financial support from the welfare system.

First collections of short stories

A Calendar of Love, published in 1967, shows startling development of technique. When we compare his early Magnus fragments with 'The Three Islands' we can see how he has moved on. He is much better at capturing the psychological dimension of a story and uses shifts in points of view to create added drama. In some stories, he takes up new themes, such as technology; in others he returns to old favourites, such as the story of Saint Magnus.

In all his collections there are stories that move across great swatches of time. Time itself, its rhythms and patterns, was to become a fascinating central theme. Whereas in his poetry he plotted the rhythms of the seasons, for example, in his stories he could add the dimensions of drama and character. He saw – and perhaps created – close connections between his prose and poetry:

> There is a close relationship between my prose and poetry. Many of the poems, for example 'Hamnavoe Market', are highly condensed stories. Many of the stories are poems from which the discipline and restrictions of poetry have been lifted until they have a life of their own in prose. This is not to say I like poetic prose. Generally that is bad prose and worse poetry. The poetry of an author who uses both forms should be ideally a distillation of the prose but the grapes must be sound before either the prose or the poetry is any good.[4]

In his notes for an interview with Ernest Marwick in February 1969, Brown says: 'I think of my stories as extended poems in prose. Many of my poems . . . are highly condensed stories. It might have been better if there had been in English, as in French, a tradition of prose-poems. As it is, perhaps, I have the best of both worlds.'[5]

Brown's identification of a 'relationship' between poetry and prose is very revealing: what characterised his writing in this period, above all, was narrative experimentation in both. There are as many connections as differences between the genres in his work.

Brown confirmed his position in the poetry-versus-prose debate in writings and interviews over the years, at least once referring to the same poem to illustrate his point, which suggests that he was used to being asked the question, and had his answer ready, and/or that he was very clear about what he was trying to do in each form, and, equally important, what he was trying to avoid.

His Foreword to *A Calendar of Love*, interesting for the wide scope of his vision of Orkney – small place, dense history – can be read as his manifesto and it is a beautiful piece of writing in its own right:

Orkney is a small green world in itself. Walk a mile or two and you will see, mixed up with the modern houses of concrete and wood, the 'old farmhouses sunk in time'; hall and manse from which laird and minister ruled in the eighteenth century; smuggler's cave, witch's hovel; stone piers where the whalers and Hudson's Bay ships tied up; the remains of pre-Reformation chapel and monastery; homesteads of Vikings like Langskaill where Sweyn Asleifson wintered, the last and greatest of them all; the monoliths of pre-history; immense stone-age burial chambers where the Norse Jerusalem-farers broke in and covered the walls with runes.

Dominating all the islands is the rose-red Cathedral of Saint Magnus the Martyr in Kirkwall, called 'the wonder and glory of all the north'.

This Magnus was a twelfth-century Earl of Orkney, in a time of terrible civil war. One April morning he heard Mass in the small church of Egilsay; then he walked out gaily among the ritual axes and swords. Next winter the poor of the islands broke their bread in peace.

Round that still centre all these stories move.

In spite of this wide range of reference, the idea of a 'still centre' focuses the collection. Peace – after great turmoil – is the key. There is, perhaps, a softening of his quest for silence here. Brown's Foreword to *Winter Tales* (1995) revealed his core idea, preserving meaning through art: 'Without the story – in which everyone living, unborn, and dead, participates – men are no more than "bits of paper blown on the cold wind".' In a 1969 interview with Marwick, Brown said that 'Orkney should be treated in depth', and perhaps this is another reason why he turned to the short story form at this time, in order to develop his ideas further.

The title story of the first collection, 'A Calendar of Love', was the first of Brown's many 'calendar' stories, its form offering scope to establish and develop character on a larger scale, with space to explore themes against – and influenced by – the progression of the seasons. In his calendar stories he drew parallels between moments in characters' lives and the seasons going on around them, often creating strong oppositions between character, event and setting. In this story Brown used the pub as a fulcrum for people's comings and goings; around it the characters move, their actions and limited utterances telling us more about them than detailed description – not provided in any case – could.

The main character Thorfinn's drinking and womanising are presented as his frustrated reaction to Jean's dutiful acceptance of responsibilities as inn-keeper and nurse; Peter's stereotypically life-denying dogmatism is in question when he sits up all night apparently to comfort Jean's sick father, unless, of course, he is only concerned about the dying man's soul. Under the scrutiny of the pub-goers and Evangelicals Peter and Thorfinn's attempts to win Jean and the prospect of a permanent, loving relationship are examined. Brown's dialogue is realistic, promoting drama, innuendo and humour and moving the story on, a fine example being the last exchanges between Peter and Jean's dying father, Snipe, and the juxtaposition of Thorfinn's comments on the gravestone, firstly to those in the bar and then to its new owner, Jean:

> 'Many a poor bloody drunkard's last shilling went to pay for that stone.'
> And to Jean he said, 'It's a credit to you, the stone you put up to Snipe.'[6]

A month earlier, as the calendar moved on to spring, serenity and promise in Nature matched the lovers' mood:

> The last of winter, a hard grey lump of snow, blocked the ditch. Silently, imperceptibly, the little rill of ditch-water unwove the stubborn snow, carried it off, a cold shining music, down to the loch and the swans.
> For a long time they did not speak.[7]

The narrative point of view focuses on the individual, at her lowest point, looking for a way out of her predicament, refusing to be kept down:

> Jean stood on one of the stone piers and watched the fishing boats riding at anchor. It was quiet here, and clean. The doctor had uttered six or seven words. It was lonely here. So the hunted animal carries her wound away to a secret water, and waits patiently for death or renewal.[8]

There is one face-to-face confrontation between the two competing male characters and one symbolic meeting in Jean's dream. Their physical conflict is dramatic, combining realistic and symbolic dialogue and description. What holds the story together is the pattern of influence characters hold over each other; their actions are interrelated; they live within a few yards of each other; they come together for social occasions. That the calendar creates what Brown called 'scaffolding' for character and action, bringing pattern and momentum, is a dimension of this story:

> And then suddenly everything was in its place. The tinkers would move forever through the hills. Men would plough their fields. Men would bait their lines . . . And forever the world would be full of youth and beauty, birth and death, labour and suffering.[9]

The original version of the passage had named people, but in revisions Brown made them more general or universal, aiming to represent eternal truths, all part of a pattern, always moving towards renewal. Each character has his or her low point, but finds a way through the situation. Each has failures and triumphs. Their stories move towards affirmation or recovery. Yet we often lose the voices of the characters, as the voice of an unidentified, but seemingly implicated narrator seeks a symbolic conclusion. The strength of these stories is this combination of character and symbolism, and it is the fascinating contrast between the two that makes them so distinctive.

In 'The Wheel' Brown created another device for moving around a small community, taking in characters' differing viewpoints. The main character is another of those Brown figures who stand apart from the community, but here for a new reason. (Stan Barstow's 'The Search for Tommy Flynn', in a collection of stories called *The Desperadoes*, is a possible source.) Only towards the end of the story do we learn why the character makes his circuit of the village.

'The Wheel' is a cycle of visits Robert Jansen pays to the haunts of his friend Walls every Saturday night. At the centre of Robert's life is the value of his friendship with Walls. Each episode adds to the poignancy of his refusal to accept Walls' absence, as his 'pilgrimage' from his bachelor home through places associated with his friend evokes a variety of emotions and conjectures about Walls. The ending confirms what the reader has already deduced: that Walls is dead.

The story's structure of accumulating detail illustrates Robert's regard for Walls and apparent dependence on him, whatever the reaction of those he seeks out. Brown differentiates their reactions. Robert's appearance in the pub stops 'the erratic jingling commerce of silver and glass across the bar'. In the pub he is 'the gorgon's head', but he is the object of sympathy from Miriam, the Salvation Army 'girl' at the pierhead, whose reply amidst 'the holy ragtime' is a predictably Christian one. Tolerance and understanding mark the response of 'H. Leask, Dressmaker', who, we infer, had been in love with Walls. Refusing to take umbrage at Robert's familiar halting inquiry about Walls' whereabouts, she appears a gentle, pathetic figure, weeping as she sews 'over the cloud of cotton, over the crumpled wings and crumpled petals'. By contrast, the next witness to Robert's search, Captain Stevens, sends Robert packing with a threat: '"You better not come annoying folk every Saturday night, asking after a dead man! There's places for fools like you!"'

Robert returns to what is obviously the final act in his Saturday routine. Preparing Walls' supper, he reads a newspaper clipping recounting his friend's life and death. The last words of the story arouse sympathy for Robert, as he adds an extra egg for Walls to the frying pan: 'Walls is always hungry for his supper on a Saturday night, after the drink . . . What a man for eggs!' Refusal or inability to come to terms with his friend's death has committed him to this weekly odyssey, whose episodes throw light on the personalities of the dead man, Robert and their friends.

'The Wheel' employs the 'processional' technique involving the central character with a range of people and moments in settings that are familiar to him, and in an atmosphere in which he seems at home and at ease, however strange his journey may be to others. They attempt either to bolster or strip away his security in his delusion.

Brown's ability to draw credible characters is evident, as are the sympathy and poetic touches with which he has entered, 'by imagination and art, the lives of those uncelebrated folk'.[10] As the 'wheel' of time and duty revolves from one weekend to the next, the 'still centre' in this instance seems to be the main character's security in his ritual. Whether this is a sign of mental illness or just his way of working through grief is not specified, and the ambiguity strengthens the story.

The story 'Witch' recreates a moment in the past, with Brown adapting his prose style to capture the voices of the characters and the flavour of the period. This technique effectively conveys the confused terror of the alleged witch and the grim determination of her torturers. From the first line, like an incantation, we know that we are in a different time: 'And at the farm of Howe, she being in service there, we spoke directly to the woman Marian Isbister, and after laid bonds on her.'

The characters are not described. Their direct speech is laid out on the page like a play, reminiscent of J. M. Synge, telling us all about them and the horror of what is about to unfold in their short speeches:

MONTEITH. Thou needest not fear me. I am a man in holy orders.
MARIAN. I fear thee and everyone. My father should be here.
MONTEITH. Thou hast a scunner at me for that I am a man of God and thou art a servant of the devil.
MARIAN. How can I answer thee well? They keep food from me.
MONTEITH. I will speak for food to be given thee.
MARIAN. I thank thee then.
MONTEITH. Wilt thou not be plain with me?
MARIAN. All would say, then, this was the cunning of the evil one, to make me speak plain. I do speak plain, for I am no witch, but a plain country girl.
MONTEITH. Thou art as miserable a wretch as ever sat against that wall.
MARIAN. I am indeed.

Perhaps neither has much to say to the other because both know exactly what is going to happen; there is no stopping the chain of events. For Marian, speech is futile, and she knows it. Anything she does say will be twisted so that it can be used against her by her interrogators, but the reader sees and hears that she is innocent, a clever effect to achieve in the first two short pages of the story. It is difficult to see, at this stage in this story, where Brown will find a 'still centre' for this character.

The agony of the witch's test is described in excruciating detail, yet with economy of style. We also have a chilling insight into the mind set of the witch tester:

MONTEITH . Stand up, witch. Thou must suffer the witch's test on thy
body.

MARIAN. I think shame to be seen naked before strange men. This will
be a hard thing to endure. A woman should be near me.

They bring Janet, wife to William Bourtree.

JANET. I think none of you would have your wives and daughters, no
nor the beast in your field, dealt with thus.

She kissed Marian, and then unlaced her, she making now no
objection.

Then the probe was put into the said Marian's body, in order to
prove an area of insensitivity, the devil always honouring his servants
in that style. These parts were probed: the breast, buttocks, shoulders,
arms, thighs. Marian displayed signs of much suffering, as moaning,
sweating, shivering, but uttered no words. On the seventh probe she
lost her awareness and fell to the ground. They moved then to revive
her with water.

The short, laconic speeches recall the style of the saga, with its spare
description – the only colours are the blue and red of Marian's toes
and fingers. Not a word is wasted. The effect is to increase dramatic
tension as the story moves towards its inevitable conclusion. Brown
could be accused of hiding behind an objective account here –
distancing himself from the attack on the belief system behind the
events – yet the style is effective in conveying the conviction of the
persecutors.

In a number of ways, Brown's style is what makes this story so
powerful. It is an approximate representation of the style of the day,
making no great pretence at reconstructing the speech of a point in
time, yet communicating the demeanour of the speakers. It evokes
pain and cruelty – and contrasting kindness – the alleged rights and
wrongs and the absurdity of the 'test' and 'trial' of an alleged witch.
The story continues with further cruelties – 'Then one by one with the
pincers John Glaitness drew out her finger-nails and toe-nails; and this
operation caused her much pain' – and concludes with the burning,
amid laughter and shouting, the day having been declared a holiday.

Brown cleverly shifted from description to figurative language in order
to convey not only Marian's agony, but also the comic image she cuts with
the public: 'with her fingers like a tangle of red roots at the end of her

long white arms, and her head like an egg'. In spite of our sympathy with her ordeal, we are made to see how she could arouse both pity and hilarity in the crowd. After the harrowing accounts of her torture, it is quite an achievement to present both perspectives, both the victim's and those attending the burning as a form of public entertainment.

In the story 'Stone Poems' Vikings and Stone Age subjects are brought together, again imaginatively recreating a point in time. The story starts in the present tense, providing the briefest of background sketches. The effect is of jumping swiftly back in time: seven Vikings break into the Stone Age chambered tomb of Maeshowe one night to shelter from a storm. They are a motley crew: a mercenary soldier, two sea captains, two poets, a merchant and a crusader-deacon. They carve runes on the walls inside the tomb, 'Their imaginations . . . suddenly quickened in that petrified womb.'

The immediacy of the opening catches our attention as Brown embarks on his favourite practice, cataloguing individual responses to a shared experience: the structure of the story is seven snapshots, one for each Viking, with dramatic interplay of their perspectives:

> Hermund who had been in five battles at places between Ireland and Russia, besides sieges and sackings at castles and seaports all over Europe, cut this on the wall with his blade:
> > HERMUND OF THE HARD AXE
> > CARVED THESE RUNES . . .

> Arkold, the Iceland poet, had fallen in love . . . with a girl called Ingibiorg . . . without this silent and almost invisible girl . . . his harp would have remained the ordinary harp it usually was. Here in the stone heart of death and winter he wrote this:
> > INGIBIORG IS THE
> > MOST BEAUTIFUL
> > OF WOMEN[11]

Brown reconstructed these different characters from short texts that were actually carved on the walls of Maeshowe. The story is short, but he creates a sense of real individuals, each different, each with his own preoccupations and motives.

Brown closed the story with a description of the 'weak yellow light' percolating into the chamber, signalling that it is safe to leave the chamber and continue their journey. They go on their way, having made a lasting contribution to history and legend by their inscriptions. While Brown reconstructed a particular moment in Orkney's history, he also created characters who convince us that they belong to the twelfth century, but who, in their motives and variety, seem timeless. Some see this as anachronistic, yet the effect is to cut across the boundary of time.

This selection from *A Calendar of Love* shows the dramatic diversity of Brown's first collection, some stories with intensely individual perspectives, others representing the community, with old names and even older stories. We move from the Stone Age, through Viking visits to modern times. Although there are few dates to guide us, we can tell roughly where we are in time in each story; the precise date does not seem important.

Brown's Foreword to this collection made it clear that he saw, and perhaps wanted us to see, that Orkney was a storehouse for his writing. Yet, it is difficult to identify the 'still centre' to which he directed us. A central theme is the individual caught up in, influenced or completely overwhelmed by forces, be these religious, historical, emotional or environmental, in any sense. The individual stands exposed and vulnerable in the face of such forces. Some struggle to assert or express themselves; others seem to have no power to do so. Perhaps this is another expression of Brown's own sense of isolation; finally recognising the wealth of culture in Orkney and the wealth of material for his creative writing, ironically, he was still isolated and even more so with his next collection of short stories. This type of 'internal exile' was a common theme in twentieth-century fiction, including, for example, the novels and stories of James Joyce.

Brown's second collection of short stories, *A Time to Keep* (1969), was equally brilliant and equally successful, in terms of sales and critical reception. Characters, themes and expressions from *A Calendar of Love* reappear in *A Time to Keep*. It is generally agreed that these collections contain some of Brown's best writing, and they remain a kind of landmark achievement, still in print long after the first edition.

Yet, the stories were not altogether popular in Orkney. Some viewers took offence at the image of themselves that they saw when three stories from this collection were dramatised by John McGrath and broadcast by the BBC. Letters to the Editor of *The Orcadian* reveal the depth of feeling:

20 May, 1971

There can be few television sets in Orkney which were not tuned in to BBC 1 last Thursday evening, some with quite young children watching expectantly. What a missed opportunity to present Orkney's real treasures! (One wonders if those people who might be attracted to our coasts by such Bacchanalian prospects would be really welcome.)

20 May, 1971

With regard to the last play, had we seen it before we decided to come and live here nearly six years ago, it might very well have deterred us. Surely, to call the sordid story of 'Celia' Orkney today is a grievous misnomer.

What seems to have touched a nerve is that the plays were broadcast under the title 'Orkney', in the series 'Play for Today', potentially leading to the misconception that these were realistic treatments.

There were also positive reviews: Angus Ogilvy sensibly pointed out that these stories were not representations of real Orcadians. As he rightly said, if the programme had been broadcast under the title *A Time to Keep*, rather than giving the impression that it was a documentary, there would not have been such outrage. However, there is always a risk for writers in small communities that their writing will be taken – by some – as a realistic representation of their community.

One of the broadcast stories singled out for criticism, 'Celia', offered insights into alcoholism. The main character's description of her first drink was powerful and convincing:

I knew who I was before I took that drink – a poor girl in an ordinary house on a fisherman's pier. I stood there holding an empty glass in my hand. A door was opening deep inside me and I looked through it into another country. I stood between the two places, confused and happy and excited. I still wore Celia's clothes but the clothes were all a disguise, bits of fancy dress, a masquerade . . . I wore the clothes of a poor girl but I was wise, rich, great, gentle, good . . .

The world was all mine and I longed to share it with everybody. Celia was a princess in her little house on the pier. She pretended to be poor but she had endless treasures in her keeping, and it was all a secret, nobody knew about it but Celia. A wild happiness filled the house.

Alcohol has a role in many of Brown's stories, but it is one of many illnesses and challenges faced by his characters. The character of Celia was based on Stella Cartwright, whom Brown knew when he was living in Edinburgh. His letters to her (in Edinburgh University Library) have frequent hints about her drinking, with touching pleas to her to take care of herself. On 15 April 1966, Brown wrote to Stella: 'The girl in the story is called Celia and a good deal of her is based on Stella Cartwright, so you can see she's a dear and fascinating sort of person.'

In 'The Wireless Set', one of Brown's most widely known stories – thanks to reviewers' and critics' attentions – the characters are up against another faceless 'enemy', technology: 'The first wireless ever to come to the valley of Tronvik in Orkney was brought by Howie Eunson, son of Hugh the fisherman and Betsy . . . He turned a little black knob and a posh voice came out of the box saying that it would be a fine day tomorrow'. Characters greet this new technological wonder with awe or scorn, the one seeming to feed the other; the more impressed Betsy and Howie are, the more sceptical Hugh becomes. It quickly becomes clear to them all that lies – as well as truth – can be spread on the radio: 'The voice was saying that German dive bombers had sunk the *Ark Royal* in the Mediterranean . . . Wasn't the *Ark Royal* safely anchored in calm water on the other side of the hill?'

Suddenly, Howie is dead, killed in the war. The postman's sympathy, as he delivers the telegram, is brilliantly conveyed in his gesture: 'He gave it to her as if he was a miser parting with a twenty-pound note.' Howie's parents take the news with stoicism, his father Hugh expressing none of his emotions to the missionary, which the latter misreads as 'callousness'. Hugh's emotional outburst comes shortly before the missionary leaves: 'From inside came the noise of shattering wood and metal', a neat play on the words, 'From inside' – 'inside' Hugh and 'inside' the house. Howie's mother then gets on with the next ritual, setting out glasses for the mourners who can already be seen moving towards the croft.

The radio brings the war to the family and this, in turn, brings death. This story is well known for its 'anti-progress' theme. Brown's was not a non-specific anti-progress hobbyhorse, but a position rooted in recent events and trends. He was obviously able to see that progress and technology brought many improvements, being the first to acknowledge that he would not have survived tuberculosis without new drugs. Yet, he was troubled by the potential for harm; he meditated on what was lost as improvements became part of Orkney's new 'rituals' and values.

This is not an unusual position; it is familiar territory for writers and artists, but some have seen it as a narrow, insular or naïve position, perhaps because of the limits of Brown's frame of reference: Orkney. Certainly, he failed to represent, substantially, for example, the impact of the Vikings on Pictish inhabitants of the islands. But that was not really his intention.

Some have confused Brown's beliefs with those of his characters, assuming he believed whatever they believed, but he seems to have been only too aware of events outside the islands and of their obvious implications for Orkney and the rest of the world. Sometimes he was not given credit for understanding the pros and cons of progress, or for having the courage to persist with the unpopular task of interrogating modern – national, international and local – 'development': 'Pollution, nuclear power, over-fishing, the continuing destruction of the wild wet beautiful places, and the unique creatures that share our habitat, our fellow mortals: there are plenty of challenges for present-day islanders to face and resolve. Writers and artists ought to be in the forefront of the struggle.'[12]

The interesting thing is that he was able to maintain his focus on Orkney and, later, to turn this potentially bleak vision into new writing and, even more surprisingly, into new – for him – forms in his first novel, *Greenvoe* (1972).

Changes Brown made to 'The Wireless Set' show his development as a writer: there are interesting differences between this version and an earlier one in the *Glasgow Herald* (22 November 1958), 'The Evil Voice in Tronvik'. In the revised version Brown dropped the use of

Orkney dialect and made elements of the story less explicit. More is left to the reader's imagination, and the story works better as a result. The last paragraph was changed completely:

1958 version
Old Hugh walked towards the beach. Howie was dead. But it must not be mentioned, not to-day or any day until the earth was over the two of them who were left. Betsy would say never a word. He had put peace to the black twisted mouth on the dresser. And as for the converging mourners, he would rather listen to the lamentation of the gulls down by the rocks.

1969 version
Old Hugh stood in the door and looked up at the drift of clouds above the cliff. 'Yes,' he said, 'I'm glad I set the creels where I did, off Yesnaby. They'll be sheltered there once the wind gets up.'

'That white hen,' said Betsy, 'has stopped laying. It's time she was in the pot, if you ask me.'

The new version emphasises stoicism, as the characters take solace, or find distraction from their grief, in the continuing rhythms, normality and imperatives of the day-to-day. These changes could be taken as signs of Brown's growing skill in the short story form. They also show his habit – even more apparent in his poetry – of endlessly tinkering with his work, even after publication.

The removal of emotional reactions, in the suppression of the mother's tears and of the dialect words, risks losing the individuality of character. Yet padding has been removed. The human tragedy may come across, for some, as wooden, but it portrays the parents' reactions. Brown removed long sentences and detail, to leave monosyllables and short interactions, in order to show, rather than tell, us what the characters feel. While the first version told us that 'Betsy would say never a word', the second shows her talking about anything but the death. Brown created a heavy sense of words not said, of the silences falling between their short speeches.

What the stories in this collection share is the recurring round of loss and affirmation. Again and again, characters achieve this through some kind of passage, be it spiritual, imaginative or physical, through the community. In 'The Wheel' the character goes round disrupting others' lives, but his circle is his own ritual and has its own meaning for him. The community tolerates this. The final note, if there can be said to be one for such a diverse collection of stories, is continuity: at each port of call, when each is back in his own home, the community goes on.

Poems, 1966–68

Brown did not abandon poetry at this time; three collections came out around the same time as the short stories. The first, *The Five Voyages of Arnor* (1966), although small, had poems Brown repeatedly selected for later volumes, including his final enlarged *Selected Poems 1954–1992*, published in 1996, indicating that he felt they stood out in his body of work. The collection's subject is life in Viking times and the main character in the title poem is a poet.

Brown provided insights into his view of the Viking ethos in *Northern Lights* (1999), revealing why he found them a fascinating subject for his writing:

> The Norse Shetlanders had no notion of tragedy. There was only Fate, which was implacable and had to be endured. The human spirit reached its height in the confrontation with Fate; it was a good thing to go into the last darkness with a few witty words that would be repeated, with wonderment and laughter, beside the winter fires for generations afterwards. A great saga character seemed to carve his own epitaph with his last breath.[13]

The narrator of the poem 'The Five Voyages of Arnor' had left Orkney on four occasions: for Ireland, Norway, Iceland and Jerusalem. A Viking expedition inspired his first poem. Then he journeyed to fetch a girl he won at draughts. Arnor wrote a handful of poems about her which passed into the repertoire of Christmas song. Iceland was visited in pursuit of a vendetta which was not satisfied because Arnor preferred conversation on metrical innovations to violent action. The holy voyage to Jerusalem provided more stimulus to composition, as 'The Mediterranean/Was richer by a hundred love songs.' Finally, close to his 'straw death', he regrets not perishing in battle. Fortified by the last rites, he gives instructions for procedures after his death, the fifth voyage, his

last word a farewell to his art and an evocation of the scene which will
continue after his death:

> Drop my harp
> Through a green wave, off Yesnaby,
> Next time you row to the lobsters.

This poem is rich in visual effects, as Brown runs a red thread through
several different episodes: 'blood growing cold by the saint's well', the
stained hooves of the horse which was ridden over Arnor's brother, an
axe-blade put into a dog's throat to deceive the women urging
vengeance, and Christ's feet, broken on Calvary. Arnor emerges most
strikingly from the few monosyllables describing how his wife Ragnhild
'filled my quiet house with words' and his conviction that his imminent
death will lack the intensity of events he has witnessed and avoided:

> I should have endured this thing,
> A bright sword in the storm of swords,
> At Dublin, Micklegarth, Narbonne.

'Our Lady of the Waves' is a chronicle of the Eynhallow brothers'
devotion to Mary, the mother of Jesus Christ. Simple vocabulary and
verse-movement reflect the brothers' patient industry and the
precarious nature of their efforts to make a living. Local events, a birth
and death (the latter Arnor's, 'Tired of words and wounds'), illustrate
the cycle from infancy to the end of a life of art and conflict.

'Viking Testament' is another ordering of affairs, by a man who has
reason to regret events leading to the retribution of a blood feud. Unlike
Arnor's, reminiscing on his travels and exploits, the voice of this three-
part poem is concerned with those to be left behind by a father whose
character emerges from speculation on how useful his bequests can be,
with vengeful action against his family anticipated shortly. There is none
of Arnor's wry humour, lyricism, Christian resignation or hankering for
old Viking days in the dying man's desperate – but unconvincing –
clinging to the hope that the son of an Irish ruler will be prevented from
avenging his father's slaying by the narrator.

There is moving ironic symmetry in the conclusion which describes
the stone Arnor has been ordered to buy and carve for the dying man's

daughter. The inscription is to be a statement of love surviving death: 'Red as fire, roses, blood', a legacy which may survive the hall's destruction:

> Irishmen will read it perhaps
> Over this fated lintel,
> A fragrant stone among blackened stones.

Direct address, acceptance of personal decline, dismissal of the two brothers and the wistful conclusion make this the most emotional section of the monologue – perhaps the best example of the three in this short collection.

Bringing the values of Brown's time to a story set in Viking times works well in this poem and brings the small collection to a touching and convincing conclusion. Brown departed from the tradition of laconic Norse writing when it suited him, adding depth to the poems. He also departed from his own habits; this collection was a new development for Brown in that it focused on a single, central character, Arnor the poet.

Brown's next project, *Per Mare* (1967), was written for the 150th anniversary of Stromness as a burgh, an anniversary Brown saw as an opportunity to seek a commission to celebrate his community. Although it remained unpublished, it is important for its demonstration of Brown's personal interest in the whole span of Stromness's history.

On 18 October 1966 Brown wrote to Ernest Marwick informing him that the Town Council had approached him with the commission, listing the sequence of episodes he had in mind: 'They have approached me to write a kind of pageant on this history of the town. It's going to be a big job, and purely honorary, but I'm not complaining at all about that; one owes the place of one's birth & upbringing an enormous unpayable debt.'

Always quick to accept and discharge commissions – articles, poems, stories, acrostics for special occasions involving family, friends and complete strangers – Brown was not slow to put himself forward by proposing projects he was eager to carry out because – reading between the lines – he felt he could do better than other writers had done, or the subject was an important, untapped source. It was an opportunity to break new ground and, moreover, to pay tribute to those who had grappled with Stromness's problems in the past.

Presented from 6–9 June 1967, *Per Mare* did 'depict the main events of Stromness from the Viking era to the last century'.[14] It is worth noting that Storer Clouston and Eric Linklater had written a pageant about Saint Magnus in 1937 for the 800th anniversary of Saint Magnus Cathedral. Brown's own commission could be seen as the younger writer stimulated to emulate the established writers, or perhaps even trying to compete.

The eight scenes give faces and voices to characters who played key roles in the fortunes of Stromness at home and abroad, across the centuries. It is unified by the chorus of Stromness women, punctuating the piece at the start of each scene:

CHORUS OF WOMEN – 3
The village took root, Hamnavoe grew and flourished.
Soon six hundred people lived
Between Brinkie's and the harbour.
Tall houses, with gardens and piers
Where the stylish merchants lived,
Small slipways for the fishermen,
A new kirk, inns and ale-houses.
The street uncoiled like a sailor's rope from north to south.
And closes swarmed up the side of the hill
Among gardens and clouds,
And closes stepped down to the harbour
And the nets and whitemaas.

. . .

Six happenings from the web of Hamnavoe
We have stretched out.
And still the web unfolds.
Pray that the end may be good, and we ourselves,
With all the dead of Stromness and the unborn,
With witch, explorer, pirate, poet, hero,
Shine in the silence of that heraldry.

The production was warmly received by the 1,200 people who attended the performances in the Stromness Town Hall, making Brown the object of much attention and comment. A contemporary reviewer (almost certainly Marwick) assessed the impact: 'It gave dramatic shape to a whole series of key incidents in the town's history . . . It was a fine flowering of local mythology, history and poetry, as varied as the strange story of Stromness: at times grave and elevated, at times farcical; in places candid and robust, in other places inexpressibly tender.'[15]

Brown's next collection, *Twelve Poems* (1968), was published by Festival Publications, Queen's University, Belfast, as one of a series. Although most of the contents were reprinted from periodical or anthology, there is unity of content, expressed in a variety of metrical forms. 'Deor', closely following the Old English poem's spirit and sequence of events, is remarkable for the way in which Brown transmuted the original's bald statement into new imagery:

> Beadohild wept when death
> Cold on her brother was snowing.
> And sorrow grew. No gown
> Could hide from public showing
> The glebe of her body rich
> With Weland's reckless sowing.
> *That sorrow withered, so may this*

After going through the historical events, heavy with suffering and foreboding, Brown added to his source the poet's personal sorrow, as Deor describes his own eclipse by a rival poet before the final refrain is given universal application: '*All sorrows wither, so may this*'.

The final poem, 'Black Furrow, Gray Furrow', provides a fitting conclusion to a series of local and national rites of passage. The 'furrows' bring together the subjects of farming, the sea and death:

> From the black furrow, a fecund
> Whisper of dust.
> From the gray furrow, a sudden
> Gleam and thrust.
> Crossings of net and ploughshare,
> Fishbone and crust.

There are seeds of new ideas here, which will emerge in Brown's later collection *Fishermen with Ploughs*, where the duality of sea and earth is explored in much more depth.

An Orkney Tapestry

'. . . it is the work of a man who seems not so much a manipulator of experience as the medium for a whole way of life.'[16] What Seamus Heaney said of Brown's poetry in this review of *An Orkney Tapestry* is substantially true of the whole book, including the prose. Brown mediated historical and legendary stories for a modern society which he saw as over-committed to material gain. This book also marked a new departure, a hybrid form that allowed him to weave poetry and prose together.

An Orkney Tapestry contains much diverse information about what Brown saw as Orkney's key features and main attractions for modern readers. He conveyed his sense of localities, giving his response to the stories that had grown up around characters, famous or known only within their small circle. It was a composite of 'a more imaginative and varied approach, with plays, poems, fragments of history, and real characters in it'.[17]

If Brown's choice dictated the book's substance and arrangement, it was his style and constant focus on 'the roots and sources of the community, from which it draws its continuing life' that gave *An Orkney Tapestry*'s 'sequence of vivid patterns' coherence. That style includes playful anecdote, outraged declamation or imaginative recreation of vanished people and their customs, but constant and explicit is Brown's conviction, quoting from the then unpublished *A Spell for Green Corn*, that 'Art must be of *use*'. His own art was designed to benefit Orcadians, past and present, as he offered affectionate recollections, inveighed against 'a new religion, Progress . . . a rootless utilitarian faith' or described the 'endless ballet of the weather'. The 'use' he saw for his own art was to combine the aesthetic, historical and material. It was not just to record; nor was it simple self-expression.

The people in this book embody his theme of regret for lost communities. There is some invention here, with Brown freely filling in the gaps. He may have leant heavily on the *Orkneyinga Saga* and ancient ballads, but threaded through the essays, 'Vikings', 'Lore' and 'Poets', are poems of his own, which imaginatively recreate the times he was celebrating. These add another dimension to the prose.

The way to read this is as an introduction to Orkney, both the real place and the Orkney of Brown's imagination. There are enough arresting Orkney images and scenes to capture the imagination of the reader and sudden changes of subject and form to keep it interesting. It is light, anecdotal, and in places mildly amusing. His account moves over time, including both 'events and imaginings'.

The book is out of print, but worth getting hold of. Although Brown overstates his case against 'a new religion, Progress', a compelling urgency is expressed in his mission to keep the 'roots' and 'the word' alive:

> It is the word, blossoming as legend, poem, story, secret, that holds a community together and gives a meaning to its life. If words become functional ciphers merely, as they are in white papers and business letters, they lose their 'ghosts' – the rich aura that has grown about them from the start, and grows infinitesimally richer every time they are spoken. They lose more; they lose their 'kernel', the sheer sensuous relief of utterance. Poetry is a fine interpenetration of ghost and kernel.

There are many fine poems in this book; one of the best, and most frequently anthologised, was later titled 'Dead Fires'. After the abandonment of crofts – each named carefully, one by one – in the valley of Rackwick on Hoy, with the shadow of nuclear war threatening total dereliction and the Stations of the Cross drawing a parallel with the death of a community, Brown offered a kind of prayer:

> At Burnmouth the door hangs from a broken hinge
> And the fire is out.
>
> The windows of Shore empty sockets
> And the hearth coldness.
>
> At Bunnertoon the small drains are choked.
> Thrushes nest in the chimney . . .
>
> The fire beat like a heart in each house
> From the first corner-stone
> Till they led through the sagging lintel the last old one.
>
> The poor and the good fires are all quenched.
> Now, cold angel, keep the valley
> From the bedlam and cinders of a Black Pentecost.

Powerful images of fire harnessed to domestic use are balanced by emblems of individual crofts' desertion: the unlit fire, bird-choked chimney, 'fire of rust'. Each croft is described in turn, its accretion of loss and regret part of an inventory of decay as houses' fabric and fittings were taken over by Nature, most significantly, that focus of family life, the fire in the hearth. These stanzas bring out how central fire was to families' warmth, food and conversation.

There is a sense of inevitability in the repetition of 'stone', appearing at the end of stanzas ten to twelve, and finality, with the graveyard stone. Sanctified by generations of family use, the fire-blackened stones become relics, at once indicating the history of the valley and expressing faith in its potential future. The stones are still there, for when people return: 'I do not think Rackwick will remain empty for ever. It could happen that the atom-and-planet horror at the heart of our civilisation will scatter people again to the quiet beautiful fertile places of the world.'

The theme of Edwin Muir's 'The Horses' was echoed and affirmed when 'Dead Fires' concluded with a prayer for protection against the fires of an atomic explosion. At the outset of *An Orkney Tapestry* Brown approved how certain poets were 'more interested in essences; they have described the vision by which the people live, what Edwin Muir called their Fable.' Brown explicitly placed this book in that genre. He maintained that he was 'interested in facts only as they tend and gesture, like birds and grass and waves, in "the gale of life".' He wanted to produce a 'kind of profile of Orkney, which is not a likeness of today only; it has been worked on for many centuries. "I lean my cheek from eternity."'

Brown used to say that he did not think highly of this book and did not want to see it back in print. While we have to wonder whether this was no more than an off-hand remark about his earlier work – or perhaps it was an expression of his discomfort at the stridency of the 'anti-progress' strain – it was another of Brown's exciting formal experiments. Late in life, he was considering a reprint.

From the Contents page, Brown might appear to be offering a miscellany of items which sit uneasily together, but he fleshed out shadowy figures brilliantly, while describing their historical or imagined settings. Into their stories he wove the eternal, timeless virtues of respect for humanity, Christian and pagan, and the importance of ceremony and art, counterpointing different aspects of a theme with such style that his technique – decorative and functional, creating patterns around a few central motifs – can be characterised by the book's title. *An Orkney Tapestry* is a major work in the Brown canon.

The Scottish Literary Renaissance

Although Brown's broadcast stories caused outrage in Orkney and beyond, there were others outside Orkney who placed his work in a broader context, seeing him as part of a new tradition, the Scottish Literary Renaissance. As Brown was reinventing himself as a writer, and becoming more assured, Scottish literature was going through a similar process.

His inclusion in two important anthologies, while three more at the planning or printing stage were being publicised, gave wider currency to Brown's poetry. More than this, it confirmed him as one of the writers who had 'added their measure to the harvest of the twentieth century Scottish Renaissance'.[18] The most succinct statement of how the connotations of 'literary renaissance' had evolved since Lindsay's original influential selection (1946) was provided in his Preface to the revised second edition (1966):

> This title, bestowed by a Frenchman, has touched off a great deal of that sterile, bitter controversy in which my compatriots seem both to delight and to excel. Originally, it implied close association with efforts to revive and strengthen Lallans and Gaelic. During the past twenty years, however, it has taken on a wider significance . . . the work . . . reflects a variety of experience and an integrity of expression which enable it to stand comparison with the output of any previous period of Scottish literature. These qualities . . . are what constitute the real Scottish Renaissance.

Brown's language in the seven poems Lindsay chose for the anthology confirmed critics' impression that Brown was not part of the Lallans (writing in the Scots dialect) movement, although he did write in dialect in the mid-1950s. He had contributed poems in Lallans to the

Glasgow Herald and employed native Orcadian words and syntax to provide character in his short stories.

In another anthology, also aiming to characterise the renaissance, George Bruce took a different view. While Lindsay identified key features as 'variety of experience and integrity of expression', Bruce went further, arguing that the 'new poetry' was shaping a new tradition and a new identity. Focusing on 'the problem' of Scottish poets writing in English, he argued that 'Theirs was more a question of achieving an identity.'[19]

Later, there were those who argued that there had been no 'renaissance': 'Forget about renaissances. They end up as mannerism, where style is more important than content and everything is packaged up into designed themes. The strength of today's Scottish poetry is in its diversity.'[20]

Inclusion in several other anthologies indicated that Brown's critical place in the Scottish literary scene was assured. His growing confidence could be seen in his experiments in new forms. He had always been interested in poetic form, an interest that would continue throughout his life, but at this time he was about to try his first novel.

Conclusion

The story of Brown's becoming a writer is one of him reinventing himself and his community. He constructed a world for himself to live and write in, an enormous imaginative undertaking that brought its own stresses and strains, some of which were evident in the stridency of his early journalism and perhaps can still be heard in his anti-progress writings from this time.

There was also the sheer labour of writing poetry, such as 'From Stone to Thorn', which he thought his best poem, first included in *An Orkney Tapestry*: 'I always think of it with affection, because I had an almighty struggle with it; and it seems as it stands to distil all my thoughts about life and time that appear in more scattered form else-where in my writings.'[21] Given this artistic priority, it is not surprising that, at this middle period of his writing life, he should have veered from poetry to fiction and back again.

Brown's version of Orkney's history and legend was skewed towards his own preoccupations, and there was sometimes a sense of straining to render an event or character within an overarching framework or pattern. There may, for example, be too many Stations of the Cross poems for some readers. Yet, this is not simple repetition; instead, looking over the body of Brown's work up to this point, there is an impression of an intense seeking, striving and struggling to carve credible statements out of the raw material of life in Orkney.

When Brown discussed his work with scholars and students, awkward and uncomfortable though he felt in these conversations, he revealed what could be taken as the philosophical underpinnings of his writing:

> I think that the work of some writers is shaped by a few over-mastering images. One image I discovered when I was just beginning to write stories and poems and was having some trouble sorting out important matters from trivial matters was that part of the gospel where Christ speaks of man's life as a seed cast into a furrow. Unless the seed dies in the darkness and silence, new life cannot spring from it – the shoot, the ear, the full corn in the ear, and finally the fragrant bread set on the tables of hungry folk. That image seemed to illuminate the whole of life for me.[22]

'Unless the seed dies' seems to convey a purely religious theme, but it also shows Brown finding meaning in darkness and death – and perhaps even in depression – within the scheme of things. He continued to counterpoint pagan and natural rhythms and stories with Christian ones. Religious symbols played a stronger role in his writing, yet they too became a scaffolding within which he could continue his narrative experiments in poetry and prose.

Perhaps most interesting was Brown's fascination with the concept of the necessary death, the destruction of a community or individual, that is required for life to continue. Both types of destruction were deployed in the next phase of his writing: in his novels *Greenvoe* and *Magnus* the idea was given fuller, more contemporary and shocking treatment.

7

Confronting the Twentieth Century:
Ruin and Regeneration
1970–74

Introduction

> Our own century has brought its own confrontation and challenges:
> two world wars which have changed the whole status and outlook of
> the islanders; the discovery of oil in the North Sea; the threat, so vivid
> a decade ago, of uranium mining. My novel, *Greenvoe*, deals tentatively
> with such threats.[1]

This is a clear statement of the 'confrontation and challenges' Brown
faced up to in his writing during this period: world war, the discovery
of oil, the threat of uranium mining in Orkney and the general,
constant threat of nuclear holocaust produced darker writing, in
which the threats were no longer general and abstract but specific, real
and close to home. He engaged with these forces right up to the end
of his life, writing two poems about uranium that were later published
in *Travellers* (2001).

His was not simply a sense of personal threat; the scale and scope
of the threat were enlarged. This was not just the anti-progress
rant that we have come to expect, but a deeper study of whole
communities under threat. For example, his subject in this
period was not only the trial by fire of a witch, but the trial by fire of
whole communities. The very idea of community was itself
at risk.

There were threats from outside Orkney, which, as always, had its
'intrusions',[2] but these were of a different order. The security of
knowing who's who, what's going to happen, the patterns of events,
the cycles of the seasons and so on were replaced by massive uncer-
tainties. The twentieth-century threats, in Brown's view, had the
capacity to destroy the islands, not just theoretically or artistically, but

literally. He felt that it was his task to revive fading patterns, cycles and stories in the face of such threats.

There was the on-going degradation of culture. Brown's original argument that 'Orkney has no culture' evolved into the view that any culture, indeed all culture, would be swept away by new technologies, which had, he argued, already 'diluted our identity'.[3] A deep ambivalence towards technology remained in Brown's writing, injecting tension, as long as he remained divided about it. Given the strength of his views it is perhaps surprising that he said he addressed these issues 'tentatively' in his novel *Greenvoe* (1972). Perhaps this indicates lack of confidence, his not feeling quite at home with twentieth-century subjects, or perhaps he was uncertain that his attempts to show the rejuvenation of community – in spite of modern threats – would be convincing. Perhaps he did not want to seem to be overstating the problem. In any case, the twentieth century was a new subject for him and *Greenvoe* was his first novel. Such a huge undertaking indicates growing confidence.

At the same time he was consolidating an earlier treatment of his idea of 'black pentecostal fire' – with its religious overtones – from *Fishermen with Ploughs*, which still interested him as late as 1983, when he wrote the poem 'The Black Horseman'.[4] This also continues the subject of 'Dead Fires', the gradual disintegration of a rural community. The threats were not unique to Orkney or to the twentieth century. Brown was good at making connections and seeing parallels, across time, that are often shocking.

At this point in his career Brown could be seen as quite deliberately re-establishing the patterns that were in danger of being lost for ever. This is no idealised bonding or binding; the communities he described were by no means uniformly harmonious, but they had held together. In his writing at this time, characters often go their separate ways after a crisis has passed. There is no absolute reassimilation into the community; many leave it. Perhaps, on one level, Brown realised – and wanted to express – that this was historically the role of Orkney, situated between Scotland and Norway.

Brown countered the threats with ritual, sacrifice, symbol, service and ceremony. Destruction of community was itself part of a pattern.

This was no longer just a rant against 'progress'; it was more complex than that. Looking back over his writing from this time, we can see that it was a constant theme. There were constant threats.

Some readers will see Brown's vision of apocalyptic futures as absurd or overstated; for others, what he feared for humanity is bound to have a certain resonance in their time and place. Some will argue that it remains to be seen whether or not the ruin he envisaged for us – cultural or otherwise – does, in fact, occur; others will argue that some of what Brown feared has already occurred. Yet it was not Brown's intention to prophesy; he responded imaginatively to both subtle and dramatic social change going on around him.

Biographical notes: 1970–74 (aged 49–53)

From this point on Brown produced an increasing number of publications, and with these came a series of literary awards and prizes. They brought comparative financial security and freedom from compulsion to stay in Orkney: Arts Council Grant for Poetry (1965) for *The Year of the Whale*, Society of Authors Travel Award (1968), Scottish Arts Council Literature Prize (1969) for *A Time to Keep*, Katherine Mansfield Short Story Prize (1971) – with which he bought a radio[5] – and the Scottish Arts Council fiction prize of £1,000 for *Greenvoe* in 1972. He was awarded the OBE in 1974. He was therefore not only beginning to make a living as a writer but now had credibility as a writer, both in Scotland and beyond. In an interview in 1972 he said that these prizes would help him to live and write in Orkney.

Momentum was growing in the Scottish Literary Renaissance and Brown had an established place in this new tradition. For some years he had increasing contact with other successful writers who recognised the quality of his writing. Yet Brown's growing success and increasing published output would not have provided much to live on. As he himself put it, you 'couldn't keep a cat on what you make out of poetry'.[6] Brown's friends – and our own observations – revealed that he continued with the frugal lifestyle that he had been used to, although he was financially more secure. He still suffered from depression.

What he did have was sufficient financial security and leisure to consider larger works. Norah Smallwood, editor at the Hogarth Press, suggested that he write a novel. His positive response might, in part, have been motivated by the all-too-worldly purpose of raising more funds to live on.

While he was becoming more established as a writer, and beginning to make some income from writing, Brown was still exploring and confronting. In much of his work, his new focus was the twentieth century itself, not just in Orkney but universally.

'Long-distance running': the first novel, *Greenvoe*

Brown's letters show his gradual move towards the novel, with the encouragement of his publisher. In more recent conversations Brown revealed that he had been looking for a larger canvas for his writing. In October 1967 he wrote to Willa Muir that he was 'at a loose end . . . turning in the vacuum looking for something new to do. Maybe a novel.' In another letter to her on 21 June 1969, he wrote that Norah Smallwood had suggested he try writing a novel, although at the time he did not think he was capable of such 'long-distance running'.[7] In the same letter he gave Willa Muir an outline of his first novel: one week in Orkney, how the inhabitants react to each other, how the people of a village called Greenvoe are both 'innocent and guilty', an initiation, 'a very ancient brutal beautiful ceremony'.

His first novel was a new departure. The longer short stories 'A Calendar of Love', 'A Time to Keep', 'Celia' – the last two occupying sixty-two pages – can be seen as a kind of transition between his work in that form and the longer, more complex structure of the novel.

Greenvoe appears, from his letters, to have been written quickly. He started it in the summer of 1969. Within six months, on 7 December, he was well into it. By early March 1970 he wrote that he was producing a plodding thousand words a day. A week later he was enjoying it much more. By 21 March he was revising, hoping for 'insight to recognise the bad bits and the skill and courage to remove them'. By 4 April, a couple of weeks later, he had 100,000 words and was, again, revising in May 1970. The next year chapter one, in almost its final form, was published in *Scottish International*.[8] The completed novel was published on 24 May 1972. Most of it appears to have been written between the summers of 1969 and 1970, and he himself said that it took him about a year to write.

In this novel an island clearly resembling contemporary Orkney has degenerated into a run-down community. As the novel starts the seeds of its disintegration are well established. The message seems to be that someone needs to take the island in hand. Perhaps Brown chose this subject because he himself, having made the journey from 'Orkney has no culture' to Orkney as his subject, had exhausted his own well of inspiration and energy. Having mined Orkney for his writing, he now turned his attention to the subject of exploited small communities. What role could they have in contemporary times? How would they be brought into the twentieth century? What changes had to occur for this to work?

Then there was the challenge of what was, for Brown, a new form:

> In *Greenvoe* I am attempting to work on a larger scale than hitherto. This novel has no real plot in the usual sense. It looks at the lives of about a dozen people in a small village within a brief span of time. Every character in Greenvoe – Greenvoe is the name of the fishing village I am writing about – has his own story in the sense that a separate short story could have been written about him, but he is also part of the larger story of the community. The problem was to interweave all these stories into an acceptable, harmonious and meaningful pattern, before, as happens in *Greenvoe*, the pattern is torn forever.[9]

He used multiple viewpoints and narrations, interpolations, flashbacks, interior monologues, saga style, letters, fragments of a historical novel, archaic religious language, legal writing and interrogation to convey the many different lives in the island community. What brings them all together is the threat of destruction by some nameless project.

The action of the novel covers a week in the community's life, with a wide range of characters and numerous sub-plots, before the last scene, set ten years after evacuation of the island. Characterisation is laid down in layers, as people are introduced from different angles and in different voices by means of style shifts and imagery. The scene is set by two opening paragraphs, describing a landscape whose stillness is disrupted by the first character to appear as dawn breaks:

> Slowly the night shadow passed from the island and the Sound. In the village of Greenvoe light burned in the windows of three fishermen's cottages above the pier.
>
> A small dark knotted man came out of one of the doors. He picked up a half-dozen lobster creels from the white wall and carried them across to the pier and down a few stone steps. A motor-boat called the *Ellen* was tied up there. Bert Kerston stowed his creels on board. He untied the *Ellen* and pushed off. He swung the starting handle. The *Ellen* kicked and coughed into life. Her bow tore the quiet water apart.

This first description of Bert Kerston captures his daily routine, cleverly conveying both the almost ritualistic actions, and the sense of pent-up force of the 'small dark knotted man'. We have no sense, as yet, of the character's thoughts or feelings, just hints from his appearance. From the quiet opening, there is a swift movement to 'tore the quiet water apart', which strikes an ominous note. This, in turn, makes us wonder about that 'night shadow' in the first line: is that ominous too? It suggests the safety of night, the cycle of day and night, but also the threat of metaphorical darkness or unidentified menace.

The story continues with new characters appearing on almost every page. Intersections between characters are then rapidly drawn, as if they cannot move without running over each other's tracks. For example, one character picks up the cigarette stub dropped by another. This may seem a trivial example, but the effect is almost claustrophobic. It can also be comic, an ironic commentary on the previous scene. In addition, even when characters are not visiting the village shop, the shopkeeper metaphorically brings them all there, when she gossips about them.

As the chapter progresses, the characters are more fully developed by the use of prose that echoes their own voices, either external or internal, or both. An effective example of this technique is the first appearance of Timmy Folster:

Timmy Folster emerged, as he always did since the burning, through the window. He ambled towards the pier. He bent down and picked up a cigarette end that Ivan Westray had dropped and put it in his pocket. He sat down on a soap box outside the general store and poked the tobacco from three cigarette ends into a pipe. He spoke to himself amiably all the time. 'Timmy's a good boy. Timmy never did harm to a living soul. They can't put Timmy in the poorhouse. Timmy can look after himself. Timmy's no fool. Timmy knows a thing or two. He does so.'[10]

Five sentences beginning 'Timmy' convey the character through his internal monologues, recited aloud, and in free indirect speech: the characters in *Greenvoe* are often described in the third person, but with the language they would use in their own speech. In choosing this modernist technique, perhaps more familiar to readers of Virginia Woolf and James Joyce, Brown had an ideal method of combining different viewpoints and styles. For example, the words 'put it in his pocket' convey the character's childlike mentality, as does Timmy's use of the third person.

This image of Timmy contrasts sharply with the profile of him, written by an outsider, on an index card discovered much later in the novel:

FOLSTER, Timothy John. b. 21/7/17. 5' 4" 104lb. Eyes blue. Hair dark brown. Bachelor. Third (only surviving) issue of John and Mary-Ann (*née* Linklater) Folster, Greenvoe: both deceased. No distinguishing physical characteristics. A casual harvester on farms, a casual beachcomber (we find that he has never declared any flotsam or jetsam to the relevant authorities). In receipt of state assistance. Education: Greenvoe Primary School ad age 14. Property – one house 'Sea View,' village of Greenvoe; in poor condition consequent on a fire 1/12/65; value approx. £10. Relatives: one first cousin (male) once removed, believed to be in Queensland, Australia, emigrated 6/7/23. Medical note: occasional methylated spirit drinker. Winter bronchitis. General health surprisingly good all things considered, possibly on account of a sufficient diet of greens, fish, seaweed, and an open-air life. Black Star potential (ex ten) Nil.[11]

Some characters seem to be based on real Orcadians, people whom Brown knew. For example, the character of Timmy brings to mind an inhabitant of Stromness, whose house still stands derelict after a fire. Others were based on, or seem to be composites of, real people, a conjecture confirmed by Brown's admissions in conversation. In 1995 he mentioned them by name, quickly adding that he had to be very careful when drawing on local people for his characters. He also made efforts to conceal identities by changing details.

These similarities go some way towards refuting the accusation that *Greenvoe* is a pastiche of Dylan Thomas's *Under Milk Wood*, a link made by several reviewers on the publication of Brown's novel. Brown illustrated his method in conversation on 29 February, 1996: 'Timmy [Folster] was modelled on a man Mansie [substitute name], who lived oot the town – more up towards the Loons way. And one day the local Councillor came by and said to Mansie, "It's a fine day for a run in the car, Mansie." Mansie thought that was a grand idea, so off they went in the car. And they got to Kirkwall, and, as happens in *Greenvoe*, they got to this place and the Councillor said, "Isn't this a grand house? Let's go in for a cup of tea!" And Mansie thought this was a *splendid* idea. They went in and he never came oot again . . .' At any rate, Brown said that he had no thoughts of Thomas's work as he was writing *Greenvoe*. The potential influence of Thomas must be explored further elsewhere, but it is important to remember that *Greenvoe* grew out of Brown's earlier work, both his preoccupations with Orkney's 'culture', the themes and subjects of his poetry and short stories and his observation of life around him.

Brown's use of real people was not about exposing the great and the good in his community to public scrutiny – always risky while he lived there – but perhaps about his curiosity regarding their lives. He was interested in pushing people he knew into a particular situation imaginatively, and exploring their reactions, while weaving in what appear to be issues arising from his concerns about his parents and, perhaps, their concerns about him. There was also his enduring sense of unease at the impact of the outside world on small communities. In the novel he was able to explore different characters' different reactions to potential threat.

Perspectives on the village in *Greenvoe* include those of Mrs Olive Evie, the inquisitive shopkeeper; Johnny, the Indian seller of silk goods; Skarf, the local, idiosyncratic historian; the unnamed outsider working for Project Black Star. There are also touches of humour, such as the description of an upper-class couple talking to each other as if they were 'shouting into a gale'. The Skarf's history of Greenvoe is itself full of different views on the life of the village, since his version of history is coloured by socio-political perspectives. Local historian, chronicler, Marxist, he fills in the history of the island, his 'arrogant slanted rigmarole' or imaginative recreation, inviting obvious comparison with Brown himself, even to the asterisk placed at the end of a day's writing, one of Brown's writing rituals.

The most interesting, and arguably the key, character in *Greenvoe* is Mrs McKee, suddenly introduced in the passage below, which appears with no explanation. Beginning with the peaceful atmosphere of the village, it shifts to her disturbed interior world; deploying a stream-of-consciousness technique similar to Virginia Woolf's, the text slips suddenly into her internal voice:

> Afternoon was always the quietest time in the village. The fishermen were still at sea. The crofters had not yet unyoked. There was little sound in Greenvoe on a summer afternoon but the murmur of multiplication tables through the tall school window, and the drone of bluebottles among Mr Joseph Evie's confectionery, and the lapping of water against the pier.
>
> In the manse parlour old Mrs McKee knew without a shadow of a doubt that with her it was once more the season of assize. On every bright and dark wind they came, her accusers, four times a year; they gathered in the manse of Hellya to inquire into certain hidden events of her life. The assize lasted for many days and generally covered the same ground, though occasionally new material would be led that she had entirely forgotten about . . . the tribunal was secret; nobody in the village or island knew about it but herself, not even her son Simon who was the parish minister; though Simon shrewdly guessed, she felt sure, that something preoccupied his mother sorely on such occasions; and moreover – this was very strange – the assize usually assembled when Simon was bearing or was about to bear his own little private cross.

As with the opening paragraph of the book, the opening tone of a quiet, sleepy village quickly becomes much darker. What is startling is how real this 'assize' is to Mrs McKee. The silence and peace of the village accentuate the pathos of her private, imagined sufferings. Then there is her tragic reflection on how beautiful the day is, although she is not free to enjoy it. Exactly what caused her mental disturbance is hinted at: she feels guilty for having given her son tonic wine when he was ill as a child, although this explanation is not provided until much later in the novel, leaving us wondering why she torments herself. What is clear is that she feels that she deserves her interrogations.

She has committed many minor misdemeanours, that she recalls, or imagines: a china teapot that did not belong to her being packed among her belongings in error. The detail in the Mrs McKee sections shows her almost being interrogated by silence; she punctuates her silences with interrogations. Each interrogator probes a different misdemeanour:

> There was a whole team of accusers, and it gave her pleasure to recognize their distinctive turns of phrase and the rhythms of their speaking (though some of them no doubt were very unpleasant dangerous persons indeed). It was all too plain what their purpose was: they wished to nip her as soon as possible from the tree of living, to gather her for good and all among ancient shadows and memories; and she was equally determined not to go until such time as the finger of God stroked her leaf from the branch.

The 'pleasure' she takes in her interrogation is not a good sign. That her interrogations parallel Simon's drinking bouts tells us more about their origins than she herself can know. Her individual interrogators have their own voices:

> Who would today's prosecutor be? She waited. A voice at the edge of the shadows began to speak. It was the advocate with the thin precise gnat-like voice who invariably dealt with her financial and other material misdemeanours. She did not like him, he was mean and trivial. She prepared herself for a rather wearisome afternoon.

Her masochistic self-flagellation is convincing as a psychosis. Her sections of the novel occupy a disproportionate amount of space, far more than any of the other characters. Moreover, these sections are made up of much longer paragraphs, as if her account runs out of control. Indeed, Brown did reveal, in conversation, that this is exactly what happened as he wrote: the character 'took over'. Yet the novel is well structured. Mrs McKee's physical decline is paralleled by her psychological deterioration, which in turn parallels the decline of the life of the village and the relationships between the villagers. All experience a form of 'trial' appropriate to their perceived failings.

The stranger who comes to the village in a sense operates in the same way as Mrs McKee's accusers, picking off the people one by one in his assessments, just as they pick off her 'sins' one after the other. Neither interrogators nor the stranger show compassion for their 'victims'. It is their job to act this way. It is as if they simply arrive at the right time to exploit the terrors, horrors and pernicious histories of the villagers. The inadequacies that Brown had for years been identifying in Orkney society are here represented in the characters' worlds, both internal and external. These deficiencies and flaws make the villagers vulnerable to outside exploitation and internal suffering. The novel is a penetrating reflection on the neurosis of a certain form of small community life. This is, perhaps, why Brown allowed Mrs McKee to take over almost a third of the book. He was confronting issues which were crucial to him in his society and his life. What is not made clear – and this is very effective – is whether Mrs McKee's interrogators forced themselves on her; did 'silence' generate them, or did she cultivate them herself? At times, she seems to be engaged in a creative process, letting her imagination run on to new and familiar variations, like Brown himself.

There is a clever counterpoint to Mrs McKee's interactions with other characters. For example, Johnny's commentary gives an outsider's view of her behaviour:

> Never have I felt the pressure of so many earth-bound preying ungenerous spirits. The room crepitates with them. They are offended with me – I have disturbed their communion with this gentle frightened old lady . . .
>
> What is required in this room is exorcism. What is needed is some

pure blessed deliberate ritual to rid this old woman of her ghosts. They feast on her flesh. They drink her blood, obscenely, like black bats. What can one Indian boy do in ten minutes? I am not a holy man.

It is tempting to make a biographical reading of Mrs McKee: she was almost exactly the same age as Brown's mother when she married. She too was a happy, sociable, outgoing person, but perhaps, in Brown's eyes, stifled by her husband's depression. Or was Brown guilty that he himself had been, in some way, a 'burden' to her? He described his drunken antics and subsequent shame at his behaviour towards her in an essay, 'Mary Jane Mackay – 1891–1967 (A Memoir)'.[12] He also wrote about the deterioration of her mind, again recalling Mrs McKee. His bereavement seems to have been a difficult, drawn-out, disturbing process, and it could be that it was his mother's personality and her illness, together with his guilt and grief, that stretched Mrs McKee's sections till they dominated *Greenvoe*.

In an unpublished autobiographical essay, Brown described a Christmas holiday (probably 1959): after an unpleasant evening in an Edinburgh flat, drunk and jealous, he flew home to Orkney the next day, where his mother was waiting for him, with a meal ready; he came home drunk, fell asleep on the landing at the top of the stairs, woke up in the middle of the night, threw his books downstairs, and finally fell after them, breaking his ribs. The following day brought 'that strange clarity that a bad hangover brings' and the fear that he had inherited his father's chronic depression: 'The melancholy fell on him and lasted for days. It was a depression that had nothing to do with hangovers. Those agonising anxieties had been there from childhood on. Sometimes they could be terrible. This midwinter melancholy was mild and fleeting.'[13]

Brown felt that he had experienced the condition he inflicted on Mrs McKee, but he also felt guilt at how his mother must have suffered with her depressive husband and son.

Although it was not published in the novel, Brown did write an 'index card' for Mrs McKee:

MCKEE, Elizabeth. b. 4/6/1899. 5' 2". 105lb. Eyes hazel. Hair silver-gray. Appendix operation scar (op 3/9/1912). Widow of Alan Charles McKee, d 21/2/1933. Elder child (2d.) of William Gladstone Alder, auctioneer, Edinburgh, and Thomasina (*née* Dunbar) Alder: both deceased. Semi-retired; house-keeper to Rev. Simon McKee (q.v.), minister of religion, (C. of S.) parish of Hellya. Address: The Manse, Greenvoe. Private income (insurances, investments, retirement pension). Education: Jean Dalloway's school for girls, Edinburgh, ad 17. M. Alan Charles McKee 8/5/1918. Issue: one son, Simon McK. Health: (a) Physical – anaemic; slight occ. Rheumatism left hip, l. shoulder; slight deafness r. ear (wax accumulation) (b) Mental – manic-depressive, subject to severe recurrent delusions, but no hospitalisation or treatment. Black Star potential: Nil.

Brown's typescript, showing his many corrections, suggests that while he wrote very quickly he revised carefully. Like the index cards on the other characters, this reductive snapshot is chilling, impersonal, almost an assault. The characters' weaknesses are exposed in the assessment of their suitability for the project; any strengths are diminished in the process. There is a touch of Orwell about the tone.

The non-specific nature of the Black Star Project is in some ways stronger than the more precise critique of the arrival of the wireless set in a similar community in the earlier short story which first appeared as 'The Evil Voice in Tronvik'. Although the threat is undefined in *Greenvoe*, it is all the more ominous. If we see a link between the writing and the life, we might take the mysterious dark force as an externalisation of depression. Brown's early frustrations as a writer were associated with Orkney; his later works were criticised for being fixed on Orkney; and his depression was inherited from his father. Perhaps Black Star is an image of these potentially destructive forces.

At the end of each chapter Brown introduced the ritual of the Horseman's Word, combining Christian and pagan imagery. It is a structural device, echoing elements of each chapter, yet starkly different in style from any of them. The fact that it is practised by men from the village of Greenvoe implies continuity and faith in the ancient ritual. As the village sleeps, in the remote privacy of the Bu farm another facet of the life of the community is revealed:

> Inside the stable of The Bu farm three miles away, Tammag Brown of the Glebe and Leonard Isbister of Isbister pushed the great door shut and bolted it. Dod Corrigall of Skaill and Andrew Hoy of Rossiter were helping young Hector Anderson off with his jacket. 'I bet,' said Dod Corrigall of Skaill, 'thu would rather be having a bonny lass to take thee claes off.' Andrew Hoy laughed. Sandy Manson of Blink-bonny opened a battered brown suitcase and took out a parchment, a horse-shoe, a black blindfold, a lantern, a half-dozen sackcloth sashes and a long apron. He hung the horse-shoe on a nail at the east wall of the barn . . .
>
> 'I'll thank you all,' said the old man, 'to behave as solemn as if you were in a kirk.' He spread over a stall the master's regalia – an apron crudely stitched with yellow wool in the form of a blazing sun. The other men put their sashes on; a more modest decoration, plough and sickle and quern stitched with black and grey wool.

Their activities demonstrate respect for ancient tradition. The Horsemen's ritual dress has agricultural symbolism, as does the ceremony, with its six rites, in the initiation of a novice. Brown himself said that the men were based on real people, and there is evidence that the ritual was practised in Orkney,[14] but Brown was sure that none of them would be able to recognise themselves.[15]

Each section takes us further into the rite, until, in the last chapter, seven figures recognisable as inhabitants of Greenvoe, ten years previously, complete the ceremony, having broken into the fenced-off island. The completion of the ritual is ambiguous, expressing celebration, valediction and regeneration:

> 'There is nothing,' said the leader of the Master Horsemen. 'There is darkness. There is silence. There is a silence beyond silence.'
>
> A long low wail trembled on their lips.
>
> In the north-east a little colour seeped along the gray of the horizon – a tarnish of yellow, jet, a flush of rose. The sea made instant flawless response. The colours multiplied.
>
> The Lord of the Harvest took the black cloth from the niche where

the horse-shoe had been secreted. The horse-shoe had vanished. In its place was a loaf and a bottle.

The Master Horseman raised the Harvester to his feet. They put a white cloak over his shoulders. They brought him over to the niche where the whisky and the bread stood.

Slowly the sun heaved itself clear of the sea. The cliff below was alive with the stir and cry of birds. The sea moved and flung glories of light over Quoylay and Hrossay and Hellya . . . The smell of the earth came to them in the first wind of morning, from the imprisoned fields of the island; and the fence could not keep it back.

The horse-shoe is gone and in its place there is a loaf of bread and a bottle, suggesting Christian symbolism has replaced pagan rite. The word 'Resurrection' has the same associations. The ritual consists of eating and drinking together. The people who were expelled from their homes, effectively ending the ritual, have rebelled against the bureaucracy that kept them dispersed for a decade. Fittingly, they have chosen for this restoration of, perhaps, settlement and the affirmation of their faith in 'Resurrection', the site where their earliest ancestors fortified themselves against attacks from the sea.

Given that the village of Greenvoe was destroyed, the ritual carries extra resonance: is it possible for these men to return, or does their return merely remind us of the faith that binds them together? The ritual's survival is reassuring:

The Lord of the Harvest raised his hands. 'We have brought light and blessing to the kingdom of winter,' he said, 'however long it endures, that kingdom, a night or a season or a thousand ages. The word has been found. Now we will eat and drink together and be glad.'
The sun rose. The stones were warm. They broke the bread.

Perhaps the ritual has meaning beyond the place, Greenvoe; perhaps it is more important than the place itself. Larger forces are at work than the industrial project or its bureaucracy. Larger forces are at work in the minds of these men, since they make such efforts to return to complete the ritual. Their ritualistic speech, which might seem incongruous when it first appears at the end of Chapter One, acquires dignity and meaning in this last scene.

There are echoes of the other characters, no longer in Greenvoe, in the final scene: 'rose' reminds us of Alice Voar, 'silence' reminds us of Mrs McKee's and the description of the sea takes us back to the opening of the novel. Silence is again used as a symbol. The importance of the idea of silence to Brown continues to appear in his writing and in his writing about writing:

> I think the only perfect poem or piece of music is pure silence, and a very good poem or a very good piece of music approaches this silence. But the silence that comes after a good poem or a good piece of music is quite different from the silence that went before it. The silence which follows a beautiful piece of music or poem is richer and more perfect – something towards which the music or poem aspires but never quite achieves.[16]

Is it the state of mind of the listener – who has just heard a good poem – that Brown is trying to capture? Does it mean peace, appreciation, recognition, insight? Or perhaps what Brown was expressing is a renewed sensation of solitude:

> *On the one hand you are concerned with the Pool of Silence and the interrogation of silence, and on the other hand you are concerned with the relationship. How do you see the interplay between the two?*
>
> Of course there must be relationships because life wouldn't continue without them, but all relationships and all words end in solitude and in silence. I am interested in human relationships, but in the end it's the solitude which is my destination. I am trying to say something which is almost impossible to say. I cannot explain silence in words.[17]

In a book that concerns itself so much with people and their interactions, the ending towards which Brown moves *Greenvoe* is still the idea of silence. Where Brown's many other expressions of the idea of silence seem to mean the failure of artistic expression to capture or improve on the essence of the artist's subject, in this interview and in *Greenvoe* the idea seems more positive. This silence brings a self-consciousness that is pleasurable, a feeling of being more alive and an affirmation of identity.

the silent chorus

meekly *back them* and crept up the stairs.
When the mother and sister *went* into his
room, cautiously, ten minutes later, Jock
lay in a cold exhausted sleep.

An hour before breakfast he was in
Sunniva's room. "Please", he said in the
small bleak voice *she knew* whenever he
wanted something. "I haven't done the
geography lesson, Sunniva. I forgot. Can I
copy yours? Please. Miss Willes, she'll
kill me if I turn up again with a blank
jotter. You can have my Saturday penny,
Sunniva. Oh, thanks, Sunniva *will you*. You're the
only one in the whole world, Sunniva,
that likes me — you are. I know it" *but you forgot it.*
"Tomorrow's Saturday", said Sunniva. "Go back to
bed, Jock. Don't worry".

"A classic case of Loss of
Memory", said Dr MacRobert. "Nothing to
worry about. He'll be all right."

But the island children greeted Jock
on the Monday morning like a friend who
had come back from a long exile : but
their respect and awe only lasted till
the dinner bell.

Jock had 2 more years of school. *
All that time he was a model
pupil. 'Couldn't wish for better', said
Miss Graystone.
He was more of a loner than
ever. No more football — no more
cowboys — and — Indians with the other
boys. He took long lonely walks over the

hill to the desolate part of the
island. There the tinkers saw him
more than once sitting on a stone,
interrogating silence

The conclusion of Part IV of *Fergus/Tales of a Bad Boy*, an unpublished
short story sequence (1977–86), 1978, in which Brown writes of
'interrogating silence'.

Brown's autobiography, *For the Islands I Sing*, has six pages on *Greenvoe* and *Magnus*. That Mrs McKee is central to the novel is clear; Brown suggested that at some level he identified with his character: 'Occasionally, over a glass of whisky, I take *Greenvoe* off the bookshelf and commune for half an hour with my friend Mrs McKee. She is a consolation. We have things we can say to one another.'

There may be a glimpse of what Brown was aiming to achieve in *Greenvoe* in a review of David Vogel's *The Dark Gate* which he wrote in 1977: 'There is no hint in this book that outside the enchanted gate all the monsters and devils of the twentieth century were prowling.'[18]

'Spectacular sacrifice'

The confidence and financial boost generated by *Greenvoe*'s success may have been a factor in Brown's decision to write a second novel a year later. Yet, a strong argument can be made for *Magnus* (1973) being the novel Brown had been contemplating for many years, given his earlier treatments of Saint Magnus's story described in Chapter Two and in his note at the start of the novel:

> Readers of *An Orkney Tapestry* may notice that the two old tinkers of the 'Martyr' chapter appear, more full-fleshed, in this novel. Those who saw, in Orkney in August 1972, the play *The Loom of Light*, written for the St Magnus Cathedral Restoration Fund, may also notice certain resemblances.

Magnus is as technically impressive as *Greenvoe*. Brown himself judged that his second novel was superior to his first, although he came to acknowledge that this view was not shared by most critics. His vision of events and values in twelfth-century Orkney is compelling, but his main achievement was setting these in contexts which resonate with modern readers: '. . . it occurred to me that the whole story would strike a modern reader as remote and unconnected with our situation in the twentieth century . . . The life and death of Magnus must therefore be shown to be contemporary, and to have a resonance in the twentieth century.'[19]

While unity of inspiration is provided by the focus on Magnus – the man of peace embroiled in civil war – Brown's variety of narrative method demonstrates the relevance of the Magnus-Hakon story to convulsions in societies remote from them in time and place. Far from being a compilation of previous pieces, as Brown's prefatory note suggested, the novel is a coherent indictment of political ambition and 'necessity'.

The book begins and ends with the common people, whose faith in their sense of community receives many shocks. Their suffering, resilience and dependence on personal relationships become a kind of comment on events. Their aristocratic cousins, on the other hand, regularly split the island's loyalties, and their constant interruptions of the agricultural rhythm by which the peasants and tinkers live, lower the people's morale. Brown's account of the earls' supporters ruining the crofters' patiently cultivated fields and, hence, destroying their attempts to sink roots and build a community, is a striking illustration of the need for *someone* to take Orkney in hand. In this, *Magnus* develops the themes of *Greenvoe*, but there is no prospect of a peaceful end to the competition between two Orkney earls.

One of the most dramatic moments in Brown's fiction occurs in Chapter Seven, 'The Killing', where an abrupt, unannounced time-shift creates a striking modernisation of the killing of Magnus, updated to the context of a Nazi concentration camp, a connection that was quite deliberate: 'The truth must be that such incidents are not isolated casual happenings in time, but are repetitions of some archetypal pattern.'[20] The narrative voice also changes, passing to Lifolf, the cook, an unsophisticated man who distances himself from the atrocities of war going on around him, but who is forced to execute Magnus.

'The Killing' chapter is further broken up by style shifts, from saga style to modern journalese and back to saga style. The chapter opens with the arrival of the Viking ships at Egilsay and the prospect of battle between Magnus's and Hakon's men:

> I must tell now concerning the jarl Hakon Paul's son, how he summoned about him an host, and set them in eight war-hungry ships. Then those tryst-men heard a great boast, how that from the meeting in Egil's Isle but one jarl would fare him home at sunset, and that not Magnus. A death-lust on listening faces about the mast, a weaving of warped words. Sigurd and Sighvat were the blackest mouths in all that hell-parle.

There follows description of this twelfth-century setting in a modern style:

> There had been little sleep for Earl Magnus the previous night and now, with the regular strike of the oars and the gentle onset of the ship through the firth, he began to be drowsy . . . Earl Magnus dropped his head on his chest and yielded to the images that besieged his consciousness (but not for a moment did he cease to hear the swiltering of water and the grunts of the oarsmen as they dug the sea and flung the sklintering flashing blades behind them).

Then there is the jarring journalese of a modern media report:

> Rumours of new dramatic developments in the peace confrontation between the Paulson faction and the Erlendson faction have been coming from this lonely isle all through Sunday night and this morning. The parties themselves are maintaining strict secrecy, but that something unexpected has happened is beyond doubt. There is a black-out of news. Neither of the parties is willing to give anything away. Through interviews with crofters and fishermen and their wives we have been able to build up a fairly definite picture.

This is followed by description, reflection and meditation, full of abstractions, including an authorial voice mediating the character's thoughts:

> The end and the beginning. All time was gathered up into that ritual half-hour, the entire history of mankind, as well as the events that have not yet happened as the things recorded in chronicles and sagas. That is to say, history both repeats itself and does not repeat itself.

The narrative shifts back to twelfth-century setting, in reported speech that creates a distance from the events:

> This was what had happened. The previous Thursday night they had all sat down together in Earl Hakon Paulson's Hall in Orphir to formulate some kind of an agenda for the business in Egilsay the following Monday: more words, words, words. Havard Gunison wanted this done, wanted that said, wanted an emphasis here and a modification there. He, Sigurd Kalison, had felt, sitting there at that table, a deep stir of revulsion. Would the palaver never end, either here in Egilsay or in kingdom come?

The word 'palaver' conveys weariness with this recurring story; a new one is needed.

The following section, generalising on sacrifice, philosophising, reflecting on poetry, art and music, prompts the reader to take a step back to reflect on the story, only to be thrust back into it abruptly in the next paragraph:

> At certain times and in certain circumstances men still crave spectacular sacrifice. When there is trouble in the dockyards and there is no sound from the weaver's shed; when theologians brood over the meaning of such words as 'justification' and 'penance' beside dribbling waxflames; . . . then bread and wine seem to certain men to be too mild a sacrifice. They root about everywhere for a victim and a scapegoat to stand between the tribe and the anger of inexorable Fate.
>
> So Magnus Erlendson, when he came up from the shore that Easter Monday, towards noon, to the stone in the centre of the island, saw against the sun eleven men and a boy and a man with an axe in his hand who was weeping.

This section specifies the links Brown saw between Magnus's time and his own. The craving for 'spectacular sacrifice' is presented not as the result of any particular belief system, but as general existential frustration: 'the anger of inexorable Fate':

> . . . so that a man listening to a saga is moved to say, 'This is the same performance all over again.' It is not: the costumes have changed, the masks have changed, the gestures though similar have a new style, and the personages will soon go away into their own mysterious silence.

This gives a sense of the connectedness of the strands of the story. The words 'a new style' are almost a commentary on the novel's structure. This technique shows how the viewpoint of each character is fixed in his or her own time; it is only through the whole narrative that we see connections and patterns in what they experience as unique events.

Throughout this chapter there are subtle links between its different elements. For example, one narrative voice wonders how a character in another strand of the story might respond, while another strand tells us what the person actually thinks and does. Other continuities run across the stylistic variations, such as the references to Scripture and the ceremony of the Mass. Imagery also creates connections between the different strands; it is at once a huge time-shift and a thread of contact with the condemned earl's earlier life, when Brown invests the witnesses to the killing with characteristics we remember from earlier episodes in the novel. For example, the execution chamber's 'whitewashed cube' recalls Magnus's vision of 'a small cube-shaped interior full of hard light' during Mass.

After 'The Killing' chapter, with Magnus dead, there is regeneration in the first miracle attributed to him by two tinkers, Jock and Mary. The omens are good; Magnus is seen to be working miracles and, for those with Jock's faith, has acquired the power and authority of sainthood. This fresh source of optimism for the islands is first noted by the tinkers, again positioned by Brown as the characters in the community who look beyond the military squabbles and the religious protocols of the day: '*Saint Magnus the Martyr, pray for us* . . . Jock the tinker said it before any of you.' On the last page of the novel, therefore, Magnus brings to the islanders spiritual redemption and physical regeneration.

Some critics saw the device of modernising the story of a medieval saint as anachronistic: 'these passages sit uneasily among the rest.'[21] Yet it has to be said that this was exactly the effect that Brown hoped to achieve. It was Brown's achievement to have reinvented the rather wooden Magnus of the original saga to produce a compelling portrait of a man whose humanity in particularly troubled times showed up his contradictions.

Yet Brown wanted the *Orkneyinga Saga*'s author to be recognised for inspiring this novel and other writings, over many years: '. . . for me it was a great literary experience . . . the text itself intrigued me and has exerted a lasting fascination . . . Any apprentice story-teller would do well to come and refresh himself . . . in those clear waters . . . There will almost certainly never be a more important book in our island literature . . .'[22]

There is desperate tragedy in the fact that such events have been repeated time and again in the course of history, but there is also constant regeneration, not only in the actions of people like Magnus, but also in Brown's active regeneration of old stories. For Brown, one single telling, particularly of such important, archetypal stories, was never going to be enough. Always, he had to find a new angle.

Throughout his writing life, Brown wrote about the Magnus story in many different forms. Technically, he did something different in each. Thematically, he shifted emphasis in each telling. The Magnus story was a spark for Brown's writing – in poetry, prose, drama and novel – a test of his creativity: 'There is a progression here: from paraphrase of a saga story, in *An Orkney Tapestry*, to borrowing features of the saga style, in *Greenvoe*, to rewriting a saga story, in *Magnus*, and finally, fifteen years later, to forging a new narrative technique, in *Time in a Red Coat*, now pretty far removed from the original process of paraphrase.'[23]

The nature of this output gives us an insight into Brown's writing mind; he saw the writer's task not as 'inventing' new stories, but as creating new versions of recurring stories, until he exhausted the material. Perhaps this would produce the 'perfect silence' he was searching for: once the story had been retold so often, the writer would have nothing more to say. In the story of Magnus Brown had found something to express and he wanted to do so in as many ways as possible.

Making *A Spell for Green Corn* (1970)

A Spell for Green Corn is often referred to as Brown's first play, but he wrote several one-act plays before this. Its mixture of prose, poetry, song and imaginary island records shows Brown's by now trademark use of different forms in the one piece. Published in 1970, three years after being broadcast, it tells the story of an island community from the 'age of saints and fish and miracles', through the seventeenth century – a time of 'witches and ploughs and kirk sessions' – to the 'age of machines and numbers and official forms'.

In a twelve-page letter to Stewart Conn (who was producing the play) Brown explained what he was trying to do. *A Spell for Green Corn* is revealed as a complex sequence of realistic, supernatural and miraculous 'episodes', each character and scene a link in the chain. The drama is in the articulation of the idea: how regeneration can be brought out of ruin.

This will be no consolation to those who do not find the play sufficiently dramatic, but it will delight those who enjoy the writing. The letter tells us how to read the play – if not to view it – highlighting what Brown saw as key scenes and speeches and the ideas driving the drama: 'We know that poetry & music don't feed people, don't help corn to grow or lure fish into nets, but what I'm wishful to say . . . is that man is one, and that you can't divide body and mind and spirit in him – the hunger in any part is a hunger of the whole man.'[24]

This letter shows Brown's awareness that others viewed his preoccupations as old-fashioned. He knew that he was in danger of losing his way in an anti-progress rant: 'Episode 1 (The Miracle) is set in the Age of Faith, when people were poor, illiterate, believing (superstitious, the rationalists wd. say, but I'm not a rationalist and so I say "believing").' In other words, miracles, symbolism and superstition were all legitimate tools for writing about his themes.

That Brown had been thinking about these ideas for some time is indicated by earlier treatments of subjects and characters appearing in this play: as early as 1950, twenty years before, he published a short story in *The New Shetlander* (no. 23, May/June 1950) called 'Mansie – An Episode from a Play by Storm Kolson' (clearly Brown) and a poem in number 26 under the initials 'GMB', 'The Fiddler Stolen by the Trows after a Wedding'.

The action of the play concerns the recovery of a 'sick field' that failed to provide a crop, symbolising the evil that has been going on in the island for years: 'It's a religious play (not moral, of course, anything but) but religious – the relationship between man and nature and supernatural powers.'[25] The crops reflect corruption in island society, and a spell is required to turn the dead black corn into the living green corn of harvest. This can happen only when the islanders gradually, grudgingly, come to accept that they have to give up fishing and take up agriculture.

In a long speech, the play's spokesman for Art employs archaic diction to reconstruct the time in which blighted corn did, in fact, symbolise and testify to vices in the community – 'the green word' being imprisoned by the severe Presbyterian doctrine which denied the value of the god-gifted. For it to be rediscovered and practised, fault had to be recognised, sacrifice made and food obtained before the lost word was found: 'DEATH BREAD BIRTH BREATH circled the poem of man, in all its permutations . . . Yet the word that the fiddle found . . . was altogether different, it was the merging of all those words in the complete dance, a new and holy mystery. It was RESURRECTION.'

This incantation of death, bread, birth and breath evokes the spell the island needs. The play ends with an action that has come to caricature Brown's anti-progress persona: 'There's one thing you and I must do yet . . . we must break the machines.' This was no longer a story of the outside modern world threatening the small remote community. The forces of divisiveness and destruction were now within the community.

While Brown was reconstructing a time when bonds between people and nature were stronger, or were perceived to be concrete and real, he was looking for an antidote to the forms of social and artistic decay that he saw around him. His letters referred again and again to the destruction of Orkney and his own illness, which, for him, as for Edwin Muir, were associated with living in the industrial belt and with his depression. It is hard not to make connections between his illness and the treatment of renewal in his writing; writing offered Brown 'one hope of salvation'. Yet, the pattern of re-enactment was not entirely regenerative; the sense of events fitting into a recurring pattern was claustrophobic, verging on determinism.

Poetry collections, 1971–72

At the same time as Brown was experimenting with the novel form, he continued to write poetry. What the collections published in this period show is Brown's continuing preoccupation with poetic form, even at the expense of subject. His endless revisions, even after publication, reveal that poetry was still about seeking perfection; even the published poem was work-in-progress. His revisions may not simply be the perfectionist's tinkering with his work, but an expression of his belief that his poem literally continued to develop over time.

Narrative continued to play an important role in Brown's main collection of poems in this period, *Fishermen with Ploughs* (1971). He wrote to Marwick: 'I am trying to make a "Rackwick Anthology" . . . a collection of poems, mostly very brief, illustrating life in the valley from the beginning. Of course it's all imagination.'[26] The result was a structured collection of poems and prose poems. As in *A Spell for Green Corn*, six sections chronicle the fortunes of islanders over several centuries, beginning with their arrival on an island.

'A ship . . . sails west out of Norway in the ninth century carrying a tribe of fisher people . . . They are in flight from starvation, pestilence, turbulent neighbours.' They have landed in a remote part of Orkney and the poem cycle plots their 'slow evolution' over the next few centuries. Brown plots changes in this society, but also has 'the same people appear and reappear through many generations'. As their quality of life improves, depopulation sets in; the two go together. In the last phase of the poem cycle a 'black pentecostal fire' hits a great city and drives people back to the valley, where the narrative ends with 'The Return of the Women': 'They make themselves farmers and fishermen. The women return, unchanged yet terribly changed. But the wheel has been wrenched from the axle-tree. The great song must begin all over again, very far back, beyond the oxen and millstones and bronze throats of agriculture.' The use of the present tense gives the immediacy of ongoing action, while, at the same time, suggesting continuity, implying that this is what people always do in times like these.

Unusually for Brown, the language of Part One, 'Dragon and Dove', is not adequate for the concept. Ellipsis, inversion and excessive alliteration smother the meaning. Archaisms, expressions stale through repeated use in earlier works and repetition of images – for example, 'star-shoal', 'star wheel', 'whalequake' – give this section the appearance of Gerard Manley Hopkins pastiche:

> Hoof-fast Njal bore his manseed
> > wombfurled waveward . . .
> Nor doth hero long keep
> Lithe limb or lissomness or laughter.

This work is interesting for Brown's bringing together the long-standing influence of Hopkins, his preoccupations with saga style and, perhaps, linguistic experiments of the day. A new freedom in language had arrived in Scotland with Hugh MacDiarmid's 'synthetic Scots': words from different Scots dialects could be combined, breaking down boundaries between regional forms. Old words were recovered and new ones formed. Although Brown was never interested in the Scots language to the same extent as MacDiarmid, perhaps the spirit of the latter's linguistic innovations rubbed off on Brown, who did have his own 'Lallans' period.

There are refreshing touches of laconic humour – 'Our guest is generous with his flames' – and an attractive kenning – 'one huge gale-lover', with 'The Net' being perhaps the one poem in this section which rates with the best of *Loaves and Fishes* and *The Year of the Whale*:

> The first day from the weaving of the ling net
> Three cod lay on the deck, gulping.
> A careful gleam was put in their bellies.

The poem goes through a week's fishing, showing variety in repeated small events. For example, each type of fish caught is described in a different way:

> The second day from the net weaving
> A dogfish slapped the scuppers.
> He barked at the women soundlessly.

After the urgency and effort of landing a catch, the fourth stanza's single line is a clever evocation of the weariness and futility of probing an unresponsive sea. Worse still, on the fifth day they catch a corpse in the net, graphically described. The objective narrative tone is replaced by a flood of sibilants and two emphatic final comments, echoing the skald's nausea, heaving over his harp and gulping for breath like the cod in stanza one:

> Skald sullied harp with sickness.
> The skull splayed streams of hair. And smiled. And sank.

This poem owes its effect to the abundance of concrete detail within a strong story-line. There is none of the bardic stance and diction of the earlier sections, except for the last two lines of stanza five where they cleverly work as parody.

In Part Two, titled 'Our Lady', the new islanders escape from the

'Dragon' of pagan times to security in Rackwick, content in their Christian faith and the community values it engenders. In their prayers they seek modest improvements and prosperity, yet these are so important to the small community that the requests have an urgency the florid litanies lack:

> May cuithe and codling
> Hang in the chimney-smoke . . .
> Guard the labour of
> thirty-five ewes.

These terse petitions relieve the poem from the repetitions and catalogues threatening to muffle the community's plea.

Part Three, 'Hall and Kirk', Brown's huge leap forward in time from 1151 to the early nineteenth century, occupies 140 lines: its seven poems demonstrate the continuing importance of religious and feudal authority, although the Catholic faith has been dislodged by witch-hunting and Bible-bound Presbyterianism. The egalitarian society has become stratified. Still, the work of crofting and fishing goes on, punctuated by deaths on land and sea, the laird's exactions and organised justice taking the wandering tinker, Ikey, to rigorous account for a series of alleged offences. Families renew themselves for generations in spite of regular crises running through the family line: James Leask of Reumin from 'Witch' has a namesake in the same croft more than two hundred years later.

Part Four, 'Foldings', is much closer to Brown's notion of 'illustrating life in the valley', although a third of its eighteen poems record islanders' withdrawal from participation in valley life. One by one they have aged or died. Offsetting these losses is the survivors' determination to stick to their tasks until they too

> have unyoked out of the sun and rain,
> Our brutal wheel of bread,
> And are lords of legend, beyond change or chance;

In Part Five we see 'the wheel slow down and stop'. As Brown warned in his introduction, improvements in living conditions erode commitment to island life. Seeking more of the goods and services which have percolated into it, in consequence of Brown's old abomination, 'progress', people migrate to the mainland. The older generations reject young people's interests: 'The croft girls are too young./Nothing but giggles, lipstick, and gramophone records'; the sea's rewards are significantly less as 'The valley divides the meagre miracle'; ale-house, merchant and tractors obstruct the fishermen's return with their catch and make the horsemen's traditional skills redundant:

> The horsemen are red in the stable
> With whisky and wrath.
> The petrol-drinker is in the hills.

This is an example of the rune poems that Brown had been writing since 1963. He typically followed a short, clear statement with an arresting detail and a forceful summary. The short runes neatly provide cameos of experience and attitude, giving substance to the longer poems and being interesting variants of them.

Of the last section, 'The Return of the Women', Brown said that it was a kind of prose poem, written for seven women's voices, not meant for the stage. It takes us back to the beginning of the sequence and imagery of the wheel appears throughout. This section describes how the 'atom-and-planet horror at the heart of our civilisation'[27] has forced the thirteen survivors of 'A Black Pentecost' to search for a haven, paralleling the journey of the occupants of the ship *Dove* eleven centuries before. There is a sustained intensity to this section, which the opening lacked, conveying both the search for a haven and the dark intimidation of the group by one man who reinstates traditional hierarchies, turns himself into the Laird and his cottage into 'the Hall' and deliberately, symbolically breaks the one bowl containing all that they have to show for their year's harvest of ale.

The poem has an enigmatic ending: will the people give in to the new Laird or rebel and go their own way? Further questions are raised by the absence of four of the community from the final meeting: are they making plans to follow their own inclinations and expertise? And what exactly, finally, is the 'Dragon'? As elsewhere, Brown did not specify the destructive force, so tied up was his idea of some sort of 'holocaust' with internal forces and patterns in this specific community and in humanity generally. Similarly, he represented the process of regeneration as the sum of individual courage and an underpinning set of values and customs that a select few would labour to recover. As a whole, this poem conveys hope for improvement and recovery on all levels, as another cycle of ruin-and-regeneration begins.

Narrative compression and personal courage also feature in another new poem from this period, published in the collection *Lifeboat and Other Poems* (1971). The title poem, 'Lifeboat', is a study of men prepared to confront the elements and to risk their own lives in order to save others. The obvious parallel with other sacrifices is used by Brown to underscore his point – 'offered himself' – but these are real, not symbolic, heroes:

Lifeboat

One stumbled on a gray hill, very steep.
One drank deeply, and found himself at
      a carousal of angels.
One whispered in the secretest cell of salt.
One (young) exchanged many untasted
      Aprils for a brief ecstasy.
One who had turned hundreds from the door
      of The Salt Mother knocked at
      her window that night, alone.
One wrote 'amen' on a spindrift page.
One offered himself for all commerce
      seareft, taking of fish.
These seven returned in their circuits.
One wandered in many countries of the sea:
      he crossed the frontiers of whale
      and lobster: he troubled horizons:
      he swam by nets, he had dealings
      with pearl and kraken: he drifted
      through a sea forest at the time
      of its blossoming: he offered
      himself to many crystal querns.

Brown said he intended their life stories to be condensed short stories, told in one line of ten words or less, further expression of his interest in narrative at this period of his writing. The first seven 'stories' are overshadowed by the last one, which is more developed. What Brown intended in these last lines is indicated by his revisions to the poem. Less than a year later, on 20 September 1972, he reworked the last section, in his own copy, to make the Christian symbolism more overt, linking images of sea and seasons:

> One offered himself for all seareft.
> These seven returned in their circuits.
> One harnessed the sea stallion. They trampled horizons down.
> He sowed his substance under a gray furrow.
> He entrusted his music to shells.
> He made peace between the whale and the iceberg.
> He suffered black flails.
> He offered himself among the crystal quernstones.

Brown strengthened the theme of redemption after sacrifice. Four years and further revision later, 'Lifeboat' appeared as 'The Lost', the third part of 'The Sea: Four Elegies' in the collection *Winterfold* (1976), striking a new tone of wondering on the possibility of the deaths being sacrifices in atonement for crime and pain caused by those using the sea. He reduced the crew to seven and condensed his imagery. He pointed out the irony of deadly storms being followed by prolonged fine weather in one of his most graphic conclusions:

> Were they offered for all sea-reft-piracy, pain of fish, the black and
> gold cargoes?
> A storm-ripened one went swiftly that March among
> Sea-scythes, flails, winnowings.
> After the third wave, the sea-querns had him.
> The Atlantic was veined all summer with slow pure glitters.

Brown was his own most exacting critic. These serial textual changes illustrate his determination to wrestle with detail and language, sometimes, as here, to the extent of changing the central idea of a poem. In 'Lifeboat' we have another glimpse of how he conducted his search for the 'perfect' poem: 'A poem exists in its purity, as the perfect statue is hidden in the rock. Silence is best: poetry is forever striving for the unattainable perfection of silence.'[28] Each version has its own appeal, while study of the series gives insight into Brown's dominant idea at the time of revision and into what might be called his artistic conscience. There is also no little pathos in the poet's inability to find satisfaction in his work.

Poems New and Selected (1971) brought together poems from earlier volumes. Many of the poems in the 'Selected' section have been discussed in our previous chapters. The 'New' section included sixteen poems, though some had been published in pamphlets and magazines that very few would have seen.

Typically, Brown made changes to the published poems. For example, he dropped the sixth stanza of 'Hamnavoe', thereby losing the children from a poem that originally covered every group of people in the town:

> Blessings and soup plates circled. Euclidian light
> Ruled the town in segments blue and gray.
> The school bell yawned and lisped
> Down ignorant closes.

When asked why he did this he responded that he was not happy about 'the quantities', by which he meant the rhythm of syllables and vowels. This shows the importance he attached to the process of improving poetic effects, even at the expense of a key subject; he was content to settle for less comprehensive coverage of the community if unable to improve the rhythm of the line.

What characterised *Poems New and Selected* was the mixture of new and old, in both form and subject. In a letter to David Morrison written while he was putting the book together Brown described it as 'rather eccentric in style and form – at once archaic and ultra-modern'.[29] It is interesting to observe this degree of self-awareness; those who were later to comment on archaisms in his writing might be surprised to see that the 'archaic' was a deliberate effect; what later appeared to be anachronisms in his fiction can now be seen as the deliberate placing of new and old side by side to strange or uncomfortable effect.

A poem in the 'New' section, 'Tinkers', was one of Brown's best on the subject; tinkers, or travellers, had an important place both in Brown's world view and in his writing: '"The drunk" and "the tinker" move through nearly all my stories and plays and poems; symbolical figures who are both in and out of the story, for they . . . are not bound to one part forever, but come and go at their own wild sweet will.'[30] It is difficult to read very far in Brown's writings without encountering tinkers, the 'ga'an aboot folk' whose appearance introduces a new perspective, 'free on the outer fringes of society',[31] often counterpointing the drama of a story or poem. Sometimes they were central figures. Tinkers, wandering fiddlers and tramps might be at the bottom of island hierarchy, but they were represented as shrewd and resilient. From time to time they might deserve – and receive – less than sympathetic treatment, yet their freedom of spirit made them more attractive than the 'getters and spenders' condemned roundly and regularly by Brown.

A feature of the collection was a dramatic narrative, 'The Wedding Guest', Brown's best prose poem. The central figure is distracted and delayed as he makes his way from Hamnavoe to Birsay, without abandoning his purpose. As he goes through the parishes 'to the summons and the ceremony . . . dutifully . . . a far behest . . . towards the consummation . . . a ghostly bride cup . . . the kirkyard', it is evident that the wedding he approaches is not a secular one. His pilgrimage is towards Heaven.

Sympathetic, virtuous and humble, this 'guest' resists temptations – of flesh and drink – as he registers the beauty of a spring morning, nature's fertility and danger, attack by sea-birds, encounters with tinkers, the sea-watching women, a publican and a croft family, until he is waiting on the Birsay shore for the changing tide to allow him to cross to the Brough:

> Hamnavoe of water and granite and sky, at gray daystart I say
> farewell to you, I make an end now . . .
> . . . in a secret set-apart
> morning, a triune welling of dayspring and April and
> youth, when fire and earth have their way one with
> another, a lovely spurting of seed and egg and spawn . . .

Each section is a sentence of up to twenty lines, except for the penultimate one, whose paragraph structure enables Brown to build suspense before, in the last, gradations of the sea's withdrawal are reinforced by the religious rituals heard across the water as the guest waits to cross over and by the appearance of half-a-dozen brothers to begin their daily tasks:

for the sea has
lain with his two arms about the island all night, and
glutted every cave and fissure, and now turns slowly from
the island, glutted, and begins to ebb from the island
with a sound like a struck harp, and *Lauds* glimmers,
a frail hidden monotony, and fades, and sea lapses from
crag and shelf, and from seapink to sand to washed rock
advances the foot of the pilgrim.

Brown did not specify where the guest's journey's end lay, although the imagery suggests that he had come to the end of his life.

This is an excellent example of Brown meeting his own criteria for the prose poem: 'continuous waves of suggestion . . . Every word and line must . . . have significance . . . distilled short stories, with all the powers of the lyric to surprise and strike with wonder.'[32] By these 'continuous waves of suggestion' Brown makes each of the seven episodes in this poem gather to a climax before another facet of island life overtakes it. The cumulative effect is of a relentless series of tests for the 'guest' and, on another level, of the spectrum of island life itself, with each scene rolling into another in endless waves.

While *Poems New and Selected* provided an opportunity to polish a few earlier poems, the new ones in this collection are an accomplished and varied addition to the body of Brown's work, presenting a cross-section of modes and themes to which he would return. In spite of echoes of other contemporary writers in some poems, certain subjects and themes were, by this stage in Brown's writing career, clearly marked out as his own, while he continued with what some might consider idiosyncratic experiments with poetic forms.

The next collection that Brown featured in was *Penguin Modern Poets*, indicating that, by 1972, he was perceived as a major figure in twentieth-century poetry. The volume included poems by Iain Crichton Smith and Norman MacCaig, poets of well established reputation and following. Curiously, a note introducing Brown's poems (written by him) stated that the main influences on his work were 'Norse sagas, Scottish ballads and the ceremonies of the Catholic Church', yet many of the poems published here did not fit these criteria. In others whose subjects and treatment did, Brown had a distinctive way of exploiting the influences. Overall, however, this was a collection which owed as much to the poet's experiences and imagination as to the stories and rituals he acknowledged as sources.

It is interesting to compare Brown's selection with that of other editors in anthologies of the Scottish Literary Renaissance, although it has to be said that other collections brought valuable readerships and positioned Brown in the wider literary movement. Since fourteen poems from this collection were printed in the final *Selected Poems* chosen by Brown, we can take this collection as a clear representation of what he felt to be his best work after forty years of writing poetry.

'George Mackay Brown's masterpiece'

Brown's collection of children's stories, *The Two Fiddlers* (1974), was received very favourably by authorities on children's fiction within two weeks of publication. Marion Lochhead hailed it as 'George Mackay Brown's masterpiece . . . unique in beauty and evocation, with the salt of the sea and his own humour about it' (*The Scotsman*, 7 December 1974). Jill Paton Walsh claimed that *The Two Fiddlers* could 'stand the comparison' with Hans Christian Andersen's fairy tales and stories (*The Guardian*, 15 December 1974). Margery Fisher saw it as 'a robust mixture of humour and enchantment offering good reading to adults as well as to the young' (*The Sunday Times*, 1 December 1974).

While attempting to acquire a share of a profitable new market, Brown was affected by what he sometimes called, smilingly, 'patriotism', by which he meant the desire to keep alive memories of older times in an era whose media were hostile to the story-telling of previous generations: 'Now, alas, the story-making gift is waning in the islands; and will wane increasingly as we watch our television serials on a winter evening, and read sordid ugly "real" stories out of the newspapers.'[33]

Both in style and content this book is demanding reading. All the stories have a dark side to them, with several themes and characters that would not be out of place in works for adult readers:

the supernatural, ill-fated love, a mother's murderous 'revenge', occult ceremonies, a woman–seal relationship and all-consuming greed. Not only does Brown not shrink from confronting young minds with harsh aspects of life, but he leaves no doubt of his determination to avoid sentimentality.

For a book aimed at young people, *The Two Fiddlers* has stylistic features which make no concessions: the periodic sentence, with long suspensions, frequent passages in brackets, sometimes of considerable length, for various purposes, polysyllables, 'literary' and archaic expressions, dialect words and the repeated use of 'this . . . that'. Yet the plots keep moving forward. Skilfully sketched characters interact towards familiar endings, while superbly realised locations provide a timeless background: 'the cluster of knolls . . . blazed a vivid green in the twilight . . . the knolls smouldered under the midnight sky like broken emerald . . . He . . . walked towards the glimmering knolls.'

Bernard MacLaverty's judgment captures the effect: 'Mr Mackay Brown is not writing for children, he is writing in a way that makes it easy for children to understand and feel.'[34]

Apart from the ten stories in this first volume for children, others were prepared but left out and, subsequently, never published in Brown's lifetime. (Some were included in the posthumous collection, *Northern Lights*.) Others await collection, including several inventions of incidents purporting to be the origin of local landmarks and tales.

This was another new departure for Brown in this period, not only writing for a new audience, but strengthening his affirmation of the value of history and primitive virtues. These had become his preoccupations at this time as he was working on his *magnum opus*, 'Idylls', the work unifying Orkney's history and consolidating the 'history' of his own writing, now taking shape as a substantial body of work.

Breaking new ground

Hawkfall (1974) was an advance on Brown's first two volumes of short stories, *A Calendar of Love* and *A Time to Keep*, in range of subject and technique. Still finding subjects in history, he showed mastery in the long, multiple viewpoint narrative. He broke new ground with a ghost story, and later went on to write over twenty more. Although the first two collections had more immediate impact, *Hawkfall* was in many ways a stronger book.

The meaning of the title can be traced in an earlier story: 'The voyage was rooted in pure intention; it was to be a pilgrimage, a penance, a God-faring, to redeem the time, to delete from history the Viking hawkfall.'[35] Alan Bold interpreted 'hawkfall' as a Viking kenning – a metaphor similar in form to Hopkins' composite nouns – for death. If it was, this collection could be read as an Orkney book of the dead. However, it also conveys the suddenness and ferocity with which invaders swooped on vulnerable communities. 'Invasion' takes many forms, including technology, and Brown's continuing exploration of how remote communities dealt with destructive 'progress' was as much the subject of these stories as destruction itself.

There was always the possibility of renewal and rebirth, a pattern working across many of the stories in this collection. Love, power, social change, the function of art and the search for truth are themes in *Hawkfall*'s eleven stories, particularly the title story which describes how inherited characteristics affect different generations' responses to testing situations.

'Sealskin' is about a composer's speculation on 'the use of art', leading to understanding and affirmation. Parts One to Seven are an account of domestic and parish tensions brought about by the selkie (seal woman). As the narrative voice concedes, the final part 'is really about a man and his music', as Magnus Olafson muses on the artist's function. This concluding section stands apart from the rest of the story. It is a sustained meditation in which the grand design of a social purpose for art is supported by convincing characterisation. Wrestling with a modern problem – search for faith – requires this Magnus to return to the environment and values which, long taken for granted, might offer meaning and help him counter the undermining effects of urban progress.

From autobiographical writings and conversations we know that there is a close correspondence between Magnus's life and Brown's. Magnus, the seal woman's son, is isolated by his art from fellow islanders and from educated society by what he sees as the artificiality of cultured circles:

. . . he was caught up in some meaningless charade in which everyone, himself included, was compelled to wear a mask. He would take part in their passionate midnight arguments . . . But deep down he was untouched . . . He was glad when the maskers had departed and he was alone again, among the cigarette ends and the apple cores.

There is a distinct echo of 'The Poet' here, fixing that image of the artist at the centre of Brown's work; rather than thinking 'artists are the sensitive antennae of society', Magnus is moved to the view that 'art is, rather, the ruthless cutting edge that records and celebrates and prophesies on the stone tablets of time'. Finally, he sees that art has an important role in the modern world whose inventions and values come in for strident denunciation in familiar terms: '[Scientists] were the new priesthood; the world went down on its knees before every tawdry miracle . . . that they held up in triumph.'

In the course of his meditation Magnus not only defines the role of the artist but also accepts the artist's weighty responsibility of 'keeping the roots alive'.

In this story, therefore, the character plays out the drama that Brown had internalised, revealed in his autobiography, as a fusion of artistic and moral motives: 'Everything we do sets the whole web of creation trembling, with light or with darkness. It is an awesome thought, that a good word spoken might help a beggar in Calcutta or a burning child in Burundi.'[36] Brown made a moral connection between art and religion, while chiming with the modern perspective that sees such connections between peoples across the world.

Brown denied that there was ever anything autobiographical in his writings: 'My own life strikes me as a gray uninteresting thing – I think I've never been moved to write by any personal experience.'[37] Yet throughout *Hawkfall* there are many details drawn from his life and developing beliefs. 'The Tarn and the Rosary' contains several, most notably the story of young Colm's first acquaintance with Wordsworth's poem 'Fidelity' – a poem whose effect on Brown he described frequently over the years in essays: '"Poetry", said Miss Silver. "William Wordsworth. 'Fidelity'. Page 35 in your books."' Brown had kept his school poetry book, Part Two of J. C. Smith's *A Book of Verse for Boys and Girls* (1927 edition) till his death in April 1996. Stamped '27 Aug 1929', it does, in fact, include 'Fidelity' on page 35. Similarly, Brown's facility in essay writing – 'composition' – is echoed in the description on pages 183–4. Likewise, the story of Corporal Hourston is a version of the anecdotes told by a real Stromness character, 'Soldier John' Johnston, the Stromness bellman whose talks on his foreign experiences attracted large numbers, including Brown's brother, to Stromness Town Hall.

In another example, the list of Colm's father's reading is an often-repeated inventory of Brown's father's reading tastes and his father's characteristic expression, 'She looks at me like the far end of a fiddle' appears here. Equally, recollections of a tinker woman he met when he was a child and a bite from a dog are scenes detailed by Brown in written and oral anecdote, taken from his own life. Finally, Jock Skaill's diatribe against 'Progress . . . the modern curse' and the men's dialogue in the smithy originated in Brown's memories of people meeting in Peter Esson's tailor shop and the [Army] Shelter (a hut the men used to gather in, of an evening, for a chat).

What is most significant about this collection is that Brown singled out these stories as a summary of his view of the artist in the modern world:

> I find it very difficult to comment on my own work, except in some imaginary context. I have recently finished a short story called 'Seal Skin' [*sic*] about a musician. He reads, in Dublin, an old Celtic manuscript, about 'the intricate web of creation' that men are mindlessly exploiting and tearing; and he is much moved by it. The last paragraphs are as follows:
>
> > He . . . thought of the men who had thrown off all restraint and were beginning now to raven in the most secret and delicate and precious places of nature. They were the new priesthood; the world went down on its knees before every tawdry miracle – the phonograph, the motor car, the machine-gun, the wireless – that they held up in triumph. And the spoliation had hardly begun.
> >
> > Was this then the task of the artist: to keep in repair the sacred web of creation – that cosmic harmony of God and beast and man and star and plant – in the name of humanity,

against those who in the name of humanity are mindlessly and systematically destroying it?

If so, what had been taken from him was a necessary sacrifice.[38]

The theme of 'necessary sacrifice' was central to Brown's persistent story of ruin and regeneration. It is striking how many personal references were incorporated into this theme at this time.

Conclusion

Greenvoe and *Magnus* show the impact of human beings on landscape and community; some bring violence, others peace. Both novels reveal cycles, with images and actions resurfacing to show patterns in history across the centuries. This does not mean that the characters are mere ciphers or shadows servicing some larger theme; instead, there are layers of narrative, each resonating with the others. Not that each moment is depicted in historical detail – and in that sense these are not 'historical novels' – since that was not Brown's aim:

> I used to reproach myself with being too lazy to research a situation thoroughly . . . But now I am sure that this is not how the creative energies work. All that is required is a suggestion, a flavour, a rhythm, an aroma. The imagination seizes on such intangibles and creates upon them living forms that are more real than a first-hand account by the best journalist – I was tempted to say, than history itself, but the reality of history and the reality of literature are quite different, each being one facet of the truth.[39]

While we might be prompted to debate definitions of 'realities', this passage does give us an insight into what Brown intended to achieve with his patterns of redemption, symbols of sacrifice and sequences of ruin and redemption. It also makes the case for the lighter touch on historical 'fact'; while other novelists incorporate the fruits of extensive research, this was not Brown's way. That is another genre. His approach had much in common with Virginia Woolf's novel *Orlando*, and it would be interesting to compare Brown's views with those of Robert Louis Stevenson, with regard to his novels *Kidnapped* and *Catriona*.

With a wide knowledge of world literature, Brown was aware of the range of choices open to him in subject and technique. That Brown had read and thought about Woolf's writing is evident not only from the fact that he owned her books, but also from his invention of 'The Orkney Common Reader' column – excellent concise reviews of Orkney writers – probably taking the title from Woolf's *Common Reader* volumes. Brown seems to have been very clear about what he was – and what he was not – going to achieve in his fiction. He was, above all, concerned about the survival of community.

These patterns had become more and more important, even at times insistent, in a proposed wide-ranging collection of works to be called 'Idylls'; he was pulling all his works together into one great literary scheme, but had no one volume to put them in. Perhaps, however, the idea of such a collection imaginatively provided the unity he needed at this time.

Had Brown resolved his tensions about Orkney? At one point Orkney might have had 'no culture', but time had moved on, its culture was regenerated and Brown had matured. The interaction of degenerative and regenerative forces was now pictured in Brown's work, particularly in his novels, and there were to be more of these.

PART THREE: 1975–1996

'Keeping the roots alive'

8

'Through the eye of the needle of Orkney': Experiment and Consolidation 1975–80

'Dedicated to extinction'

Brown's lifetime study of the tension in Orkney's island communities between internal and external forces and, increasingly, internal and external audiences, produced various resolutions. The tension was itself a recurring theme throughout his life and work and in his vision of himself as a writer:

> Writers that have been born and nurtured in a small community invariably want to break the circle and to reach a wider audience. It is not necessary, to try to achieve 'universality' . . . to break away from the native roots and sources . . . But there is always the danger that at last a writer might, without wishing to do so, appeal to the wider anonymous readership and forget, to some extent, the reader by lamplight in Hamnavoe or Hoy.[1]

Brown was not sufficiently disturbed about the critical stereotyping of his writing as anti-progress archaic rhetoric to make any radical changes to his subject or style. Instead, he used anachronism as a literary device, continuing to weave together different strands of time. In fact, he did this to such an extent that regular readers would have formed the impression that temporal unity was of no importance to him.

This period, particularly 1975–76, was relatively fallow; Brown wrote very little new poetry. It has to be admitted, as critics and reviewers pointed out, that he was covering over-familiar ground in his writing during this period, and some thought his themes had gone stale. Part Three of this book, 'Keeping the roots alive', considers the persistence of Brown's themes: had he become 'Johnny One-Note with a vengeance',[2] or was it that he passed everything, as Seamus

Heaney put it, 'through the eye of the needle of Orkney'?[3] What could he do in this period to keep the roots of his writing alive?

What marked a distinct new departure was the 'Idylls', the grand design that would let him bring together works already written as Idylls and new works stimulated by the scheme. This project would have taken up a fair amount of his time and energy, although to this day, there is very little to show for it as a collection, in the public domain. At the time, a grant from the Arts Council was based on his proposal to produce the 'Idylls' collection, and it therefore remained a priority. In spite of his new literary goals, it would be some time before Brown turned back to ideas, and experience, of stability and continuity; in his published work, during this period, there was little of the implied idealised unity of his earlier or proposed works.

Biographical notes: 1975–80 (aged 54 to 59)

There was continuing ill-health, including depression and bronchitis. His life at this time was uneventful, as he settled into his writing routine. There was an increasing number of visitors and researchers, whom he had to fend off in order to protect time for writing.

A long unpublished essay, written about this time, 'Sanatorium, 1941', is a fascinating description of his experience of his tuberculosis diagnosis and subsequent hospital experience, beginning with the words, 'How long have you been coughing?' There are also passages on his adolescent morbidity and terror.

There was not much time for poetry in this period, although he did find time to publish ten books. Instead, his writing time was taken up with poetry reviews and essays on Orkney life for *The Scotsman* newspaper, work on the unpublished collection of 'Fergus' stories and planning the ultimate collection, the 'Idylls'.

Idylls: a 'history of Orkney'

The 'Idylls' project presented the new challenge of holding together a wide range of writings. The 'Idylls' concept indicated Brown's growing sense that his work was all part of a great theme, or that he wanted it to be so. He held to his central subject, the search for the perfect poem. He was also looking for new, larger and more complex unities. While in other aspects of his writing he was marking time, with this project he was still moving forward, still as ambitious as ever.

There is a resemblance between Brown's 'Idylls' idea and Wordsworth's *Prelude*: in his Preface, Wordsworth explained that the lesser poems were the little cells and 'oratories' on the periphery of the main structure, part of the structure but not the main dominant structure. In Brown's scheme there were individual stories, but all moved forward in one large sweep of history.

Brown's striving to pull his work together was perhaps a response to his critics. He might have been aware that he was running out of time to complete such a large project as the 'Idylls' was intended to be, but its value – and unspoken purpose – might have been that it would take him further than his previous projects. In addition, his new literary goal brought some affirmation, unity and the prospect of completeness, and he continued to work on it from 1976 to his death in 1996. It would have helped him to see his work in a different light, exactly what he needed at this time.

Traditionally, the idyll involves a particular form and story: 'each idyll contains an incident in the matter of Arthur and his knights which is separate (or framed) but at the same time is connected with the central theme'.[4] The characteristics of the form are that it is a framed narrative, from the Greek *eidyllion*, meaning 'little picture' or 'framed picture'. It is bounded in some way, closed, but there are no formal requirements. Brown's idylls are compact, focused and pointed.

The classical idyll was a form of pastoral, used to describe idealised landscape and life. Tennyson used the idyll form for his poems about the court of King Arthur, elements of which are far from ideal. Brown used it for more realistic depictions of Orkney life. What both Tennyson and Brown had in common was a desire to write about a life and time away from, and apart from, contemporary society. Both conveyed a longing for a place and time separate from the contemporary context. In the idyll the search for an ideal, or a solution, was triggered by social or health problems.

The 'Georgic' idyll, a tradition developed in the eighteenth century, but going back to the poet Virgil, focused on seasonal toil, while the idealised idyll yearned to be a description of ideal reality beyond time. It is perhaps this potential for representing both seasonal time and an ideal beyond time that appealed to Brown, given his constant playing with time in his fiction.

Most readers who recognise the word idyll will perhaps associate it with 'idyllic', and there are examples of Brown drawing ironic contrasts between the form and the far from idyllic subjects, as Edwin Morgan did with the sonnet form in his 'Glasgow Sonnets'. We know from quotations Brown used, and from his book collection, that he had read idylls by other writers, such as Theocritus, Shenstone, Wordsworth, Maupassant and Tennyson. Nearer home, Burns and Fergusson also wrote idylls. As a literary form it is not practised much nowadays and was considered archaic even in the nineteenth century. Associations of idealisation arose when the selected moments in time appeared to be only the best moments. Yet, the idyll can also highlight a moment of psychological crisis. This raised the question of whether Brown selected his moments in time for a purpose, in order to draw out some underlying theme that tied them all together. Unifying them all in the Orkney setting, which he saw not simply as a unity of place, made the point that there are universal motives at work.

Brown's intention was revealed in an unpublished, and as yet undocumented, draft of his application for a bursary (23 May 1981). Brown outlined his scheme, his plans and his published works to date: 'I have been working for 3 years on a long series of poems and stories (provisionally called *Idylls*) that seeks to explore imaginatively the history of Orkney from its earliest stone-age period up to the present and beyond. About half has been completed or is being worked on; in perhaps 2 years the work will be finished, if all goes well.'

The construction of closed moments in time recalls Brown's use of images of closed societies: the rural community cut off from the urban complex, the tubercular patient isolated in his room, the Newbattle students absorbed by literature, with their group identity, a hermetic community at one remove from the outside world, cut off from family and friends by their illnesses or interests. This was a theme running throughout his earlier works.

If Brown's 'Idylls' are to be taken as a kind of collection, they can be characterised by quotations from his short stories 'The Wanderer's Tale' (written in summer 1982) and 'The Scholar' (published in 1989):

> I, Alexander Sweyn the laird, have written the above account. I have reasoned, 'The story, or anthology of stories, will be forgotten, if someone doesn't record them soon, somehow . . .'[5]

> The schoolmaster folded the sheets with reverence and gave them to Mr Sweyn the laird. The laird stowed them in the great chest of writings where all the transactions of the island, with official seals and stamps and ribbons, had been hoarded for centuries against the uncomprehending slow siege of time.[6]

As the 'Idylls' was a collection which Brown sketched and worked on over a number of years, he expanded the list as he wrote. His idea seems to have been to capture a moment in time, particularly a moment of social change that creates tension: a son in the story 'Love Song' refuses to join his father on the farm, opting instead for university education and a budding relationship with a woman on a neighbouring island. In others, an educated youth finds conflict and friendship in a 'gap' period aboard a whaler; a laird goes round the houses of tenants suffering from consumption; another laird's young widow considers asserting feudal 'rights' over an attractive fisherman. There are many other examples of this type of story.

Brown was, like other writers more frequently considered modernist, such as Woolf and Joyce, simultaneously engaging with time in two different ways: there was synchronic treatment, in his 'moments in time', and diachronic treatment, in his ongoing, chronological, transhistorical time scheme.

We know Brown's precise intentions for inclusion in the collection from a list of dates and titles, headed 'Idylls', in his handwriting (not previously published), from manuscripts and typescripts on which he wrote 'Idyll' and from discussion with him about his use of the word in this way. He seems to have had in mind a collection of unpublished works that he had laid aside with the intention of publishing at a later date. Many of these stories and poems are apparently complete.

Brown's handwritten manuscript, dated 1978, listed twenty-eight 'Idyll' titles in manuscript (MS) or typescript (TS) or appearing in magazines and some were later published in collections. For each, he noted the date or time period in which it was set. Where he left line spaces they are reproduced here, as they may indicate gaps he intended to fill later. Those Idylls which were published appear in bold and the place of publication is noted.

Idylls 1978

Title	Time	Printing/publication
Hunters	Stone Age	In *Scottish Short Stories*, 1981
Pictures	Broch Age	MS/TS
Meditation	800	TS
The Earl: Two Elegies		Corrected TS
Hair Like the Sun	1127	'Working' TS
The Summer of the Young Men	1150	In *Vinland*, 1992
1588	1588	Completed typescript
Gallowsha	1650	In *Portrait of Orkney*, 1981, 1988 and *Travellers*, 2001
Shore Dances	1760	In *Temenos* magazine, 1981 and *The Masked Fisherman*, 1989
The Horseman	1790	Completed TS
The Fires	1800	Corrected MS
The Scholar Gypsy	1810	Incomplete MS
Father & Daughter	1830	Corrected MS
Saul Scarth	1846	In *The Wreck of the Archangel*, 1989
Hugh & Anna	1850	In *A Second Scottish Poetry Book*, 1985 as 'A Country Tale'

Visionary	1860	Corrected MS
Mistress Eliz Sweyn (Letters)	1870	On BBC Radio 3, 1981 and in *Travellers*
Spinster	1878	Corrected typescript
Whaler		MS as 'Whales'
The Fight Between Jeck & Johnny	1900	TS
Winter Song	1910	TS
The Airman	1917	MS
The Winter Song	1920	*The Scotsman*, 1980 & *The Masked Fisherman*, 1989
Miss Instone	1923	MS
The Rose Bowl	1925	MS incomplete?
The Road to the Kirk	1928	MS
Fisherman	1930	MS 'Andrew'?

One feature that most of his Idylls share is the name Sweyn. Brown's determination to use this name is indicated in corrections to manuscripts. All these pieces, almost all prose, were either listed by Brown as Idylls or he had written 'Idyll' on his manuscript. Dates written on the manuscripts suggest that Brown had been working on these pieces around 1977, though some of them did not appear in print till 1989.

In addition to this list of almost thirty works, there is another list of thirty, including new works, in Brown's handwriting, dated 1982. In other words, Brown's 'Idylls' clearly represented a grand scheme of work that he returned to over an extended period; however, the question of which works should or should not be included in this scheme must remain open to debate. It would be possible to make a case for 'Tithonus' and 'The Lairds' Story', for example, and it would be interesting to see what the whole picture of Orkney would look like then. In total, there may be up to a hundred, or even more, works in Brown's 'Idyll' scheme.

What is different about stories and poems marked out as Idylls is the shift of focus to the event in time. Frequently, there is little development of character or imagery. For example, the opening page of the first on Brown's list, 'Hunters, An Idyll', set in the Stone Age, introduces several characters, none of whom is more than sketchily drawn:

> Woe to this people. The boar has taken the young man Swa. The hunter Swa is dead with breached belly.
>
> Swa left us. A tusk sent Swa on his way to winds and earth and waters. Swa, not looking back, was visited by the rat, the black-backed gull, the worm. Farewell, our sorrow.
>
> Ingil, make us a dance, with true steps, for Swa. Honour Swa with songs. Let the women grieve deeper than handwringing.
>
> Ingil sat, his back turned, at the mouth of the Cave of Making.
>
> The friend of Swa, Hotil, sat all night by a fire. Between Swa's friend and the fire a new long stone of battering, well fashioned, lay. The friend of Swa groaned. In the morning he laughed, putting the club to his shoulder. The friend of Swa went out against Konderka the boar.[7]

The story is framed by the lament for the death of the young hunter, at the beginning, and the old people's rejoicing at a boy's killing of the boar at the end.

Orkney's more recent history, 1920, is represented in the story 'The Winter Song' (*The Masked Fisherman*), again in the form of a snapshot of the island's history. The story is framed by a song sung by a young boy at the beginning and end of his island tour. This is a familiar structure for Brown: a journey round the community giving insights into the different characters who live there. The boy knows all these characters, yet stands apart from them. He gives a running commentary on the community, person by person. His New Year Song is a long-standing cultural tradition, expressed by a contemporary child, who selects words appropriate for each person he meets. His observations are complex and subtle, mingling the innocence of the child with the half-understood gossip of the adults. It is a solitary enactment of the ritual. There are fourteen stages on his tour, recalling the Stations of the Cross. He sings for money, but not just for money; there is some recognition of the tradition of singing this song at this time:

At Nessvoe, Willie and Jessie set me in their great straw chair, legs dangling. Willie looked at me solemnly through owl spectacles (price one shilling from the wandering hawker). Jessie gave me a cup of ale. I sang till the cups on Jessie's dresser shivered. The ale had made me reckless and gay. I uttered all kinds of blessing, half the song.

> May a' your kye be weel to calf
> And every ane hae a queyo calf
>
> May a' your mares be weel to foal
> And every ane hae a mare foal
>
> May a' your yowes be weel to lamb
> And every ane hae a yowe and a ram . . .

'That's not likely,' said Willie, and he eyed me like a friendly owl.[8]

The Sweyn family appears again. We have a fleeting glimpse of the old laird asleep at the fire, his wife stitching an alphabet on her sampler. Most of the community are ageing. There is only one new family. As the boy enacts the tradition, he adapts it to the real people who live in the houses he visits.

The 'Idylls' collection incorporated the kind of work that Brown had been writing for some time; they were not new subjects or new forms for him. The central character is still the place rather than the people who live there; what certain characters think or do has less importance. Not that these are fatalistic pieces, but the characters' motives are buried in the action of the story. For some, they are even hidden from themselves.

The theme is not progress, or anti-progress, but that moments in time can appear self-contained, even though they are part of the great sweep of all time. The effect is to convey that imaginative reconstruction – of traditions and habits of thought and action – can and should be part of the life of the community. Given that Brown continually drew parallels across time and has been stereotyped as 'anti-progress', it is interesting to find this focus on change, on moments of crisis for communities, turning points that stand out like freeze frames in time. This is not an idealised pastoral, but a search for the ideal in the history – real and imaginary – of the place.

Most of the unpublished Idylls appear to be complete, corrected versions. The short story is most common, but there are also diary, poetry and prose poems. The project looks to have been formed after he completed the short story 'Tithonus' (another Tennysonian subject), his contribution to Collins' *Scottish Short Stories*, 1973 and the title story of his collection *Hawkfall* (1974). Both these stories feature a laird, part of a long tradition, caught in time and place, yet paradoxically free-standing and in some ways apart from his community. The laird was a symbol of the community, yet over time could see that his traditional role was changing. He could therefore be used as an expression and embodiment of both continuity and change.

This is what Brown was moving towards at this time: trying to create unities. The idyll was the ideal form to show the distinctiveness of each story while also showing how all the stories were interwoven in time, place and theme. That he kept the 'Idylls' project going for the rest of his life shows how important it had become, vastly outgrowing his original Arts Council project. The word 'idyll' also appeared in one of his last poems:

> Between idyll and epic
> The soul of man moves forever.[9]

New stories

The Sun's Net (1976), a slighter body of material than Brown's outstanding early collections, is dominated by dark themes – darker than *Hawkfall* (1974) – which hold the collection together: it is full of betrayals, punishment, disillusionment and people hiding from their problems.

> My eyes, some morning,
> Will be caught like two fish in the sun's net.[10]

Net imagery is not uncommon in Brown, but this example does not provide an obvious title for the book. Taken as an image of winter's imminent end, the phrase 'the sun's net' is appropriate, but its relevance to the contents of this collection is not immediately clear. Brown's earlier use of the image the 'Net of Time', as the original title of the story 'The Three Islands' in *A Calendar of Love*, suggests that the passing of centuries cannot obscure the high points of island history; they are caught in time, available to later writers to mediate them for their own generations:

> I am inclined to think that a really great story – [should] have a mingling of myth and legend . . .
>
> I am not an isolated storyteller writing in the late twentieth century; I draw from a treasury of narrative written and unwritten out of the islands' past; many voices speak through me; I am part of a tradition.[11]

The Sun's Net includes several stories in which Brown goes over local events and weaves in traditions, 'trying, imaginatively, to fill up a gap in time'.[12] So many people have lived and left no record; Brown saw fleshing out their stories as one of his tasks.[13] This is most obvious in the seven stories with an Orkney setting, but what these and the other three have in common is the aim of showing people trying to understand and come to terms with problems and make their way along the road to self-knowledge, pain and reconciliation.

'Brig-o-Dread' is a ghost story, one of Brown's best in the genre. The main character, Arkol Andersvik, is on a journey to find the truth about his own nature, what people think about him and the manner of his death. For a person mildly complacent, in life, about his family, making his way through a curriculum he set himself, he undergoes torment seemingly out of proportion to his foibles. Instructed to write a memorandum of his life, he has it read out by an 'interrogator' and is scoffed at by his cultural heroes, Beethoven and Van Gogh. Once he has gained knowledge, insight and acceptance, he is ready to go on to write 'the poem of his life', granting him access to eternal life. This story demonstrates not only the process of moving towards the perfect poem, Brown's quest, but also the imperfect stages along the way: 'The interrogator began with a reading out of the statement that Arkol had originally made: "trust of the townsfolk" . . . "quest for truth and beauty" . . . "intend to get to the bottom of this" . . . The interrogator was interrupted every now and again by wondering laughter . . . "The statement, it is a tissue of lies . . . You must revise your statement in certain respects."'

Arkol has to revise his 'memorandum', in a kind of purgatorial ordeal, perhaps removing his clichés, reviewing his appreciation of the arts and paying his 'debt to the truth'. He has to acknowledge that he has been suffering from delusions, with no ideas of his own, with the complacent belief that everything was fine, that he was kind to his brother, who actually murdered him. He has been betrayed but is true to his newly acquired vision. Certain values are eternal: love with no reward looked for, the beauty of true art and acceptance of Christianity: 'The poem was, as never before, a cold pure round of silence; a fold; a chalice where, having tasted, a man may understand and rejoice.' Out of this harrowing story, the main character does find his way, through his true statement, to peace. There are no more horrors to come.

Although Alan Bold[14] argued that 'the more exhilarating theme of birth dominates in *The Sun's Net*', he used only four of the ten stories to support his point. While it is true that a new life 'holds out hope of renewal', the effects are more complex, since the manner and reception of the first, a modern re-enactment of the Nativity, shows three tormented principal characters of 'A Winter Tale' in a less than hopeful light; the birth arranged as a test of virility may fit the feudal nature of the setting, but says little for the morality of a young man and his future father-in-law in 'Stone, Salt, and Rose'. 'Soldier From the Wars Returning' anticipates a child will be the result of a secret liaison, and the spate of pregnancies in 'Pastoral' leads to lynch tactics and deliberate perversion of a good man's moral code. This is the closest we get to consistency of theme in this book: integrity being strained until positive, new perspectives begin to emerge from different forms of betrayal.

'A Winter Tale', like the island of Torsay in 'Tithonus', is 'dedicated to extinction',[15] 'a dying community'.[16] The desire for social and economic improvement promotes the decline of the crofting system and emigration. In a long paragraph Brown questions the long-term benefits of moving to the towns for people who feel 'the dark earth-rhythms which had dominated their lives for generations still operant, but with nothing to glut themselves on, only the empty rituals of "getting and spending", and a more refined and empty mode of social intercourse'.[17] A number of lives are regenerated, but only once they have left illusory paths to happiness.

The question of what brings three highly educated individuals –

doctor, minister, teacher – to a remote, decaying island, whose inhabitants are leaving, is considered in this story. Brown strips away layers of appearance, self-assessment and assumption, as each observes and evaluates his peers. All of them are hiding from problems. Only one is at ease professionally; only the doctor makes the best of his skills for his and the community's benefit in which he sought 'solitude and darkness' and 'the cure of silence', yet, ironically, he has assimilated well into island life. The other two will leave in due course. They have neither found their 'cures' nor fitted in to the community.

This was not a great collection. It even had two consistently flat stories, 'Perilous Seas' and 'The Pirate's Ghost', which was unusual, giving the impression that Brown, or his editor, was eking out a thin list of adequate stories. Brown had covered these subjects better in other books and in other genres. It was as if he were struggling with the free-standing short story at this time, since he was more focused on pulling everything together for his collection of 'Idylls'. He did not publish another collection till 1983.

Perhaps Brown's loss of direction and impetus had crept into his writing, shaping both the stories themselves and the selection for this volume. The stories have a recurring theme of self-delusion. The characters have lost their way or have chosen not to address a problem in their lives. As the momentum of Brown's writing life stuttered to a brief halt, it is perhaps appropriate – and even refreshing – to come across characters who do not have a direct route to meaning and the 'still centre' that was the focus of stories in earlier collections, such as *A Calendar of Love* (1967).

What characterised Brown's writing in this period was a diminishing fascination with narrative. Although there is a narrative dimension to the 'Idylls' scheme, in a column written around this time he said that he was turning more and more, with renewed pleasure, to poetry. He had, in some sense, found poetry again and this became his main driver for a spell.

New poems

'Just when I thought the muse of poetry had deserted me, I began to write verse – I daren't begin to call it poetry until a year or two has passed – in astonishing profusion. I'll always remember 1976 for that.'[18]

Although Brown was just rediscovering poetry, he already had a volume ready to publish. In 1976 he brought out *Winterfold*, whose main themes are Vikings, death at sea and Christianity. What is remarkable about this small collection is that he managed to find the time, and inclination, to write poetry at all, given the growing number of prose projects that he was engaged in. In fact, he was still writing new poems and improving old ones.

Brown defended his now well-established technique of sweeping over large stretches of time in a note at the start of this collection: 'It should not be obligatory for poets to celebrate, as best they can, only the grayness of contemporary life. Some of the poems in this book are swatches cut from here and there in the one weave of time.'

The first five poems, grouped together under the title 'Winterfold', deal with the birth of Christ, conveying the confusion of the birth in the byre:

> A lantern, quick. Something's happened
> The last sorrow and the first joy are one . . .
> A birth? In the byre? Whose bairn?
> We give these rings and robes to a winter child.

Brown brought this sequence of poems up to date in the last of the five, 'A Poem for *Shelter*', neatly slipping from the time of Christ to His modern homeless counterparts, touching on the intervening generations. The last line of the poem both consolidates the Christian theme and asserts the permanent need for basic necessities: 'But the children of time, their rooftrees should be strong.'

There are seven groupings of poems in this collection, with the effect that there is often this kind of dramatic or narrative element holding the poems together. In another example, the Viking presence continues in a series of poems about Rognvald Kolson, based on the *Orkneyinga Saga*, and three 'harp-songs'. There is also yet another series of poems on the 'Stations of the Cross'.

A highlight of this collection is 'Sea Widow', four touching poems, epitaphs for a drowned fisherman, capturing the love between him

and his wife: 'Silence', 'Lost Lovers', 'What the Fisherman Said' and
'Wedding Ring'. 'Silence' touchingly tells how she concealed her fears
about the dangers of his occupation: 'But I said nothing. Love ebbed
and flowed. We kept the feast and the fast.' In 'Lost Lovers' she
considers the more secure married life that she might have had if she
had married someone else: 'A merchant promised whiteness, a ring, a
proper blessing in the precincts of God.' 'What the Fisherman Said'
describes his lyrical, persuasive courting of her:

> I will build you a house with my hands,
> A stored cupboard,
> Undying hearth-flames, a door open to friend and stranger.

In 'Wedding Ring' she describes her year of marriage, how his promises were not fulfilled, how her fears were realised:

> There were maybe four
> Good rounds, perfect returnings, in that one year
> . . . I left him . . .
> And stayed a month at my father's place.

After several break-ups there were as many treasured reunions. But the
poem ends with her alone, having taken stock of what it had been like,
reminded of him every time she looks at their child:

> They unweave him, mackerel and gull.
> I know the man only
> In flecks of salt and grains of sand,
> And when through the drifting pools of a child's face
> Looks back the skull.

While this collection does not move the story of Brown the writer on
very far, it is interesting for the groupings of the poems. Again, the
flavour of this collection is of searching for conviction, very much part
of the mood of this period. 'Keeping the roots alive', in his own work,
was proving no easy task. His frequent use of the story of the Stations
of the Cross might have stemmed from a mixture of religious conviction
and the pursuit of artistic excellence. His artistic endeavour continued:
his best poem was still the one beyond the one he had just written.

Children's stories

Pictures in the Cave (1977), a sequence of stories, opens and ends with episodes in the life of Sigurd Bressay. Entrusted with 'the whole history of the cave' by a tribe of seals, the young truant from school remembers the stories into his sixties, when he tells them to his housekeeper's daughter, 'a new keeper' who can pass them on.

Descriptions of 'The Truant', rebelling against the constraints of school, and the old skipper, irritable from gout, finding respite in drink and sharing the cave's history with Solveig, have the vitality and unsentimental appeal of other stories in which Brown portrayed characters with similar motives. For example, there are echoes of the boy of 'Five Green Waves' and the opening of *Fergus: Tales of a Bad Boy*, a long manuscript on which Brown worked from the year of *Pictures in the Cave* till January 1986.

'Stone People' tells how the survivors of the sandstorm which buried the village of Skara Brae react to the inevitability of new danger, the Vikings; 'The Ship of Death' is a tale of how a dead farmer, head of the island, is given a symbolic Viking funeral, burned in a stone boat, to keep alive the tradition for his community, which cannot afford the trappings and ceremony of the age when they could afford to burn ships: 'The flames congregated in the pyre, whispered and crepitated, then broke out, raged and sang and leaped in the wind, and climbed, until it seemed that a silken sail of yellow and scarlet was shaking out.'

Old Bressay's outrage at the threat to mine for uranium in the cave reflects Brown's response when this was proposed in Stromness, at the time this book was being prepared. There is an elegiac note to the skipper's reception of all the characters before 'The End of the Cave' and to his statement of their stories being entrusted to Solveig. His birthday cake's being 'like a great Viking funeral ship drifting into the sunset' is a sign of mortality, although the book ends with him settling into the chair that has been occupied by generations of lairds before he purchased the Hall.

Dialogue in this collection is excellent, while clever plotting and passages of description argue against Alasdair Maclean's dismissal of a book that demonstrates Brown's sense of audience and capacity to write for it:

> George Mackay Brown is Johnny One-Note with a vengeance and the old characteristics are all on display here: the inevitable Orcadian setting; the monotonously short sentences all facing resolutely in the same direction (surely Mr Brown's only forward-looking attribute); the large number of one-sentence paragraphs; the constant rebuke to literary sophistication; in short, the notion that one can will oneself into primitivism and that an a b c sort of simplicity is the signature of it.[19]

A point-by-point rebuttal of this could be constructed, but the strength of this criticism from a fellow poet – and its sweeping scope – seems overstated. It has to be acknowledged that there are recurring themes and locations in Brown's work, but there are other qualities, identified as, for example, the quality of 'grace', for which Brown was praised by another Scottish poet, Edwin Muir, in his Introduction to Brown's first book, *The Storm*. Alexander Scott, another poet and authority on Scottish literature, saw this quality in 'How the Sabistons Came to Orkney', the original of the expanded story in *Pictures in the Cave*, 'The Man from the Armada', the very story that Maclean was criticising.[20] Clearly, Brown's repertoire of themes had begun to wear out for some readers, but there were others who saw the strength of technique that persisted even in the weaker works.

Ernest Marwick wrote a positive review of Brown's earlier collection of children's stories, *The Two Fiddlers*, in which he praised him – 'a little part of our heritage of legend and narrative has been restored to us.' He continues: 'Mr Brown has let his imagination play on his themes . . . He is always true to the truth of his material; he does not attempt to force it into his own mould.'[21]

Only three years later, with this new collection, Marwick, himself a widely respected folklorist and historian, drew a comparison between *The Two Fiddlers* and *Pictures in the Cave*, accusing Brown of taking 'all kinds of artistic liberties with his material'. Since the books are quite similar, there is no good reason why they should attract such different responses from the person who knew Brown's work so well. Marwick accused Brown of building his stories on mere hints in legend, rather than history. This will come as no surprise to anyone who has read

Brown's Preface to *The Two Fiddlers*, where he described his method as precisely that: taking fragments and creating stories from them.

While it is important to document critics' responses, particularly in this phase of Brown's work, where they appear most critical, and perhaps most justified, it is equally important to keep them in perspective. Where all this negative – even hostile – criticism came from was perhaps the critics' boredom or impatience with Brown's persistent themes. They were clamouring for something new.

His next collection of children's stories, *Six Lives of Fankle the Cat* (1980), sketched out and begun in July 1976, oddly – whether deliberately or coincidentally, we cannot know – encompasses the isolation Brown must have been experiencing at this time, isolated from both the literary community and from fellow Orcadians: 'There was nobody else on the island to share her visions and fantasies with', as he says of his character:

In this children's story, an imaginative eleven-year-old who loves to invent and act roles is given a cat, Fankle, who fascinates her by his tales. Brown makes up adventures for him, including a fight to the death on a pirate ship, a cat congress to rid Ancient Egypt of Persian rats and a position as clandestine political adviser to a Chinese empress.

Less exotically, Fankle is a local personality, killing a huge thieving rat and renewing an old woman's appetite for life by his antics – which do not include participation in the children's winter activities, as he does not like snow. Their communally built snowman, charming school essays on Fankle and the bully's receiving a shock provide a background of reality to Fankle's yarns. Similarly, Jenny as a grandmother prefaces her allegorical tale about man's exploitation and slaughter of animals with reference to 'that oil rig' and 'The uranium mine', his observable impact on the environment. There is also a swipe at 'science'.

Tantalisingly, the smoothly paced story ends before Fankle's lives are used up, but Brown has provided an assured narrative. More inventive than his earlier writings for children, which leaned heavily on familiar history, legend and setting, this book has much for older readers to enjoy.

'Quiet perambulation'

Brown continued to write weekly columns for *The Orcadian* newspaper, maintaining his journalistic mode, writing about the daily and weekly events in his local community of Stromness. At this time his columns were longer than his earlier ones in, for example, 'What the Pierhead is Saying' (*The Orkney Herald* and *The Orcadian*), and they had a more imaginative slant. They appeared under the title, 'Letter from Hamnavoe' (collected under that title in 1975); from 1976 they were headed 'Under Brinkie's Brae' (collected in 1979), the name referring to the hill above Stromness; a second collection of 'Under Brinkie's Brae' columns was published as a book in 1992, as *Rockpools and Daffodils*. In these pieces Brown consolidated his focus on Orkney in regular writings. These are little gems, amounting to almost a quarter of a million words in the three collections, and far more than that if we include the columns that were not selected for publication in these volumes. They contain some of his freshest writing from this period.

In the issue of 18 February 1971, Brown sketched out for *Orcadian* readers the nature of this new column:

> It is proposed each week to write a letter to some Stromness 'exile' in Auckland or Vancouver or the Falkland Islands (or anywhere else) letting him know some of the things they are saying along Victoria Street and Franklin Road.
>
> It is a queer time, when you think of it, to begin letter-writing, because the postmen have been on strike for a month now, and this is almost certainly the only letter being written in Stromness today.
>
> We miss the postmen grievously – we never really appreciated them till now. Every morning regularly I was awakened by the rattle of the letterbox and the whispering fall of letters on the lobby floor; and that more than the thought of breakfast made me get out of bed . . .
>
> We Orcadians feel very isolated these days as one of the most precious things in life, the communication between friends, has dried up.[22]

The conversational tone – 'when you think of it' – is typical of these pieces. For some, this may seem a bit couthy, but these little essays are a study in economy and structure, often elevating the commonplace to the thought-provoking, finding in the familiar something curious or making a virtue of repetition, when he pointed out that, though he had dealt with a subject before, there was still something new to be written about it. This predictability was part of the challenge and the charm of these columns, which still appeal, and are even more impressive in their collected form.

Brown thought his articles on local topics were the best things he ever wrote, an assessment that we might take issue with, but there is a rich variety of beautifully written pieces in these collections, and it is true that they might be among the best things he wrote during this period. On another occasion he said that he stopped writing them in order to recharge his batteries, suggesting that he took the task very seriously and devoted considerable energy to it; he did not simply scribble them down in an *ad hoc* way or see them as a routine chore.

The weekly newspaper column was, after all, the literary form in which Brown had had most practice over the years. The subjects ranged from changing times, changes in Stromness, journeys into his childhood, school, Christmas, the holidays, the seasons, Saint Magnus, Robert Burns, each dealt with at the appropriate time of the year, anything except the 'barren scuffles' of politics and religion. Instead, looking back, in 1975, when extracts from the columns written over the previous four years were gathered together in one volume, *Letters from Hamnavoe*, Brown described the typical one as 'a brief, quiet perambulation'.

Over the years the writing changed dramatically from light news to extended essays, not a rag-bag of items, but columns separate from the other main news articles, each with its own architecture.

Under Brinkie's Brae covered three years of writing. In his Introduction Brown focused less on the subjects covered and more on the technique he had developed for writing them: 'I might be content to call the best of these little essays "prose poems", and leave the matter there . . . I have a weakness for overlaying plain prose with a wash of lyricism.' Much later, the last column that Brown wrote – also the last of his writing to be published in his lifetime – appeared in *The Orcadian* on 11 April 1996 (later published in *Northern Lights*):

This morning – as I write – is April 3, and the first wash of Spring has gone over the earth.

It is such a beautiful word – April – that even to utter it lightens the heart. It is a little poem in itself. It is full of delightful images. It has its own music – little trembling lamb-cries at the end of a field. The first daring lark lost in light. You feel, in April, that you have come through another winter, a little bruised maybe, but unbowed.

Those chalices of light, the daffodils, having been sorely battered by the March storms, are shedding, one by one, their green covers and opening their vernal tapers. Soon all of Orkney will be stitched by golden threads of daffodils, a lovely spread garment for Primavera. (Goodness, I seem to have got my images all confused there – chalices, tapers, coats – but one may be allowed a little exuberance, tasting now the first wine of Spring. Wine! There's another image to add to the heap!)[23]

These columns are a good source of glimpses into his life, what he was writing at a specific time, people he met, his favourite authors, the comings and goings of visitors to Orkney and 'GMB' and, above all, the changes he saw in Orkney year on year. In these columns Brown had another means of preserving, in a different form and in a fresh presentation, aspects of Orkney life, its times, customs, history and its people. There is no sentimentality about this; he simply recorded these subjects and succeeded in giving them immediacy. Rather than preserving events like fossils, he brought them to life, in their bustle, heat and colour.

More importantly, the columns and the collections contained seeds of work he was to publish later, sometimes providing the main story or theme in miniature; in others, he might try out a slightly different tack on the subject. For example, in 1972 (13 April) he wrote about the triple threats to Orkney of 'Oil, Gold, Uranium' – a direct, unsentimental title for a column dealing with contemporary developments. At the same time he had just finished his first novel *Greenvoe*, although these threats were not named there:

We had better relish the flavour of every day we live from now on, because very soon the life of the place is going to be radically altered. Oil is going to change everything . . .

... between oil wells, gold mines and uranium mines, we can bid a swift farewell to the Orkney we know ... That Orkney is about to vanish as drastically as Pictish Orkney once the Vikings arrived.

Much that is wonderful and precious and irreplaceable will be no more.[24]

This short piece, with its dramatic subject, touched on the elegiac theme, but then jumped to the attraction of the impending mineral discoveries, in all their material enchantment:

Yet there is a certain amount of hypocrisy in those nostalgic backward glances. 'Suppose,' I keep telling myself, 'you were to be walking out beyond Warbeth, and you kicked a pebble – and, impressed by its hardness and heaviness, picked it up and found that you had an uncut diamond in your hand – and later found two or three more diamonds in the same place – what then? There would be less talk of the wistful past of Orkney; your mind would be one wild delirium concerning your own private jewel-strewn future.

This was quite a range to cover in less than four hundred words: from 'wistful past', to 'oil wells, gold mines and uranium mines' to 'wild delirium'. Although Brown, in his Introduction to *Letters from Hamnavoe*, disclaimed the imaginative element – 'Look for no odysseys of the imagination in 400 weekly words of journalism' – he could be seen as misrepresenting his writings, since this is exactly what they delivered. Above all, what these pieces showed was precisely how 'The outer world has intruded all too successfully into our silences and secrets'; Brown made a more credible case for this, to some, unremittingly nostalgic position. Taken as a whole, the columns plot the progress of this transformation of life in Orkney.

In fact, the strength of these pieces is that they provide in miniature a less strident, more balanced picture of progress. He allowed himself less room here for railing against progress; in this short form, events were left pretty much to speak for themselves, with very little commentary. Strikingly, Brown also made space for the positive side of the argument: he includes the pros, as well as the cons, of modern inventions, recent discoveries and new technologies.

Perhaps the most important lesson we can learn from these pieces of journalism is that we should look more carefully at his literary treatments of these subjects; there is much more to Brown's novels, poems and short stories about progress than naïve ranting. There is always a study of loss, certainly, but there is also an awareness of the inevitability of change.

Conclusion

In 1977 a volume of *Selected Poems* was compiled from five earlier collections: *The Storm* (1954), *Loaves and Fishes* (1959), *The Year of the Whale* (1965), *Fishermen with Ploughs* (1971) and *Poems New and Selected* (1971). The selection included several poems from the first three volumes, only eleven of the sixty poems in *Fishermen with Ploughs* and almost all of the new poems in the fourth book. Arguably, some of the better poems were left out, such as the elegies for Thorfinn and J. F. Kennedy, and the selection was hardly a balanced choice: none of the poems from Parts I and II of *Fishermen with Ploughs* appeared, and only one each from Parts III and IV, nine from Part V and nothing from the prose poem. This selection disrupted the carefully planned structure of the original collection. There were only two poems from his first collection, *The Storm*.

The implication of this selection is that he was far from attached to his earlier poetic schemes and sequences. In fact, he had moved on from them considerably. His focus, during this period of his writing, had clearly shifted to the much larger scheme of the 'Idylls'.

Yet, the Orkney connection was still there in his writing, in many forms, including Brown's statement of the importance of Muir's encouragement, in *Edwin Muir: A Brief Memoir* (1975). This little volume, neither profound nor analytical, provided an impression of Muir in keeping with Brown's other written and spoken accounts of his Newbattle Abbey College mentor. Muir's lecturing style, encouragement of Brown through comments on his work and successful attempts to have him published were brought out clearly, as were the personality of Willa Muir and Brown's gratitude to her husband: 'I think that without Edwin Muir any seeds of poetry in me would have died through sheer discouragement'. Published in an edition of 160 copies, this tribute is worth tracking down as a sincere, elegant piece of writing which reveals as much about Brown as his subject.

The period covered in this chapter fell between two productive periods, the early 1970s and early 1980s. Later, a new creative burst would produce *Beside the Ocean of Time* (1994), an ambitious novel that Brown said had a section that was '*Greenvoe* all over again'.[25] Yet there was more to it than that. What such remarks, and some of the writings of this period, tell us is that Brown, hardly surprisingly, was conscious of mining the same sources repeatedly. He was willing and able to engage with those who criticised him for doing so, ready to persist with his artistic vision and to preserve his sense of the value and meaning of his writing. After all, he knew that he was not the first to write about one small place; other successful writers have focused on a narrow range of subjects and scrutinised a small community again and again, such as George Crabbe, J. M. Synge, William Faulkner, Willa Cather and Carolyn Shute. He knew that this need not in itself be a flaw.

Perhaps his 'Idylls' scheme was created to express another version of Orkney's fractured, and constantly changing, history, one that could not convincingly be moulded into one unified whole. Perhaps fragmentation, rather than unity, was his real theme at this time.

Having come through this testing phase, Brown was revitalised. From this point on he was much more productive. Perhaps this testing period was just what he had needed; his output certainly increased enormously in the next decade. As he continued to experiment in poetic and narrative forms, he remained committed to his favourite themes.

9

The Recurring Journey
1981–91

Introduction: 'Orkney is a microcosm'

Writers like me who live in a group of islands might seem to be cut off
from contact with other writers and with the market-places of
literature: Edinburgh, Glasgow, London.

That may not be such a drawback as it appears. Even if it is a
drawback, there are more than adequate compensations: for example,
the imposing of a work pattern without distraction, but – much more
important – the possibility to see life as a harmonious whole. A place
like Orkney is a microcosm of the inhabited globe; here meet and
mingle most of the 'types' that compose the human race. They can be
seen in all their shifting relationships and patterns; not only do we see
the islanders who live and go about their daily businesses, but we have
knowledge of their roots in the past, we have stories . . . about their
origins and ancestry and kin . . .

. . . a small community is not at all insular, a mere scattering of
yokels and beachcombers. It is a rich and diverse entity: all of
humanity reduced to a scale that can engage our sympathy, satire,
imagination.[1]

This was not just Brown's view of his islands; he saw it as a well
established literary technique:

Looking at the great wheel of human life in a small segment is an
ancient literary device. Chaucer chose a random company of pilgrims.
James Joyce wandered about Europe but wrote entirely about the city
he had exiled himself from, Dublin.[2]

This was a far cry from the man who at one time was desperately
sure that he had to get out of Orkney. By this time he had made it
his own, his source of subject and inspiration. Accused of mining

George Mackay Brown with the 'Pierhead Parliament' of Stromness in 1970. Taken by Ernest Marwick.

it too often, he maintained that he had not yet exhausted the material:

> I got sort of tired of people saying Oh, sooner or later he'll begin to scrape the bottom of the barrel, you know, he can't do anything more, he's exhausted the whole subject . . . But I don't think so, you know, there's so many themes here that you could live to be quite an old man and still only be a quarter the way down the barrel really . . . So I said to myself, just to show these guys, you know, I'll wander a bit further afield in my imagination.[3]

Brown returned to the novel during this period, with his first one in eleven years. He also returned to the Orkney setting, but in a new way; the whole world was taken up in the sweep of one story. Recurring journeys across time had created a fluidity in his narratives; with his next novel, *Time in a Red Coat*, the nature of time itself became the subject. Time became a character.

Brown's continuing connection with Edwin Muir was signalled by his edition of *Edwin Muir: Selected Prose* (1987). Brown selected and introduced the works and wrote a memoir for the centenary of Muir's birth in a volume that divided its reviewers. Several regretted the inclusion of substantial extracts from widely available books at the expense of selections which would have reflected the variety of Muir's prose. Lack of editorial information and comment on historical and literary contexts for Muir's experience and ideas troubled others, as did Brown's brief Introduction and what they saw as the uncritical adulation of his concluding essay, 'Edwin Muir at Newbattle' (which had already been published in *Akros*, 16, 47, August 1981). Yet these were features which held most appeal for some critics. Neither a scholarly nor satisfying work, this hurriedly compiled book was still a gesture for a man Brown continued to venerate.

This was to be one of the few performances of Brown the literary commentator. During this period, instead of arguing for his ideas and preoccupations in journalism or guide book, he expressed them in event and character, in his prose fiction, and in form and structure, in his poetry. The critics' challenge seems to have motivated him to concentrate on giving artistic form to his values and themes. This is not to say that he had been diverted by the critics, but that, from now on, the works expressed his ideas more directly. In terms of his development as a writer, this stage marked a strengthening of his commitment to his recurring ideas and closer scrutiny of the very notion of a recurring idea or journey.

Biographical notes: 1981–91 (aged 60–70)

There were three main strands in Brown's life at this time: writing, illness and artistic collaborations with the composer Peter Maxwell Davies, the photographer Gunnie Moberg, and young Scottish artists.

His contribution to the Gale research project took up a fair amount of his time. This was a long, 10,000-word, double-column essay by Brown on his life and work. Published in 1988, it was the most 'personal' of his writings in print until *For the Islands I Sing* appeared posthumously. Brown's growing reputation brought an increasing number of interviewers, such as Isobel Murray and Bob Tait whose

1984 interview was not published till 1996. There was also an increase in commentary and scholarly research on his work.

Ill-health took him to Balfour Hospital in 1981 and Aberdeen in 1990 for surgery. A cataract operation in Aberdeen in 1988 resulted in an unpublished essay, 'The Cleansing of the Eye'. Throughout this time, he continued to produce his regular journalism. In 1985 he was very pleased with a letter from Ted Hughes. In 1987 he won the James Tait Black Memorial Prize for best novel for *The Golden Bird*. Unusually, for him, he visited London, and was taped for BBC Radio 4, on 7 June, for the book programme *Kaleidoscope* in 1989. The year before he had made a visit to Shetland that produced writing offering insight into his composition process.

By 1984 Brown was secure in his vision as a writer, had financial security, had attracted the attention of scholars and students and was the subject of much literary criticism. His writings indicated a new level of self-awareness, with self-commentary, technical development and an increasing number of commissions. He was sufficiently confident to take a risk with his next project.

The recurring journey

Time in a Red Coat (1984) is the story of a girl who follows wars through Europe and across the huge expanse of time. The story is not set in real time and is a hybrid of history and fantasy. None of the events is specified in terms of time and place, but there are hints to help us work out roughly when and where she is; wherever war is, that is where she will be. All wars are presented as one repeating tragic pattern of human behaviour. It has been described as 'A Fable Against War':

> I was born in a burning palace. I was taken and hidden away like a butterfly in a box. I came to the Well. I'm here now, on the River. I must come to the Inn, then the Forest, then the Town, then the Burning Mountain . . . I can't see further than the mountain. Wherever war is, that's my place. It's all written out for me. In the end, there's the Dragon to meet.[4]

As she travels, it is not clear whether her journey is a quest, a form of self-sacrifice or a pilgrimage. One way to understand her journey is to see it as an individual's search for meaning and peace in a world filled with destruction. Elements of this tale are darker than Brown's earlier works, as the theme of constant renewal is replaced by constant war. Some elements of this story seem like an extension of 'The Wheel', where a committed, perhaps confused, individual acts out grief by returning to old haunts, trying to find a lost friend and a reason to continue.

There are a number of ways in which we could read *Time in a Red Coat*. Firstly, it is an anti-war story, taking us up to the twenty-first century, showing human beings as unable to break the pattern of conflict. Brown represents the world wars of the twentieth century as too awful to describe, leaving readers to their own imaginations. This is a clever variation, since he described so many war scenes.

It is also a story in which Brown was aiming to put new life into a 'worn metaphor'. This was a new way of writing about affirmation for Brown, since it involved describing so much death and destruction. All metaphors have the life crushed out of them in the context of war – what purpose can they really serve? – and so he set about recovering them. It was always his intention to focus on keeping the language – rather than the soldiers – alive. The iteration of this theme shows how easily the power of metaphor can be eroded – by anything from cynicism to inattention – and how determined Brown felt he had to be in order to recover the language he thought was being eroded. In the main character he represents the personification of an idea that cannot be eroded by time.

As the novel progresses it becomes more and more fantastic, a feature of many of Brown's writings in poetry and prose at this time. At one or two points we are not sure what type of story we are reading: is it all a dying soldier's dream or an old woman's foggy daydream? Or is it a fantasy about a girl who wanders unscathed through many war zones, through many centuries, and finds a simple peace at last?

Because one of the characters is a poet, there is another echo of the Viking skald, with one telling difference: the heroine is not celebrating war, but takes the wider view, noting all the damage to people, property and values. The purpose seems to be to undermine the excitement of war, even to undermine the idea of writing stories about it. The way the story is told ensures that any ideals attached to war are quickly dissolved.

Several chapters begin with the dissection of 'old metaphors'. The 'sure and sweet monotony' of the countryside is swiftly undermined by the opposing view. It is made quite clear that the heroine of the novel is 'not in search of country idylls'.

The most striking difference between this book and Brown's other novels is the shift away from the Orkney setting. There is no single setting. Brown did not locate the story in Orkney until the last chapter which appears to return to an Orkney-like place, but it too is no idyll.

War is a timeless story, endlessly recurring: 'These are matters that our children and children's children will have to endure.' The image of this repetition is perfectly captured in the museum of war in Chapter Fourteen. There is also a comment on the artists who have depicted war: 'Artists who had never seen a shot fired in anger had expended utmost skill to satisfy the aggressiveness that lies buried deep in the minds of the most pacific of men.' An odd rationale for war is presented: 'a flawless goal beyond the trash of materialism', an old Brown theme in a surprising new form.

Even the simple peace that the main character finds at the end of the novel has potential threats: there are the fisherman who has been press-ganged and a new mining project in the area. The little village is never safe from the outside world. The idyll is not sustainable. The small community will always be part of the larger world. The true task of those seeking peace, it seems, is to find ways to interrupt the pattern of recurring war and conflict.

Reflections on the 'worn metaphor' punctuate the war narrative; although the subject of the novel is unmistakably war, each war story is broken up by these non-narrative moments. This clever device prevents the reader from becoming caught up in the narrative of any one war, any one soldier or even the main character's experience of any of it. In what are almost 'asides' the narrative voice takes up a completely different tone and style; whatever the drama of the bloody or 'blood-boltered' scene, it is punctuated by this detached narrative voice:

> It is a worn metaphor, surely, that sees life as a river issuing from high mountain snows, with cataracts and torrents, down to a fertile plain and then, with many windings and turnings, finding its way to the vastness of the sea . . .

And by an extension of the metaphor, the river is not a figure for the life of a single individual, but the life of the whole tribe, the whole nation, the totality of the human race, and indeed of all creation . . .

It would be tedious to follow the river any further, though in the course of this tale – which is like a river too – we will have to go downstream a little.[5]

What is particularly deft about these reflective moments, recalling John Fowles' metafiction, is that while they are detached from the scenes of war around them, there are subtle echoes of the wars. For example, one battle which takes place on a hillside, with all the soldiers running up and down, in their assaults and retreats, is ironically echoed here in the mountain-river metaphor.

Brown risked destroying everything he had built up in his writing up to this point: his imagery, his Orkney and his trademark literary devices, such as numbers, seasons, Stations, religious rituals and natural cycles. Remarkably, the narrative voice in this novel wearily rolls out each of these and explicitly comments on their tedious familiarity. They can, however, still be recovered, as Brown showed when he switched from the almost cynical to a more hopeful tone:

And yet, when it was new-minted, the metaphor must have seemed beautiful and true.

Doesn't life begin with the high snow-bright innocence of childhood; and have great mountain tumults and sonorities in adolescence and young manhood; and afterwards there are the slow fertile turnings of maturity, when the river becomes ever deeper and wider; until at last it empties itself into the bitter immensity of death, the ocean of the end?[6]

Several chapters are 'enveloped' with these meditations on familiar metaphors; that is, they appear at the start and at the end of these chapters. They make the case that humanity – rather than George Mackay Brown – has worn out these metaphors.

This broken narrative is disconcerting and intriguing, even arresting: it is dramatic when we are caught up in the story one minute, only for it to stop abruptly the next. Allied to the question of who exactly the main character in the red coat is and what exactly she is doing, this creates layers of ambiguity. Everything changes all the time. There is still a sense of narrative momentum – and the nagging question of the girl's safety – but there is no pattern. There is no outcome. Although the wars end, or continue, there is no resolution of the central problem they present. There is no closure to the story of war; perhaps this was exactly the point Brown wanted to make in this novel.

Has anything been created out of the chaos and destruction of war? Is there anything that can endure? The answer is love and acceptance in a community. Again, the community is not unlike Orkney, but one of the smaller, more remote parts of the islands. This story comes down to how people treat each other – in times of war and peace – and this seems to be Brown's main theme. The girl's journey has been as much about that as about the action and aftermath of war. Nothing and no one exists in isolation, however isolated the community.

Was Brown being ironic? He had been publicly accused of wearing out metaphors, but in *Time in a Red Coat* he showed that it is not possible to do so; metaphors can be resuscitated. Was Brown saying 'Let me show you how I can rise to this challenge, write about an international subject, set it in a range of national settings, provide a collection of literary references, a menu of classic metaphors and still lead you back to Orkney'? If he was being ironic, then *Time in a Red Coat* is one of the most creative responses to critics in recent times. It is as if he has mapped out the route to his writing, plotting his literary recurring journey.

Orkney has become, in this novel, a metaphor for whatever place and time human beings can get to in order to rebuild relationships and communities, with the proviso that they have to want to go there. In its form, *Time in a Red Coat* is like a novel trying not to be a novel; yet it is very much about the process of Brown's imagination and his writing.

There were hints of this novel's theme in an early column in which Brown meditated on the 'most natural and time-approved method of welcoming the returning service-man' with 'a kiss and a big feed of bere bannocks and clapshot . . . simply, naturally, and spontaneously. In this degenerate age money steps in and spoils everything, dirties all relationships.'[7] The end of *Time in a Red Coat* has echoes of this scene, as the soldier returns to his village, is duly kissed and then interrogated by the factor about payment for his house and boat. There are also, in the column, traces of the healing powers of the Orkney setting: 'there definitely is some natural influence in the atmosphere of these islands, which, properly contemplated and assimilated, induces a calm and serene temperament in the inhabitants.'

In the closing pages of *Time in a Red Coat* this effect is seen working on the girl now that she has stopped following wars: 'she seemed to be utterly absorbed in the small summer curling waves on the beach . . . There was silence in the village, but for the gulls and the small breaking waves . . . "It's a peaceful village, this . . . Is it the end of the road? Maybe I'm home at last."'[8] Once again, we are back in Orkney, but in such an innovative and distinctive way. This glance back at Brown's early journalism shows how far he had travelled in almost forty years of writing.

Voyages and *Wreck*: new poems

During this period, and from this time on, Brown's output was a mixture of all genres and in each genre he continued to experiment and innovate. He wrote novels, poetry, short stories, plays and works in many other, often hybrid, genres.

His first collection of poems in this phase stayed with the image of the journey, *Voyages* (1983). Brown obviously thought highly of this collection, since he included almost all of it in his *Selected Poems*. Its themes are affirmation, the permanence of art and the universality of love.

In his typescript, dated 16 January 1979, providing a commentary on one of the poems in *Voyages*, written for a schools radio broadcast, he continued to engage with and refute allegations of parochialism:

> What pleases me too is that the story the poem tells can have any setting and any period. It would have been quite easy to write about an Orkney fisherman and his proud beautiful sweetheart who had dreamed of the wealth of Vikings. But then, if I had written that, the

critics would have said: 'See, we told you – he can never escape, George Mackay Brown, from his few North Atlantic Islands!'

It was unusual for Brown to take any interest in what critics said at all. He used to put all his press cuttings of reviews on the top of the dresser in his spare room – only collecting them because he had a friend who liked to read them – and did not usually pore over them for hints on how he might improve.

'Tired of being imprisoned for life in the Orkneys by critics', he took satisfaction in writing what he thought was a story in verse that could have had any setting in time and place, 'Letters to the River'. Theme and setting were not the only areas in which Brown innovated at this time; he also worked for new cadences in his verse: 'I have tried to move away from the rhythms of the north, which are stark and abrupt. The verse moves quietly, as though the scene is pervaded by soft perfumed mist.' This new rhythm features in the second section of 'Letters to the River':

> I have never been better off.
> I have three coats, large butterflies, across the bed.
> I have a purse with a silk cord.
> Gifts are left at my door.
> A poet I have never seen
> Is, they say, praising me in the villages.
> And the children imitate my dances.

Sadly, this is one of the few poems that Brown decided not to reprint, apparently more out of sensitivity about the subject matter than for its literary merit, since it is a fine poem. However, it deals with sexual relations, and this is one of the subjects that Brown censored in his work when he prepared the 1991 *Selected Poems*.

'Seal Island Anthology' comprises twenty-seven poems with ample space for scenic description, reflection and intertwining themes. In contrast, 'Bird in the Lighted Hall' depends for its success on a four-part structure: an old poet's words to his lute; images of life passing; his regret; final affirmation of how the instrument keeps music alive. The brevity of existence is stated tersely, in an echo of Bede:

> Bright door, black door,
> Beak-and-wing hurtling through,
> This is life.

Brown's joyous evocation of innocence and expectancy is tempered by a prosaic section, before nature provides emblems of old age and dissolution:

> (Childhood lucent as dew,
> The opening rose of love,
> Labour at plough and oar,
> The yellow leaf,
> The last blank of snow.)

The elegiac cadence in which Brown reflects how short-lived are a person's existence and contribution modulates into affirmation of music's power to endure over generations:

> Too soon
> The song is mute,
> The spirit free and flown.
> But you, ivory bird, cry on and on
> To guest and ghost
> From the first stone
> To the sag and fall of the roof.

The poem 'Voyager' contrasts the vigour and aspirations of youth with the jaded resignation of later years:

> After ten thousand mornings
> Of rain, frost, larksong
> How should I find a way back
> To the waterfront of Trondheim?

It is interesting to see Brown actively exploring the theme of imprisonment in one place, which is not Orkney.

Many of the poems in this collection deal, unsurprisingly, with voyages, one of the best treating marriage as a kind of voyage: the poem 'The Star to Every Wandering Barque, for a 25th Wedding Anniversary' won the Cheltenham Festival Poetry Competition, out of 21,000 entries (one of three winners, along with Charles Tomlinson and Edwin Morgan). The title is from Shakespeare's Sonnet 116, in response to a request for a poem for setting to music inspired by that sonnet. Brown's poem deals with an epic voyage. Men may be exhilarated by striving against the elements until 'The prow crashes/Into a new time', but women's resentful acquiescence seems a more mature attitude than seamen's venturing 'for more than bits of gold', as the voice of experience warns:

> 'It is that slut, the sea
> Always
> That has their hearts.'

Rather than finding stimulation in potential threats and obstacles to a secure marriage, the couple whose union has lasted twenty-five years had an uncertain beginning, described in terms of a sea journey, fraught with danger from the elements and environment, symbolising human contacts and relationships. Declaration that their freight of love has carried them through to their silver anniversary provides a positive and grateful conclusion devoid of complacency and sentimentality:

> How could we have doubted?
> Like a lantern in a barn door,
>
> Like the roof-furled familiar dove,
> Upon our voyage hung the homing star.

Brown's next collection was *The Wreck of the Archangel* (1989): 'Is poetry then a fraud? Or is it a quest for "real things" beyond the sea-glitters and shadows on the cave wall?'[9] While Brown's prose Introduction to his first major collection since 1983 stated his disinclination to travel on such a 'quest' to remote lands that had been a fertile source of inspiration throughout his writing life, it revealed his fascination with values and relationships which he reconstructed imaginatively.

As Brown noted, voyages provided the main theme of several poems at this time: 'the blue road to Jerusalem' in Earl Rognvald's crusade; Magnus on his way to sainthood via the ordeal on Egilsay and the journey of the Magi through settings as different as the desert, with 'all day the barren gold of the sun' and a northern island with only one door not closed against the travellers, 'And it a shelter for sheep'. The most successful of these combinations of narrative and description may be the title poem, dramatising the rescue of 'Archie Angel', sole survivor from the ship which gave him and his descendants their name:

> He endured there
> The seventy ploughtimes, creeltimes,
> Harvests of fish and corn.

Whatever the time or scene, Brown demonstrated his gift for condensed poetic imagery relevant to his topic: the sign of the Cross is 'in the air like a shield going before them'; a lobster is the 'Mercenary in the dark blue coat of mail'; and

> Twilight
> Silently
> Battered a bronze nail (a star)
> In the west.

The capacity of modern life to destroy the environment is the subject of several poems, spanning countries and generations to bring out the vastly increased scope of weaponry, contrasting with the qualities of life that it threatens:

> London is burning and breaking . . .[10]

> Poets of machine and atom,
> A last bird at a tidemark
> Announces the death of the sea . . .[11]

> A thousand missiles were hurtling here and there . . .[12]

> The sun goes dark.
> It falters and falls from the blue, the light-drained lark.[13]

Less explicit, perhaps, to those who do not know the landscape of north-east Scotland, the most chilling of these references is early in the book, where the nuclear installation at Dounreay features in a poem about Agricola's ships in the Pentland Firth in a prophetic conclusion which was a late addition to the typescript:

> Dawn flashed from the silver orb
> Further on, where forbidden fires smouldered.[14]

These are only a few examples of Brown's continuing 'quest "for real things"', as he said in his Introduction, trawling past, present and prophesied future – his ongoing attempt to define the essence of things, as in his earlier collection *Stone* (1987). Ten of its original sixteen poems were printed in *The Wreck of the Archangel*, with a new one introduced and changes made to a number of others, as in 'A Stone Calendar' and 'Milestone', where the conclusions are strengthened: 'Are on the sea' is revised to 'Three sea kings/Seek the House-of-Bread'. The focus is altered dramatically, becoming more powerful and graphic than the relatively empty original which appeared in *Stone*:

> How many miles to the daffodils?
> The child
> Is there always, lost among dews-and-gold.

was revised to

> How many miles to the lost children?
> The stone
> Cries in a daffodil surge, with spindrift of dew.

By contrast, loss of the last line of 'Song of the Stones' may seem like one revision too many: 'The wave harps the stone to sand and whispers.' Yet Brown's new version was better at capturing time, movement, sound and atmosphere:

> Stone in hourglass
> Whirls, scythes, sinks upon silence.

Appearing after several slim volumes, *The Wreck of the Archangel* was substantial collection, his most satisfying since *Fishermen with Ploughs* (1971).

Selected Poems 1954–1983 (1991), by contrast, was a surprisingly disappointing selection for three reasons: the number of excellent poems omitted, the nature of certain changes to the texts and the allocation of only 135 pages to twenty-nine years' work. While accepting that constraints of space forced difficult decisions on Brown, it is difficult to justify omissions of some of his best work, while inferior poems were included.

Some of the omissions can be attributed to Brown's apparent self-censorship of, for example, poems with sexual content – however slight – or connotations of anything suggesting wildness or irreverence. Poems were dropped altogether or modified, losing their original vitality. For example, nuances of the beachcomber's cheeky perspective were lost when his reference to how fear of church Elders forced him not to work on a Sunday changed from: 'Sit on my bum' to 'Smoke on the stone',[15] as if Brown were afraid of offending those who observed the Sabbath. Similarly, the 'big wind' which 'Whirled up Merran's petticoats round her head' became, after revision, 'whirled rose-petals, spindrift, round Merran's head'.[16] An object of gossip changes gender: 'A black lamp in a window there. Look./But after nightfall/Moths and men flutter her flame. The slut', became 'A black lamp in the window there. Look./A good skipper once,/All but ruined with aquavit and rum.'[17] Around thirty of the two hundred textual changes were of this type, fifty others being small changes in spelling and punctuation and the rest attempts to improve the sense or metrics – nearly all successful:

> A poet's drafts represent his rough pilgrimage towards the final grace of the poem. They chart a voyage of discovery during which words mutiny, lines are keel-hauled and stanzas are occasionally made to walk the plank. Sometimes the whole craft is suspended in the doldrums. Sometimes it skims home with just the slightest tacking and veering.[18]

The best example of this sensitivity – or squeamishness – was the way Brown changed 'Hamnavoe', arguably his perfect poem: 'A stallion at the sweet fountain' became 'A cart-horse'; merchants 'holy with greed' were now 'rosy with greed'; the fine snapshot of a crofter woman trudging 'through the lavish dung/In a dream of cornstalks and milk' was replaced by the town bellman's bread and butter announcements with a poor pun. The effective original stanza six was omitted and 'lovers unblessed by steeples' who 'lay' under the moon became 'Ploughboy/And milklass' who 'tarried' under it. 'Hamnavoe' remains a fine poem even with Brown's revisions.

In spite of these disappointing changes, the 1991 *Selected Poems* still has much to admire. It was reprinted in 1996 in a new, 'enlarged' edition as *Selected Poems 1954–1992*, with the addition of three poem cycles, 'Tryst on Egilsay', 'Foresterhill', 'Brodgar Poems' and two other poems. Many of Brown's collections seem unsatisfying because of their limited selection. This one remains a meagre representation of his published poetry over thirty-eight years. Many important poems are omitted, while inferior ones are included. Moreover, the many limited editions, which contained some excellent poems, would not be seen by many readers. The *Collected Poems* (2005) put this right.

Legend and fantasy: short stories

In *Andrina and Other Stories* (1983) twelve of the sixteen stories have familiar elements, such as the Orkney setting, but with striking new nuances and techniques, such as ambiguity and fantasy, as Brown began to go deeper into the psychology of his characters. This may be why he started to write more ghost stories, myths and metamorphoses.

The main character in 'Michael Surfax, Whaler' is developed in letters he writes, which reveal a startling fluency, in several styles and tones for different readers. The hard-headed skipper is shown to have other qualities. The idea of there being more to someone than meets the eye recurs throughout this collection. Characters are transformed, as unexpected facets of their natures are disclosed. Some are transformed into different beings in fantasies.

'A Winter Legend' is a fairy tale with a moral lesson. A princess, imprisoned and forced to live on a diet of worms and dried grass for fifty-one years, has passed the time reciting, singing and scratching on the floor stories remembered from her childhood, all except one story, 'a winter legend that was a white confusion in her mind'. Released by a snowflake that turns into the key of her cell, she changes into a swan: 'And now the swift-moving hands of the snow spun and wove about the princess a seamless vesture. Soon she was no longer a chaste statue in the barracks square. Her arms were sheathed in heavy flocculence. Her bosom was a white powerful curve.'

While she was imprisoned, history had overtaken the outside world, whose people have 'all gone into stories'. Before she suffers the same fate, in this 'last winter of time', she has her wish granted – seeing her parents in the form of two waves which break on the shore and withdraw into the ocean: 'The swan-princess rose, hovered, tried to follow the two torn waves. But all those innumerable strands and drops were mingled inextricably with the ocean.' Now that she is a swan, she remembers the lost legend, which she sings: '"Once upon a winter . . ." The swan-princess sang at the shore the lost legend. A silver key turned in her throat. Silent, unmoving, she was gathered into the pure crystal of time.'

She is now ready for death, ready to follow her parents into the waves.

'Poets' consists of four stories, defining and illustrating the gift of poetry. In one of the stories five poets show their various motives, some satirical, some documentary, and the forms in which they work. The idea of interrogation – as defined in Brown's key poem 'The Poet' – is included, as one poet is asked by a mock jury, in seven questions, how he works:

> *How came you, in all this House of Man, to this one forbidden door?*
> A dark and devious way, instructed by ghosts, listeners, knowe-dwellers.
> *Who gave you the key?*
> It is my own forging . . . I forged my own key in silence and in secrecy . . .

He defines poetry as a 'secret language . . . essences of language known to the poet alone . . . so that men with ordinary speech are moved often to tears or to joy'. Poetry has the power to move to anger, tears and joy and can bring the poet recognition, but may require sacrifice and separation from the community of others.

Taken together, these four stories define the effect of poetry on different communities. Given the range of the poets' experiences, this is not an idealised view of poetry. Only one of them can be aligned with the 'interrogation of silence' described in 'The Poet'. What is new is that alternatives to this position are presented here, making the 'interrogation of silence' just one of several possibilities.

'Andrina' is the major achievement of this collection. Torvald is the hot-tempered crusty old narrator whose relationship with a young woman who calls every day to care for him is complex. As the story progresses, he relishes her attention more and more, to the point where 'A few words from her would be like a bell-buoy to a sailor lost in a hopeless fog'. He becomes emotionally attached to her: 'What claim have you got . . . on a winsome twenty-year-old?' He falls in love with her: ('What I dreaded to hear was that Andrina had suddenly fallen in love.') One day she fails to appear.

The time scheme is also complex, as the sequence of events seems distorted, moving backwards and forwards in time: at the start of the story Andrina's visits seem to be ongoing, but the story shifts abruptly back in time, more than a year, to the first evening on which she failed to appear. There follows the skipper's illness, interrupted by his memory of a dark incident from his past and sense of let-down amounting to betrayal, in his self-dramatising mood. He identifies with 'Captain Scott writing his few last words in the Antarctic tent'. On his way to the village to find out why Andrina has not called at his house, his thoughts of how much she loved his stories trigger Torvald's recollection of how he gave a cavalier, fragmented, boastful account of a still painful story. This prompts a further flashback to his first romance, fifty years before. Responses to his inquiries about Andrina disturb and bewilder him: no one has seen her. We are then taken back in time to the love story when a letter arrives from Australia.

Torvald's treatment of his first partner, rejecting her when she becomes pregnant, shattering their summer idyll, is described in a way that conveys both the contrasting cruelty of his actions and the extent to which it still haunts him:

> At once the summertime spell was broken. He shook his head. He looked away. He looked at her again as if she were some slut who had insulted him. She put out her hand to him, her mouth trembling. He thrust her away. He turned. He ran up the beach and along the sand-track to the road above; and the ripening fields gathered him soon and hid him from her.

This contrasts with his image as the vulnerable old man. The repetition of 'He' and the short staccato sentences create a very different effect. The emotion of loss of Andrina – who has become part of his everyday routine – and the guilt at his rejection mingle.

The letter from Australia is from the lover he rejected, informing him that the daughter she bore had herself had a child, Andrina, who died suddenly. She tells him that Andrina had wanted to look after the grandfather she had never met. Andrina must be a ghost, a reminder of both the sweetness of the love of his youth and the pain of his loss. A single, stark line, separated from the surrounding paragraphs by line spaces, dramatically conveys Andrina's absence:

She did not come again on the third afternoon.

Initially, the story seems to be a simple fantasy – the old man imagining that someone has come to look after him – but gradually, the darker past intrudes. In the end, it is one of Brown's best ghost stories.

Isobel Murray read 'Andrina' as a 'parable',[19] suggesting that there is a moral to the story; is it that the captain learns from his earlier cruelty, or that love and caring will prevail? As a collection, *Andrina* is surprising for its use of myth, fantasy and ambiguity. While there are familiar Brown characters, themes and settings, there are also reflections on the nature and impact of story and poem. There is also consideration of what it is about communities and individuals that generates – and even requires – stories and poems. However, Brown himself, writing informally (in a letter to Rowena Murray dated 16 November 1985), revealed that he did not see it as a unified collection, except for the use of myth: 'possibly some of the *Andrina* stories move deeper into myth than most of the stories that have gone before. Then time and place obey the laws of *The Tempest*, where the imagination only rules.' The starting point for 'imagination' was, as ever, his idea of 'silence': 'I sometimes think it's a bit like a séance: into the silence some words come. And everything starts from there.' While this is written in a personal letter, it does ring true, reinforcing many conversations and Brown's published writings about his work, its inspiration and process.

In his next collection of stories, *The Golden Bird* (1987), Brown regarded the longer of the two stories in this book, 'The Golden Bird', as a novel and the shorter, 'The Life and Death of John Voe', as a novella. The book won the prestigious and lucrative James Tait Black Award in 1988.

Can only do one's best.

I meant to look out a more representative bunch of typescripts for you, instead of that rather random lot, whose worth I can't estimate: at least, not yet.

Interesting, what you say about _Andrina_. I agree that it's not a unified set of stories. But critics, either for or against, have never influenced me. Kevin Crossley-Holland asked me what drift or direction my poetry was taking? Honestly, I never think of such things. It's as prosaic as this: I sit at the table after breakfast and think, "How about a story today, Mr Brown?" — tho' Mr B's mind is quite empty. Often enough, though (and this is strange) a story does come, usually with an image, which sets up a rhythm, and other images and incidents cohere. The same with verse. I sometimes think it's a bit like a seance: into the silence some words come. And everything starts from

here. I hope that doesn't sound pretentious, or daft.

Masked Fisherman is based on a brief incident in _Orkneyinga Saga_, a thing I find very moving. The sudden change in Guthorm's mood — he has been very frightened, now he is safe, and rich in fish for a day at least; he finds relief in rating his benefactor, especially as there is a mystery about him (possibly sinister.) This complex kind of reaction I think is true of human nature.... As for anyone is liable to slip and fall, even a friend of sea and shore people walking on seaweed

I think. Possibly some of the _Andrina_ stories move deeper into myth that most of the stories that have gone before. Then time and place obey the laws of _The Tempest_, where the imagination only rules;

What you have said in your letter I do find stimulating and valuable. And I much look forward to read further portions of

Part of a letter from Brown to Rowena Murray, 16 November 1985.

'The Golden Bird' concerns a long-standing feud between two women and their families. In spite of them the community goes about its business: '. . . it could be said that they lived in a kind of willed harmony . . . If there had not been this state of perpetual compromise, of "mending of nets and fences", life in such a small community would have been impossible.'

In addition to the feud, there are two other strands to the story: the figurative birds, Eagle John the school teacher and a boat called the _Golden Bird_; and the decline of traditional values and way of life in the island community. There is tragedy in so many people being caught up in a feud, but hope in the catalogue of island produce, making concrete the idea of sustainability. While internal divisions and external forces changing the way of life always present a strong combined threat, the action of 'willed harmony' persists: the men, aware that their wives keep their feud going – killing a lamb here, smashing a boat there – choose not to react: '"Go back indoors, woman," said Amos sharply. "Most things you see under the sun are lies and darkness . . ." Rob went inside. He said, "It's a good thing the child is asleep and can't hear a word of the things you say."'

Their story shows that 'willed harmony' requires patience, persistence and courage. Although the men are not willing or able to end the feud, they do not join in, keeping themselves to themselves instead. Ultimately, when the feud has run for three generations, the two warring women decide to make up, but, ironically, both die on the way. The next generation will put an end to their 'ancient quarrel'.

It is intriguing to see Brown focusing on social forces. Barriers between people living so closely together – the protocol of who can wash their clothes together in the stream and who cannot – are established in such feuds. Social interactions are circumscribed by histories of disagreement. Mutual dependence – bartering for food, for example – is threatened by both the internal feud and the arrival of the grocer's van. Perhaps the internal divisions are a reaction to externally driven changes; there is no longer any need for the bartering economy in this community. Its day is past. This change unravels social bonds. If these people really had to rely on each other for food they surely would. This change threatens their identity and, in some cases, fractures their families.

The second story, 'The Life and Death of John Voe', chronicles a man's life, its episodic structure assembling a steady stream of memories of his past. It gives a vivid description of Stromness, thinly disguised, and some of its inhabitants, likewise disguised. Returning from South America to a maelstrom of noise, movement and emotion, he hopes to slip quietly home, but instead finds himself at the Lammas Fair. The blind fiddler's music follows him through the town, evoking memories of his travels and emotional responses to the beauty of the music and, by association, the beauty of a woman he loved:

> And now it seemed that a sudden spell was being put on the fair. A soaring exquisite thread of melody rose from the heart of the throng. It was so beautiful and pure it made all the other noises cheap and tawdry. The crowd parted. The blind fiddler passed through, wooing his fiddle to him, caressing it, conspiring with it to put bewitchment on the holiday crowd. The sightless eyes looked at nothing. The varnished bird cried and swooned and triumphed as the bow flashed about the strings. The music dwindled, it died; the enchantment lasted for half-a-minute maybe. Then the blind fiddler put his cloth cap on the causey, and pennies rattled and rang in the street around it, and fell softly into it. The crowd flowed again about the blind fiddler and hid him from Jock's view.

The theme of continuity is represented in the cutting of peat. The same peat bank has been cut for generations:

> They laboured all afternoon to give the buried compacted forest back to the sun and wind . . .
>
> Jock sank in his tuskar. What was this, a sudden white curve in the vertical thrust of his cutting? He eased the earth from the whiteness with his tuskar. It was a long thin bone. He eased away more peat: another thin bone, at the end of which was a hand, a small articulated cluster of bones. More scrapings – a rib cage, a thigh bone – and there crowning the column of the vertibrae [*sic*], and fallen slightly apart, a small skull . . .
>
> A small hoard of flint arrow-heads had been buried at the child's side.

Recalling similar episodes in *Greenvoe* and Lewis Grassic Gibbon's 'Clay', this conveys continuity of dwelling, occupation and exploitation of the land. It contrasts with his own travels away from this place and, later, with his son's emigration to Australia. John Voe wants to put roots down in this place where his travels started.

The longest incident in the story describes an interrogation: John Voe, in his sleep, is called to account by every girl and woman in a 'court' where he is accused of raising their expectations of love and then breaking their hearts. His real crime, however, seems to be that he did not take up the work of the croft, but, instead, set off to 'unlock new horizons' in California, panning for gold, then on a whaling ship. Extravagant accusations are brought against him, like Mrs McKee's in the novel, *Greenvoe*. Both are required to defend themselves against persistent questions about their motives and their accusers' scornful reactions to their responses. None of the latter is ever sufficient to silence the interrogators. While Mrs McKee appeared to take perverse pleasure in her punishing, imaginary schedule of court appearances, John Voe is clearly bewildered. This demonstrates his innocence to the reader, but makes no impression on his interrogators.

Perhaps this is an insight into John Voe's conscience: he wonders if he should have stayed at home and helped his father on the croft; this is the only 'case' that his interrogators can build against him. Since he is interrogated in a dream, it might be the workings of his conscience. The real drama of this story is the internal conflict John Voe faces when he returns to the island. He has no regrets, but he is aware that there are those who think he should have. Perhaps there are parallels here with Brown's life. In any case, internal interrogation is clearly a strong image that recurs in Brown's work.

In the end, Brown assesses the main events of Voe's story and gives a rounded account of the whole life, right up to Voe's death. In this last section there is a new narrative device: thirteen very short paragraphs, followed by a long prose poem, of more than five pages, a total of fourteen elements, possibly a Stations of the Cross sequence. It draws the whole story together.

Voe's story is, therefore, told in more than one way, setting up a kind of interrogation for the reader: which version rings true? Is each version, in a sense, true? True to the character's experience? True to those sizing him up as he returns to the community? The construction of the story undermines the idea of one essential truth. In the last lines, John Voe's vision of his son's life again takes us beyond his real existence to the pattern of generations, as the dying man imagines his son carrying away his ashes:

> He opened his eyes.
> A young man was standing
> in the open door. He carried
> a jar on his shoulder

The young man turned
once and greeted him – then
in the heart of that winter
he went out into the
harvest-hoarding sun

John Voe said, *That is
my son. He is carrying
away the dust of my
death*

The fact that the story ends with myth is a key to Brown's emphasis; this is a story of individuals, but they can also be archetypes.

Brown's third collection of stories in this period was *The Masked Fisherman and Other Stories* (1989): 'Winter, season of storm and dearth, is still a mighty quickener of the imagination. The stuff of narrative lies thick everywhere, but in the past rather than in the present. Now the mind is too easily satisfied with the withering pages of newspapers and their "stories", and with the fleeting shallow images of television serials.'[20]

Brown's focus here appeared to be on winter but, in fact, the word 'quickener' is the key to this collection: regeneration and rebirth are its themes. It is no surprise, then, that six of the stories in this collection are Christmas stories. This is one of Brown's most uplifting collections.

The characters are all well drawn, all different, but the way in which they are interlinked is fascinating. For example, in 'The White Horse Inn' the linking device is the lamplighter going along the street, meeting all the other people in the village, so that we find out about them through their reactions.

This collection is invigorating for its catalogue of many different forms of regeneration: as street lighting comes to the town, the pub lights up the social scene; the school teacher stands up to his school board Chairman; a house and garden that have been neglected are reborn, as if reinstating the kind and loving personality of the previous owner. The writer finds regeneration at the edge of despair:

He was filled with slow disgust and resentment as the hollow characters and contrived situations of his novels heaved like jetsam through his mind . . .

The sketch of the fable he must write now – a long tale of a kind utterly new to him – filled his mind suddenly like an illumination . . . He wrote the sketch down in the writing-pad, and the images came in an ordered solemn sequence, as if they had been waiting for a summoning bell.

While he has his 'illumination', the very slight changes in light, as the winter solstice ends, are magnified:

Some snow had fallen in the night. When he awoke, he saw through the window part of a great purple-black cloud, freighted with snow. He got up and walked down to the shore. The horizon to the south-east was clear. The sun rose, a point further east than two mornings previously. The sun plucked this morning a brighter string on the great harp of the light.

So profound are the depths of despair, disgust and darkness that such moments of healing, hope and light seem like miracles. These are set on a par with the Christmas story that hovers in the background of some stories, in the foreground of others, in this collection. Several stories deal with this moment, each in different terms, when the sun is glimpsed through the winter darkness, bringing the promise of summer: 'the winter was over and done for Jamie and for the whole island. He was caught up in a green gathering wave of grass and daffodils, larks and herring shoals, that would presently break over the bewintered world.'

It is not just about the seasons turning; the characters have their own internal darkness to shake off. Because the external world is also changing at this time of year, there are some marvellous descriptions that capture at once the literal changing of light, but also the magic of the moment of change faced by each character. What they see, as they look around them at the end of their stories, is that the world itself has changed:

The islands glittered, low dark emeralds, all around.[21]

The first star glimmered in the dews of the cut stone.[22]

Outside, under the silver star-web, the ox bellowed once. A goat snickered.[23]

The little one slept in his crib in a corner; time pulsed softly through him, like fish in the fathomless depths.[24]

The croft was a little secure summer in the heart of perpetual snow. My mother sang to the child. I nodded off to sleep, my head like a bee-hive.[25]

Moments of peace are, in these stories, hard won. There is no idealised, predictable path to peace. Darkness has to be endured before the light comes. Each of the stories is an assertion of rebirth, not in pain, but in relief, replacing disgust and despair with renewed joy in life and love. Brown now expressed his themes and ideas through his characters' journeys.

Limited editions

Although some of Brown's pamphlets are modest collections, others are significant, and there is fine writing in all of them. Some of the limited editions are sumptuous, expensive, hard-cover publications, for which the word 'pamphlet' hardly seems adequate. They are neither well known nor widely accessible, but it is important not to omit them from an account of Brown's body of work. While some of them can be found in later collections, others were dropped.

All of the short pamphlets are included here in order to show how many shorter projects Brown was working on at this time – in addition to his longer works – and the different ways in which he was gathering his poetry together, in these smaller collections, with illustrations, in collaboration with artists and musicians and sometimes with a personal dedication.

Christmas Poems (1984) contained seven poems that later appeared in the substantial section of Christmas lyrics in *The Wreck of the Archangel* (1989, pp. 92–109). Just as the anniversaries of Burns' birth and Saint Magnus's death stimulated Brown to celebrate these figures he revered from his earliest knowledge of them, the approach of Christmas was sure to herald poems and stories on the Nativity, in addition to those appearing in Christmas issues of *The Scotsman*, the *Glasgow Herald* and *The Tablet*.

Whenever these poems are set in time Brown's principal characters are placed in testing contexts: burning desert, perilous sea voyage or freezing croft. Common to all these poems is the act of faith represented by the attendance of travellers (Magi and shepherds).

Two poems stand out: 'Dance of the Months' and 'Christmas Poem'. The first is a calendar poem, each month in a single line, before 'December with snowflake and star' is given a three-line stanza to make the Christian point:

> In the inn of December, a fire,
> A loaf, a bottle of wine.
> Travellers, rich and poor, are on the roads.

The final poem is best, taking us through the agricultural year until Christ's birth seems both necessary and inevitable. Brown hung framed copies of both poems on his wall, suggesting that they were particularly important to him. This may be because these poems, and the point in the year at which they were written, brought together a number of his personal themes:

Christmas Poem

> We are folded all
> In a green fable
> And we fare
> From early
> Plough-and-daffodil sun
> Through a revel
> Of wind-tossed oats and barley
> Past sickle and flail
> To harvest home,
> The circles of bread and ale
> At the long table.
> It is told, the story,
> We and earth and sun and corn are one.
>
> Now kings and shepherds have come.
> A wintered hovel

Hides a glory
Whiter than snowflake or silver or star.

The themes dealt with here were to form his 'poetic year' and he returned to these subjects at the same time each year.

The Hooded Fisherman (1985) is a limited edition, illustrated by Charles Shearer, containing a vigorous short story, later reprinted with four alterations, including a change of title, in *The Masked Fisherman* (1989). Retelling an episode of the *Orkneyinga Saga*[26] it is faithful to its events and mood, and presents an attractive picture of Earl Rognvald's skilful fishing in the dangerous Sumburgh Roost.

Brown explained his purpose in this story in the letter of 16 November 1985 to Rowena Murray:

> *Masked Fisherman* is based on a brief incident in *Orkneyinga Saga*, a thing I find very moving. The sudden change in Guthorm's mood – he has been very frightened, now he is safe, and rich in fish for a day at least; he finds relief in rating his benefactor, especially as there is a mystery about him (possibly sinister). This complex kind of reaction I think is true of human nature.

The four *Christmas Stories* (1985), published in a slim paperback, were included in *The Masked Fisherman* (1989). Three of them appeared first in newspapers or on the radio and are pleasant variants on the Nativity, but 'Christmas Visitors' is a much better crafted, more moving work, reminiscent of the tender, but unsentimental 'Sea Widow'.[27]

Keepers of the House, a book for children not published until the expensive limited edition of 1986, then in a general edition the following year, was written in 1976. Brown was quoted on the back cover of the 1987 edition: 'Some might call it a children's story but it ought to appeal to mature people and graybeards as well.'

Seven guardians of house and garden have their activities described in four thousand words. Each little story is lively enough, as Brown tells of 'small moon-tranced cats . . . their mad fiddles' and describes the moon as 'a new silver gondola . . . a fat Chinaman blandly admiring himself . . . a cold cinder crumbling into last gray ash'. Intimations of time passing and damage caused by a mischief-maker are provided in a 'seven ages of man' form and a humorous account of repairs to the roof. While children of up to eight years old are likely to enjoy these fantasies, older readers, including adults, will appreciate the hints of larger issues below the narrative surface and the manner in which they are dealt with and reinforced by Gillian Martin's excellent illustrations. In the light of Brown's comment it is interesting to note that he carried over into the later story 'A Winter Legend' (1983) the imagery of the moon: 'a gondolier, a fat smiling Chinaman, an old woman over fading cinders'.[28]

The Scottish Bestiary (1986) is a collection of nineteen poems, a deluxe edition of sixty copies costing £1,500 each, produced in collaboration with several young Scottish artists. In a format larger than A4, the poems came with original prints, presented as a boxed set. It is now a much sought after collector's item. While it is difficult to get hold of a copy, five of the poems were reprinted in *The Wreck of the Archangel* three years later and feature in the *Collected Poems* (2005).

The bestiary is a literary form going back to the Middle Ages: a collection of descriptions of animals, usually a mixture of natural and unnatural creatures. Brown's chosen subjects are harnessed to human beings' needs and whims, pursued and destroyed for food or sport, along with legendary creatures who are representations of human forces of destruction, and, finally, the human beings are, in turn, menaced by animals. He also included a symbolic element: the creatures' beauty, freedom and touching acceptance of their lot.

The long opening poem, 'Raven', describes the privations suffered by a ship's crew until the bird fulfils its task – discovering land. 'Field Mouse' dies before its time. Busy in its house, the creature's contentment, comfortable below the farmer's plough, is shattered – 'Then the earthquake struck' – in a clear echo of Robert Burns's poem. This inadvertent slaughter is followed by human beings' deliberate pursuit and killing. Wildlife has to fear a formidable array of threats in 'nets and hooks', 'blunt club' and 'thunder and smoke' of guns: a whale 'surges up,/A sudden fountain flowers from his skull'. There is here and there a curious mixture of fear and anticipation, as the animals wait for deadly meetings with their predators: 'the hare and the grouse and the vole. With joy and terror they wait for the tryst.'

One creature, the Unicorn, seeks to be sown into a tapestry where, immortalised, it will outlive its creators:

Gravely, there, for centuries, heraldic,
He sports with the lion.
One by one the royal ladies have withered and died.

Tapestry also features in the story of the 'Lion', scoffed at as an incredible creature by a far-travelled skipper whose scepticism disappears when he receives the gift of a magnificent specimen of what will become the Scottish national emblem.

This collection is therefore a traditional literary form with a Scottish accent, including indigenous animals of Scotland: grouse, whale, seal and spider, the last of these not typically Scottish but famous in Scotland from the story of Robert Bruce. Bruce learned from the spider's pertinacity 'once more to spin the web of policy and statecraft'.

The wolf, like the raven, is harnessed to the service of human beings, as it licks the chief's hand in what seems to be the wolf's decision, less a process of domestication and more a kind of reconciliation orchestrated, not by human beings but by the animals as a self-protective mechanism: 'And the great smoking tongue of the wolf curled about his fingers: the kiss of peace.'

The case is made that the life of animals may be better than that of humans in 'Eagle'. Brown conveyed the freedom and beauty of the creatures which do not have to face 'Ten thousand brutish days/Yoked with clay and sea-slime'.

What is distinctive about this collection is the way Brown related legendary creatures – part of Orkney lore – to modern times: 'The spirit of the Stoor-Worm is immortal. To-day we know it as nuclear war.' Brown set up in opposition Assiepattle – an idle dreamer – 'the spirit of poetry, music, art, dance': 'Now that the scientists and the mathematicians – those modern seers and heroes – stand impotent before the monster they have summoned up, let the imagination begin to work its spells.'

While this was a strong, familiar Brown theme, in this collection the interplay between real and imaginary animals works as a kind of exercise for the imagination, thereby engineering the effect he thinks is so important. This is more than a plea for the arts; it is a demonstration of their power.

A Celebration for Magnus (1987) was written for the year-long celebrations marking the 850th anniversary of the founding of Saint Magnus Cathedral. Another deluxe edition, it features a short play that is quite static, occasionally enlivened by choruses. There is music by Peter Maxwell Davies to accompany Brown's words. A recording of the words and the music is available on audio-cassette.[29] This publication was part of an Orkney-wide celebration: children from each parish brought a stone to be placed in a central position and there was a *son-et-lumière*, with stained glass windows, paintings, music and chant. Photographs of these feature in this lavishly illustrated commemorative volume.

The book contains over thirty pages of poetry, prose and verse drama, photographs, drawings and facsimiles of Brown's writing. The language is incantatory and the story is familiar to readers of Brown's work. He himself said, in his Introduction, that it was a sequel to his *Loom of Light*.

The first poem is a moving piece called 'The Death of Magnus', which Brown himself must have seen as a highlight, since it alone was included in a later collection. It tells the story of Magnus and Hakon. What is astonishing about this poem is how Brown retold a story he had used many, many times, still finding a way to make it touching:

The Death of Magnus

What's this? I'm bidden to a great feast?
But here I stand, lost
On a dark moor, and I can hardly move
For the heavy coat-of-state on my shoulders.

Men pass me on the moor. They wear masks
Of wolf and of raven.
They *seem* to pass me, then come about,
They stand in a yelping circle.
They are the ones appointed, I think,
To bring the earl to the feast.

How have I, of all men, deserved a feast?
The islands are in trouble.

Fire in the thatch, blood on the shore,
The tables and cupboards empty,
Weeping at every doorstep.
And I who am set over this people
Bidden to bring them with me to the banquet.

The women go by with clay pots to the spring.
Where is the golden bowl?
A man stands before you, Magnus.
He is poor. He's in tears.
The axe shakes in his hands.
The spring morning is very cold.
Put your coat-of-state about him, Magnus.

Quick – let the silver cord be loosed . . .

The dark waters rise up into my soul.
Here's your ship of death, Magnus.
Those bright ones? They ferry you over to the Feast.

This poem conveys the humanity of a man facing his death: from the first line, with the abrupt question registering his surprise and the informal contraction to 'I'm' – instead of 'I am' – then the second line shifts suddenly into a darker tone, showing his vulnerability and uncertainty – 'I think' – and throughout the poem, there are subtle touches that make us hear Magnus's human voice. His observations on those around him suggest the strangeness of looking at things for the last time. Although trappings of state are mentioned at the start and the end of the poem, these serve only to contrast poignantly with his sense of himself as 'lost', in every sense of the word: lost to his earldom, lost to this life.

The poem has many echoes (the Bible, Bunyan, Lawrence, *Orkneyinga Saga*), yet the presentation of the text makes it visually very much his own: along with the facsimiles of Brown's manuscript there are his notes on the action of the play in the margin. There are also echoes of his previous work.

The poem is a technical exercise in what he called 'salt mathematics', by which he meant that he set out the lines of his poems to echo the rhythm of the waves of the sea. He had explained the technique in the short story, 'Sara' (1971).[30] When he wrote the seven stanzas, he gave each one a number of lines from one to seven: the first stanza has four lines, the next has six, the next seven, the next two and so on. This is, therefore, one of his patterned poems.

Although 'The Death of Magnus' conveys the individual experiences of Magnus, the cook and others, the book, taken as a whole, makes it clear that, both at the time of Magnus's execution and at the time of the anniversary celebrations, these events were not just individual dramas; they were major events for the islands. This was not just another 'GMB' preoccupation; it was a turning point in the islands' history.

The play of which these poems are part is sober rather than dramatic, perhaps requiring a particular type of interpretation to work in performance. In any case, Brown saw much of his drama as 'plays for voices', rather than for stage performance. Having said that, there is fine verse throughout:

> Rejoice. Saint Magnus kirk
> Is launched on the ocean of time.
> The dove sits furled in the stone rigging.

All the other art forms in the beautifully decorated volume provide interpretation of Brown's words, so that this book works well as a celebration, as was intended.

The next limited edition, *Stone* (1987), although in many ways a 'stone Book of the Dead', is not a doleful volume. Sprinkled references to childhood innocence, the fulfilment of love, lively description of the shore's changing moods and surface, alongside ample evidence of people coming to terms with the fruits and dangers of the sea and the inevitable progress of time make *Stone* a reading of life which is thought-provoking and brilliant in expression. The oldest feature of the seashore, the stone, is approached from many perspectives, including that of stone itself, when the shore speaks its 'stone music,/One grain removed/From silence'. Stone is cast in the role of apparently permanent observer of human existence, outlasting the green, rainbow, blue and grey coats of farmer, children, fisherman and spinner before 'the one in black, with a black flute' brings death.[31]

The human perspective is provided by Brown's description of how people adapt at the shore – building ship, larder, house, window, gravestone – bringing together a whole span of human existence into the sequence of sixteen poems:

> Flower of the stone,
>> A name, two dates, cut deep.

Ironically, a narrator corrects stone's complacent assertion of its continuing useful life in contrast to the mortality of plant, bird and human beings:

> Said stone to raindrop,
> 'Don't run.
> We're for the mill, you and I, to grind bread.'[32]

In 'The Shore at Daybreak' the stones, and everything else on the shore, are exposed where they have been hiding in the darkness; when the humans begin to appear, colour and texture gradually come into the scene:

> 'Childe Rowland to the Dark Tower came' . . .
> (A wave on a stone)
>
> One silver star in a tumult of black stars
> (A wave on a stone)
>
> Persephone, shepherd your seapinks now
> (A wave on a stone)
>
> Skipper, fishermen, mingle salt with silver
> (A wave on a stone)
>
> Toll, here, your seventy winters, man
> (A wave on a stone)

Repetition invokes the incessant movement of the sea, through the minutes before dawn. Brown did not dwell on individual characters – their activities seem small and pointless – but set up reverberations of the opening quotation, suggesting that a crucial turning point had been reached. He detailed the emergence of a new day in which the activity of people and nature are transitory beside the perpetually recurring wash of sea on shore in the refrain of 'A wave on a stone'.

Brown chose as his subject the inevitability of time, but without bitterness, nor is it maudlin, nor was he charting patterns through the generations. This collection creates a strong evocation of the sea's permanence, but its subject is stone: against the backdrop of the sea's permanence, stone marks out the stages of human life and its comparatively minute span. Finally, ironically, stone itself is impermanent: 'The wave harps the stone into sand whispers.'

As this was a costly limited edition, Brown included ten of these poems in *The Wreck of the Archangel* (1989).

In *Songs for St Magnus Day, The Seven Jars of Sorrow and Comfort* (1988), as in many of Brown's works, the jar has physical and symbolic importance: 'It is very symbolical, very ancient and fits all of life (and even death) and the entire human condition. The making of the first pot (for oblation, drinking, or the ashes of death) must have been as wonderful as the first wheel.'[33] This limited edition of 150 copies uses images of jar or cup to reflect mood, as events take Earl Magnus closer to his death and sainthood: 'a jar of peace ... a stone bowl ... cup of keeping', signifies Magnus's purpose, his awareness that his end is imminent and acceptance of that fate, in the first three stanzas. In the fourth stanza, communion from a chalice equips him for the encounter with his enemies, 'the jar of comfort' after a night of isolation and anguish in the cold church. In the fifth stanza, the church is described as a 'stone ship' – the church as a kind of vessel – then he offers himself to God as a vessel of salvation: 'He offers his clay to wheel and kiln once more.'

The metaphor of jar/vessel/chalice does work, but it has to be worked for. In places this poem is obscure, as Brown weaves the story of Magnus around the image. Ironically, amid all this anguish, drama and complexity, island life continues as before:

> *Ite: the voyage is over.*
> The skipper steps out of the stone ship ...
> A daffodil keeps a crumb of snow ...
> Below, a ploughman
> Follows, with a drift of gulls, his dithering share.

This is probably the best of Brown's Magnus poems; the metaphor is more convincing than his other uses of it. A great deal is compressed into forty-seven lines. There is a freshness about the natural imagery and dramatic irony offsets Magnus's dark drama. It comments plausibly on how events affect Magnus himself, the jars at once conveying his motives, his rarefied vision of sacrificing his life for peace, as well as his humanity, in his need for comfort, and his awareness of ordinary life going on around him. All three strikingly different perspectives are focused on Magnus, so that he is not simply a saint-in-the-making, or a frightened human being or just another inhabitant of the Orkneys, but all three at once. At the end, once Magnus has become a saint, we have part poem, part prayer:

> Saint Magnus, keep for us a jar of light
> Beyond sun and star.

Two Poems for Kenna (1988) is the shortest of Brown's limited editions, consisting of two poems composed for a close friend: 'A Writer's Day', written in November 1986 and 'The Prince in the Heather', written in February 1987. First published in an edition of two hundred, both later appeared in *The Wreck of the Archangel*, the first with minor changes, the second unaltered.

'A Writer's Day' is a study of the writer's labour, including movements and contacts, throughout the day, from start to finish:

Gulls

> It was a long day in his field
> Turning furrows like pages.
> He strove towards a sign, the cornstalk . . .

Sunset

> His seaward window was black and red.
> A poem might come with the first star.
> Lamplight fell on two white pages.

Tryst on Egilsay (1989), subtitled 'Hakon and Magnus/Seven Poems', is a Celtic Cross limited edition publication, set in a familiar period of history. Brown's Introduction, dated September 1988, is a skilful summary of the events described in the *Orkneyinga Saga*, but his purpose was more subtle than is suggested by the bald statement closing his brief Preface to *Tryst on Egilsay*, later reprinted in *Selected Poems* (1996): 'This seven-fold poem celebrates the events of that April day as seen by some of the people on the island.' What Brown was aiming to do here was different from his previous treatments of this story: 'In this sequence of poems . . . I try to imagine what is left out of the great story.'

Each poem features a different character, each with a different role and perspective on events. We are back to 'salt mathematics', as Brown varies the number of lines to the stanza in each of seven poems. With twenty-eight lines available in a section, he could examine characters' previous experiences, probe motives and display their roles in relation to the violent resolution of the islands' problem. Whatever their position on the page, the seven- and six-line stanzas convey the characters' reflections on and descriptions of the scene, but the penultimate stanza of the first five poems occupies a single line, in order to sharpen the focus on Magnus's vulnerability as he accepts his fate:

> Then, in the chapel, this cry
> *That they may take the wings of the morning . . .*
>
> Magnus housed long, in a seagirt cell, westwards.

In the Margins of a Shakespeare (1991) is a prose limited edition in which Brown took minor characters from Shakespeare's plays and made them central to short complete stories, for example, the doctor tending Lady Macbeth. Brown said this was only a piece of fun, but some of the pieces are quite moving. He liked to speculate on 'a stirring in the shadowy chambers where the lesser characters live' and 'listen at the keyhole or peer through curtains, and to wonder'. From the 'subtle hints and suggestions strewn about the plays' Brown gave each character a background, voice and developing role before, during or after great events.

Among the best are the Dark Lady of the Sonnets and Falstaff's page as the 'old twister' declines. These two were placed in Orkney settings, the Dark Lady becoming an island woman given to poetry, insensitive to the charms of the great poet Arnor, whose 'music and magic' she admires while reserving her affections for an uncaring fisherman. She can respond to Earl Rognvald's entreaty that she visit Arnor, apparently at death's door with lovesickness, without abandoning her love for Harald, as she sits with Arnor:

till he says a few fine words again,
    smiling,
  the wine-gleam shifting
    about his face,
    like sun and sea
in the eyes of a surly fisherman.

In 'Caliban' the moon-calf has become a beachcomber on 'a dying island', his home, the Hall, taken over by a star-gazing laird, whose demand for allegiance is rejected. Sympathy for Miranda, tied to such a father, retrieval of bodies brought ashore and the search for a missing fisherman show that the finer feelings suggested by Shakespeare have been recognised. The final passage of the story develops the beachcomber's tact and generosity. For atmosphere, treatment of character and settings that allow character to unfold from the plays' sketches, *In the Margins of a Shakespeare* is a successful realisation of the task Brown set himself.

While some of Brown's limited editions were coffee-table books – some for expensive tables – others were a different order of text altogether, giving full treatment to their subjects in writing and illustration. That Brown was invited to produce text for so many indicated his growing reputation and, perhaps, the appeal of his poetry to visual artists and musicians.

Portraits of Orkney

Unlike *An Orkney Tapestry* (1969) which took a clear stand 'with the poets', meaning that Brown was interested in the poetry of incident, rather than the 'facts', *Portrait of Orkney* (1981) is more of a coffee-table book, with all that that implies about presentation and content. There were two editions, 1981 and 1988, with two very important changes, in two new chapters. In the second edition Brown added a section on his childhood, the best and longest chapter, and substituted for a chapter on 'Culture', another called 'Song and Sign', which is an improvement on the dull, perfunctory list of the earlier version. He added interesting, though minimalist, thumbnail sketches of Orkney artists and poets. While the prose sections of this book are elegantly written, the literary pieces are much stronger. The endings of chapters are particularly well crafted; the language is beautiful.

While there is a sameness to some of the descriptions of, for example, Stromness – and how, after all these years, could there not be? – he still found a new angle:

> What can never be taken away from the town is a unique beauty. The stone web will always be there between Brinkie's Brae and the sea. The single surging twisting street is admired by all visitors to Stromness. But what they too seldom visit are the closes that swarm up the side of the hill, and the steps that seek down to the twenty creeled and salty piers, washed twice a day by cold incoming Atlantic waters.

With four pages or so in which to cover each subject, this book required strict compression. Yet, there is compensation for this in the verse which expresses a wide range of ideas in a few lines:

> The horse at the shore
> Casks of red apples, skull, a barrel of rum
>
> The horse in the field
> Plough, ploughman, gulls, a furrow, a cornstalk
>
> The horse in the peat bog
> Twelve baskets of dark fire
>
> The horse at the pier
> Letters, bread, paraffin, one passenger, papers
>
> The horse at the show
> Ribbons, raffia, high bright hooves
>
> The horse in the meadow
> A stallion, a russet gale, between two hills
>
> The horse at the burn
> Quenching a long flame in the throat.

'New forms'

'George did not really write drama as such. His gifts were those of the poet, the story-teller, the renovator of myth and the re-creator of ancient legend,' wrote Donald Campbell.[34] 'Though George was constantly intrigued by the dramatic form, he was no dramatist. He wrote choral music, settings for voices. Actors were conduits for his poetic vision,' agrees Morag MacInnes.[35]

Three Plays (1984) brought together *The Loom of Light* (1972), *The Well* (1981) and *The Voyage of Saint Brandon* (1984), providing very little to contradict these comments. As Campbell asserted, conflict, irony and character development, the dramatist's art, did not figure strongly in Brown's plays. As MacInnes continues, 'actors were . . . not movers and shakers and door slammers . . . an audience wants stuff happening'; such practicalities of stagecraft are not common in Brown's published plays.

Yet Brown's interest in the dramatic form is indicated by the fact that over fifty years, he wrote fifty plays. Several of them, though unperformed and/or unpublished, satisfy the criteria identified by the above commentators. From the many reviews of productions that Brown wrote in his journalist days and his writings about plays, it is clear he was aware of what constituted viable drama. In fact, what Brown was attempting to do in his drama was to find new forms. He had, after all, articulated his personal notion of dramatic form: 'I am interested in writing plays. Not in the traditional 3-act or 1-act mode – I think these are played out. We have to go on to new forms, I believe.'[36]

The form Brown adopted for *The Loom of Light* is, in his own words, 'more a chronicle than a developing play'. He stated that he found it difficult to write about sanctity: 'the devil has all the best stories too'. But Brown was concerned to tackle this difficult writing challenge: 'But if a writer uses the best and most beautiful language that he can, then he may, from far off, admittedly, suggest something of the nature of sanctity.'[37]

He did this by deliberately developing a previous work on the subject: '*The Loom of Light* . . . began with the last scene only, which was a kind of coda to the prose account of St Magnus's rule and martyrdom that appeared in *An Orkney Tapestry*. Then it seemed logical to cast the whole "biography" in dramatic form: hence *The Loom of Light*.'[38] The original lively scene has been transformed from the story of two tinkers, who know about the Saint Magnus story from a distance, after his death, and experience a miracle after praying to him, to the whole story of his life in the play.

Each of seven sections begins with a Chorus explaining the King of Norway's machinations and how they affect the Orkney earldom and its people. Seen to be suffering through the quarrels of their ambitious rulers, with the Church unable or unwilling to intervene, the people of the island are given a vitality that the nobles and clergy lack: the peasant Mans, full of resentment, blustering yet cowardly; his patient wife Hild, yoked to the plough; Jock the tinker, anxious and caring; and Mary, his partner, 'too fond of bright things', steadily losing her sight, but not her vigour. Always, 'the monks in a green holm sing' to illustrate the Church's continuing prayer, but like Hakon's hectoring supporters, they are pretty pallid creations, perhaps deliberately so, lacking individuality and genuine involvement in the action of the play. The metaphor of chess is used to describe Norway's scheming, so that the characters are chess pieces, not very dramatic, but conveying the idea that Brown wanted to present.

There are few surprises in this well known story, as Brown 'follows the main outline . . . as it is recorded in the Orkney Saga. It tries to give a picture of life in that brutal and extravert age, from the highest to the lowest, from nobleman to tinker. I haven't scrupled to use my imagination when I thought it might illumine some dark places.'[39] Brown's imagination did indeed illumine 'dark places', the crofters' physical conditions and the risk to their crops and lives.

The highlight of this play is the final scene, improved from the workmanlike and absorbing version in *An Orkney Tapestry*. Deservedly, 'Jock and Blind Mary' has become part of the Orcadian dramatic repertoire, performed occasionally by schools and amateur societies. The last scene draws together the different strands of the story, portraying the bishop's enigmatic role, Jock's humility and lack of resentment, the restoration of sight to the perennially spirited, irreverent Mary and public acknowledgment of Magnus's sainthood.

The 'new forms' that Brown was working towards were in evidence here. There is the chronicle, not a static tableau with a single narrator, but descriptions of points in time, defining moments in the history of a place. Brown took episodes and made them cohere, bringing together different threads, as in the dramas of the different earls, which was itself the drama of Orkney, split in two and only unified when one earl was dead.

These are short dramas which go progressively and coherently through different eras in history, bringing to life sparsely documented events. There is action, but without the pace and structure we expect in a play; instead there is excellent compression and suggestion. Some would say that this form of play works better on the radio than on the stage, and Brown himself referred to his dramatic writing as 'plays for voices' on more than one occasion. However, they could be performed in sets of two or three, like other contemporary plays, giving audiences time to adjust to and appreciate Brown's 'new forms'.

New discoveries, and people's responses to them, also featured in *The Sea-King's Daughter: Eureka!* (1991). *The Sea-King's Daughter* is another short play for voices, with seven voices unravelling the story of the Maid of Norway – the 'sea-king's daughter's' – voyage to Scotland. Six of the voices are her attendants' and the seventh is the queen herself. As the attendants offer commentaries on the weather, premonitions, the little queen's activities, running around enjoying the storm, or tell her a long story or pray, they reveal their own experiences and temperament, as does the object of their care, the queen. Margaret is an attractive, innocent and sincere person from her own speeches and what the others say about her.

Brown had the same order of speakers for each scene, the queen coming between the flirtatious girl who sees her to bed and the keeper of her clothes and valuables. This creates a sense of their routines; the audience becomes accustomed to their order. This pattern leads to the most striking moment both dramatically and visually in the layout of the page (p. 52), when the dead queen's voice is replaced by a stage direction:

> WHERE THE QUEEN WOULD HAVE
> SPOKEN THERE IS SILENCE.
> THEN THE SILENCE CHANGES TO
> THE MUSIC OF A REQUIEM.

This break in the established pattern emphasises how the queen's death has left a gap in the women's lives, a break that Brown prepared for with ominous hints in previous scenes.

In *Eureka!* Brown imagined the discovery of materials and processes which mankind has exploited for good or ill, at different times. Twenty-two are compressed into thirty-two pages of text. Brown made a few moments glow in their context, as when a stone that the characters had been tripping over is thrown into the fire:

> The stone cracked open. A net of dancing light
> went over the gray crypt walls.
>
> The faces of the old monks flushed.

Coal had come to heat the crypt Brown frequented in his 'New Botyl' (the old spelling of Newbattle) days. Other discoveries follow: Leif Erikson lands in America, gunpowder sweeps aside conventional weapons, iron is extracted and processed from rock, a duck drunk on a solution of rotted wheat discovers beer.

Brown showed how fear, scepticism or respect for tradition had to be overcome before the novelties were adopted. The focus of this story is not on the years of preparation or observation that often precede discoveries and innovations; instead, Brown attempted to capture that electric moment of first discovery, sometimes quite accidental, unexpected, even seeming magical.

Conclusion

Letters to Gypsy (1990), lavishly illustrated by Simon Fraser, opens with an essay reprinted from *The Scotsman*, in which Brown described looking after a friend's cat. This book has a link with *Six Lives of Fankle the Cat* (1980), Gypsy being Fankle's sister. (Another cat-piece is 'Augustus: A Mystery Thriller' (in manuscript, dated August 1991), an unpublished story about a cat turned detective.) Little notes to the cat fill out the text, providing a pleasant, undemanding read for cat-lovers. Brown did write letters to the cat every week, all very light, with the occasional characteristic image and echo:

> Dear Gyps,
> Thank you for sending me your journal for 1988. Very interesting reading:
> **January**: *Had New Year with voles and blackbirds. Ate one tin whisky-flavoured turkey. No hangover.*

Flashes of Brown's imagery, showing the influence of Edwin Muir, cut through the whimsy and there are moments when the language and ideas might be beyond the intended child reader:

> Oh, the horses! Such splendid heraldic creatures
> will still be here when the tractors are heaps of rust.

Brown also imagined Gypsy's letters to him: 'light ethereal insubstantial tissue-of-moonbeam'. This whimsical compilation to a cat, or perhaps to the owner of the cat, suggests that we could read it as a more personal statement, perhaps one of Brown's most personal voices. What is new here is the combination of humour and a more personal voice than we are used to hearing in Brown's work. Even as he was writing some of his most innovative fiction, stretching the genres of novel and play particularly, he could produce this lighter genre. Perhaps his growing sense of conviction in his writing gave him permission to digress from his more serious work; or perhaps this was simply another demonstration of Brown's versatility, in evidence from the earliest of his writings to survive, *The Celt*.

During this period Brown strengthened his commitment to his own agenda and territory for writing. He had by no means shaken off the critics who would continue to probe for recurring journeys and themes, but he had an interest in new forms; if his imagery appeared tired and old, he attributed that not to his failure to provide variation, but to the wearing out of language that he had predicted right from the start of his writing career. He was not going to take responsibility for wearing out images when his task was to 'interrogate silence' until he found new ones. That this was far from an arrogant position for him to adopt is indicated by his continuing revision of his own work; perhaps he felt that his published poems became worn out and needed an injection of new life.

The idea that language had become, in his words, 'played out', that metaphors had become 'worn', fitted very well with his sense of the continuing journey to find perfect expression of his idea. This coherent vision was sustainable, even if he did remain in Orkney – and it was perhaps the stimulus for what was to be the most productive period of his writing life.

10

'Perfect Silence'
1992–1996

Introduction

> But a circle has no beginning or end. The symbol holds. People in
> AD 2000 are essentially the same as the stone-breakers and horizon-
> breakers of 3000 BC.[1]

Brown held to this belief right up to his death in 1996, bringing it up
to date with his reference to the new millennium. This last phase was
perhaps the most prolific of his career.

There was a rich and energetic period at the end. He was considering
a volume of his essays and had already prepared a list of contents. He
was working on what was to be his last book, the collection of poems
Following a Lark, preparing it for press, reading proofs for it and, at the
same time, writing the text for *Pictures and Poems*. His journalism
continued, and in fact, increased, as his newspaper columns were up to
six times longer. His snapshots of Orkney life had grown into extended
reminiscences, recreating his childhood. He published a double volume
of his collected columns. Compilations of poems and stories involved
many revisions. Apart from *Following a Lark*, his first major volume of
poetry for six years and several limited editions, he produced substantial
new material in the short story. Wider recognition brought more and
more requests for commissions. He was full of plans for writing. With
so many projects in progress, he seemed to have a new lease of life. This
energy resulted in six books and seven limited editions in five years.

Brown still found inspiration, and fresh ways of communicating it,
in the values and behaviour of Orcadians. As always, there was a
particular focus on his native town of Stromness. Celebration of
social events remained a fruitful theme. For example, in *Following a*

Lark 'A Rainy Johnsmas' and 'The Old Wife and the Hill Folk' brought out communal respect for the observance of traditional customs. At the same time, everyday experience was being described from a personal stance, which took account of others' attitudes, as in 'Spring: The Kids of Feaquoy Farm' and 'Easter in an Island'. The *Orkneyinga Saga*, the Bible, Robert Burns' lore and cycles of the liturgical year were exploited compellingly, with a number of works examining the role of the artist, charged with responsibility to preserve, honour and 'hoard' language and imagery. Far from always looking backwards, he looked forward to 2093:

> I hoard, before time's waste
> Old country images . . .[2]

Brown's concern to offer faithful accounts of individuals and societies responding to their own generations' circumstances, aware of how previous ones reacted to the pressures and benefits characterising their own, found expression in a number of lively vignettes. Yet there are strong intimations of significance beneath the surface narrative and lyric: what deeper, essential meaning is there, once behaviour and emotions have been described, however vividly?

> Under the last dead lamp
> When all the dancers and masks had gone inside
> His cold stare
> Returned to its true task, interrogation of silence.[3]

Repeatedly, Brown declared his conviction that 'silence' – 'perfect silence' – was the truest poem. It is tempting, in hindsight, to take this to mean that he had nothing left to add, with his subject exhausted, or, here and there at least, perfectly treated. Yet, he clearly continued to pursue the perfect poem right to the end of his life, both in new works and in revisions of published ones.

The title of this chapter goes back to a central idea in Brown's writing and the theme of this book: 'interrogation of silence' was his 'true task'. Various interpretations of this idea were considered in the Introduction; yet the poem from which this idea emerged, 'The Poet' (1970), must be offset with a darker version of 1974:

'Perfect Silence'

The Poet

Nor did you choose, it was fated on you,
That gift.

Therefore you must fare on as best you can with it,
That scroll.

And it will be a burden to you a many a day,
That music.

But remembered love and sorrow will nurture it well,
That image.

And a kind listener in the street will lighten the pain of it for you,
That song.

And a girl perhaps will lift it from your face a moment,
That mask.

Yet many a day it will bear you in grief to your knees,
That dance.

And you will not be loved in the doorways for the light it unleashes,
That jewel.

There are those who would wish to see it unwinged and tongueless,
That legend.

It will clothe you with starkness, no coat-of-songs,
That loom.

It will utterly possess your heart and your bones,
That symbol.

Its secret is always beyond your deepest questionings,
That rune.

They will take it from your widowed hands at last,
That harp.

Think not that one line or one phrase will be ever remembered of it,
That stone.

This version, published in the *New Statesman*,[4] suggests, in its last line, that, in spite of all the writing he had done at this stage, all the prizes won and reputation established, Brown still felt that none of it would last. Since the lighter version of 'The Poet' was still being tinkered with for a later publication, in 1991, we should not see Brown as descending into darkness; instead, we can take both poems as capturing the light and dark intensity of his experience of writing – and rewriting – poetry.

What is clear is that he felt he had not exhausted this central theme. Far from giving in to the darker vision of artistic failure, he seems to have been just as motivated as ever to pursue his quest for perfection, not just in poetry, but in all the genres.

Biographical notes: 1992–96 (aged 70–74)

Growing recognition during this period was perhaps most clearly signalled by the shortlisting of his novel *Beside the Ocean of Time* (1994) for the Booker Prize. At the same time as he experienced his burst of creative energy, he was recovering from cancer, but still suffering from bronchitis and gout. The last five pages of his autobiography suggest that he was simply waiting for the end, struggling with a depression, 'So severe . . . that one longs for oblivion', yet during this time he was very much alive and bristling with projects: 'An old man withdraws into a narrower circle, just as in November the light lessens . . . This year more poems than ever have come . . . The imagination is still working, and the tools of the workshop are bright with use.'[5]

His death in April 1996 was sudden: he caught a cold, developed bronchitis and died within the week.

A new novel

Brown set out to write a boys' story of 10,000 words on the subject of the Viking voyage to America, but found that he had writer's block on this particular story. He had put it away more than ten years earlier, came across it again by chance, saw some possibilities in it and was surprised to find that it fired his imagination so that 'images and events came crowding in so fast'.[6] To his own amazement, he found that he could not put it down and soon he realised he had a novel on his hands, *Vinland* (1992).

It has been said that the title, *Vinland*, is misleading, as only a few pages deal with the Vikings' voyage of discovery to America, but the book is really about their motivation for making this and many other journeys and the different motivations of the people they meet on their travels. More importantly, this story occurs at a turning point in their history: just when they achieved one of the voyages for which they are still famous for seamanship to this day, their decline had already started, as new beliefs and faiths were coming in, not least of these being Christianity.

The description of the battle of Clontarf is a strong section, lifting the narrative above the weighty political exposition and showing the Vikings in their characteristic fighting role:

> Then an extraordinary thing happened. The tangled webs of noise – the horns, the hammers, the taunts and insults, the twanging of bows and hoof-stampings, the hucksters' cajolings and the harp-strokes of the balladmen, the shouts of the captains and the screechings of women on the hillside – all fell silent and one sound only was heard, the small ringing of the sanctus bell in the tent of the priests . . . And then once more the dense web of discordancy covered the morning . . .
>
> The faces about him were all distorted, like hideous masks. And he knew that his own face was twisted with rage and blood-lust and a kind of terrible joy.
>
> The raven fluttered over the host. Then the raven was down in a flurry, among the scrummage of men.
>
> Olaf the Shetland boy said, 'Ravens and sheep never get on well' . . . Then that shepherd knelt on the ground. Ranald saw blood coming out of his mouth. Then Olaf died.
>
> The raven was lost in the mêlée.[7]

The turning point the Viking way of life was about to confront is signalled in the reference to 'priests'. There are those who think that the old views and values are a waste of time, life and property: 'There is still too much talk of fate and the old gods here in the north.'

While voyage and battle are two central activities, two themes dominate the novel: Christianity coming in to replace paganism and the attempt to do away with the old Viking ways, in a proclamation requiring men to replace Viking raids with merchant cruises and games. It is time for peaceful trading with other peoples in the interests of the common good. Yet those still lusting for power are not going to take this lightly. There will be trouble within the community. It will require diplomacy or strong action either to see this change through or to stand in its way. There is strong, vocal and threatening resistance to the change: 'I foresee nothing but trouble.' This will only be reconciled by a battle of ideologies. In due course, the inevitable violent confrontation is described in a brutal scene.

Ranald is one of the Vikings who seek a new way to live. Disenchanted with the 'men of blood', he takes up farming, and lets his son go to the Viking council for him. He has a long discussion with the abbot about the meaning of existence, in which the abbot argues that what their society needs is a saint, while Ranald continues his meditations, in an interesting dialogue between their very different perspectives:

> Again and again they turned their minds to the shadow of fate that had hung from – it seemed – the beginning of things upon the minds and actions of the northern peoples.

The Viking's genuine belief in fate is convincingly put, showing that, although he has adapted, he retains some of his old beliefs:

> 'And I myself', said Ranald, 'am still convinced that things can't be other than they are, individual men and tribes behave as they do because their history was written down for them from before the beginning. Believing this – it is in the very marrow of our bones, it is carved deep in our hearts – bestows a kind of wild freedom. Let us wring what we can out of the tight fist of fate. Then we can go down with a certain carelessness, even with laughter, into the invisible dust.'[8]

Brown reconstructed the Vikings' world view – fascinatingly, in transition – explaining their motivations and macabre dark humour at the moment of death. The abbot responds with an eloquent case for free will, within his framework of religious faith:

> 'But there is a mystery in all this that is, I think, beyond the power of our minds to understand – there is freedom, the possibility at every moment of our lives to choose either this or that. It can be objected

that it is fate, not the man himself, that chooses in the end. But every man born is aware, now and then in the course of his life, of what you have just called a wild sweet freedom when all seems possible and good . . . sometimes only once or twice in his life, sometimes often, and I have known men who seem to have that light on their faces always.'

The abbot's speech is rendered in three pages of continuous prose, with no paragraph breaks. But his gently persuasive tone and the range of his imagery prevent this from turning into a sermon; as if to underscore this point, a sermon follows later. Instead, it gives insight into the man's world view, just as Ranald's speech did, as both men honestly share their world views in the full knowledge, and sensitivity, that the other man has very different opinions. This peaceful confrontation between their beliefs is a perfect counterpoint to the brutal battle earlier in the novel.

There are many dimensions to this novel: the violence of the Vikings, the tragic death of a daughter, the voyage of discovery and the retreat to farming life. With all the competing motives at work it is a clever device to have two characters sit down to compare notes on what it is all about. These final meditations work well to get beneath the surface of the action of the novel, to examine what drives the getting, spending, raiding, killing and the retreat from all of these.

The balance of the novel suggests that the journey across the ocean may not have been their greatest achievement. In spite of the voyage and the battle, many Vikings in this story are left with something they want to put right or have someone with whom they feel they need to make peace. A more testing journey, it seems, is to meet those with whom they disagree violently in peaceful dialogue. The perfect peace at the end of this novel is achieved through the Vikings adopting Christian faith and practice:

Soon afterwards Ranald died on the greensward above the shore.
The fishermen carried his body into the chapel.
The monks lit candles at his head and at his feet.
The chapel was shaped like a little stone ship.
At sunset they sang in the choir.[9]

He dies on the 'greensward', not at sea, and his funeral is in the 'little stone ship' of a chapel, not a burning boat. The imagery reminds us of where the Vikings have travelled from, while showing, perhaps, that some of their own lore is carried into their Christianity.

Unlimited experimentation

Each limited edition Brown was invited to write for can be seen as a discrete performance of celebration or friendship, but taken together they show that Brown exercised the freedom they granted, while keeping a sharp focus on the required topic; these compact collections contain formal experiments that might not have been possible in larger, more complex collections.

'A nuclear war is so unthinkable that I wondered if it was possible to write a group of verse equivalents of Picasso's dove,' wrote Brown in his Preface to *The Lost Village* (1992), a limited edition of twenty poems on war and suffering, adding up to an indictment of war. Brown made an eloquent plea for understanding and tolerance in a world on the brink of nuclear conflict. These poems celebrate the values of communal living, repudiating aggression in every form. The villagers go about their placid pastoral business, all too aware of the devastation war wrought on their ancestors and rejecting overtures to participate in what they see as the madness still abroad in the world.

In his Preface, written in 1991, Brown paid tribute to the beauty and power of Picasso's dove of peace, qualities evident in the language of *The Lost Village*. Each short poem is a triumph of description, with an incremental effect within the sequence, ending with 'Red Wind':

> ### Red Wind
>
> There's one wind
> Carries fire and bloodsmell about our doors.
> Here and there on earth, still,
> A page of the BOOK OF WAR is turned.

The effect Brown was aiming for is spelled out in his Preface, a 'dream' of the state of peace in the mountain village: 'Can "the global village" come to inherit the innocent joys and sorrows of our lost village among the mountains? It is a dream. May the nations of earth wake up and find that the dream is true.' Far from being 'lost' the village could have found the secret of peace. Hope and realism are blended in the conclusion.

The Lost Village, in an edition of 185 copies, was another example of fruitful collaboration; Rosemary Roberts's illustrations reinforce the text, carrying the dove motif through it.

'At once the images came swarming in like birds to one place. There is something exciting about letting the imagination go free among mysterious rites and customs and attitudes of mind, and yet the solidity of the stones, and their mathematical exactitude, prevented too much extravagance.'[10]

For Brown's next limited edition, a chance thought of the great stone circle led to a series of poems on the Ring of Brodgar's individual standing stones. The result was *Brodgar Poems* (1992). In twenty-eight short verse-paragraphs the stone-setters' society is shown from the erection of the first stone, with intervals, to fifty-two. Romance, play and beauty leave their mark on folk memory as stones take their places in the planned circle, symbolising the wish for good crops and protection not only from the encroaching years but also, running ominously through the sequence, from invasion. While each stone's installation is the cause of communal rejoicing, the process has its dangers. Exposed to all weathers on the moor, one of the monoliths is damaged by lightning and, sixteen stones later, one of the stone transporters is fatally injured:

> The stones, against the purple sky,
> Danced.
> After the thunder, sun.
> One stone has a red wound.

Time has made 'a crone now with cindery breath' of the child who threw flowers over the thirty-second stone, itself overtaken by two 'younger' stones. The movement of stone from the quarry of Vestrafiold is spectacular:

> A beautiful stone
> Is walking today across the hill
> Under a splurge of larks.

Eight stones from completion, the newest one has not prevented the drowning of a boy gathering limpets at the lochside:

> The tall stone, if it cares, has care
> Beyond the span of our caring.

Brown's recollection of how the idea of *Brodgar Poems* came to him suddenly, when he was stuck for a subject, is in the context of a piece of advice to aspiring writers: 'if you wait for inspiration, nothing may ever visit the blank page . . . If you have nothing to write, choose a subject quite coldly, and let your imagination work on that.'[11] Adhering to his own precept, Brown produced a work to show that people of the Stone Age can be identified with those of modern times. *Brodgar Poems* is a striking justification of Brown's familiar 'theory' of composition. He had the imagination and skill to make the most of whatever came to him, but his story of the poems' origin and growth suggests that his own tentative description of 'inspiration' is relevant here: '. . . very occasionally, it seems that one's own directing will is hushed and laid asleep, and then words, images, rhythms, appear on the page that the writer knows with joy to be beyond his own capacities.'[12]

For his next project he imagined a 'medieval monastic beginning' for what is now Aberdeen Royal Infirmary, formerly Foresterhill Hospital. *Foresterhill* (1992) shows the hospital's history, from clearing the site, planning the building and arrival of the first patients. As the brothers' skills become increasingly sought after, there is a need for more equipment and space, and the building goes on.

> There must be a cool place, infirmaria,
> Pines that have lately known snow
> Where they bide till the roses of sickness wither.

Written between May and June 1990, printed by Babel in Germany, in an edition of three hundred copies, *Foresterhill* is a sequence of eighteen poems. In just under three hundred lines, it expresses Brown's gratitude to the surgeons, doctors and nurses of the hospital where he himself had been treated. He spent several months there in 1990 and took up the theme of its history 'to pass the time'.

So high is the level of achievement that it is difficult to decide which of the poems is best. Sheena Pugh (1995) praised 'Homily' as 'a bleak, aching, beautiful vision of the journey of life; its delight, its essential loneliness in the end; the small ways in which that loneliness can be rendered slightly less painful.'[13]

> Look for no company of goodly folk
> No fellow pilgrims on that road.
> Loneliness is all
> And the bitter fruit of the selfhood of each man –
> Shame, regret, fear, sorrow, rage . . .
>
> We brothers put ourselves here, at the door . . .
> And one on the road outside, at midnight, with a lantern
>
> Should a soul go past bereft and weeping.

This elegant volume is far from an ephemeral compilation; every poem is an effective, condensed narrative. There are many arresting images, whose unifying themes are sympathy for the unwell and respect for their healers. Vivid character-sketches and brilliant style make this a rich, satisfying volume which says much for Brown's courage, resilience and will to write, given the seriousness of his illness.

The Sea and the Tower (1994) is a limited edition sequence of twelve poems dealing with the story of Troy.

> There should be
> One far-fetched golden thread
> Through the pitiful rags of age.

The 'golden thread' which gleams through this book is Brown's mastery of image and diction, providing motivation and vividly drawing scenes experienced or prophesied:

> Gulls are jostling
> Like miners at a new shaft . . .
> Sunset, the trodden garlands, gules and gold! . . .
> Keel and oars
> Tore the blue silk . . .

Despite being a section of what was intended to be a much larger work, provisionally entitled *Atlantis*, on which Brown had been working for twelve years, *The Sea and the Tower* has its own unity. Seeds of conflict are sown as characters meditate or act on their responsibilities during the long voyage to Troy. Encounters with 'Thirst', 'Rain' and 'Fog', each the subject of a section of the poem, are described lyrically at the same time as these sections advance the narrative.

Brown used his 'salt mathematics' here: each of the twelve poems contains seven stanzas and is twenty-eight lines long. There are stanzas of seven, six, five, four, three, two and one lines in each. 'The Deepening Ocean' is the only poem to follow the pattern in strict descending numerical order. The others are varied to avoid predictability and mirror the motion of the waves. Vocabulary and tone are matched to character: 'How is it with Xanthe at the well' captures the wistful harking back to domestic scenes at home; kennings – poetic formulae – describe sea and ship as 'the whale-acre . . . the sea horse . . . the hollow bird' and 'the proud horizon-trampler'. Echoes of the Old English poem *Beowulf* suggest epic qualities. Direct speech gives immediacy to a situation and individual traits to a character.

This is a fine edition, rich in imagery and offering enough insight into characters to whet our appetite for the complete *Atlantis*, whose shifting between ages is foreshadowed here, when the Greek sees a modern ship in a vision:

> The ship smoked skywards
> From a tall tube . . .
> The heart of the ship
> Thudded, thudded. It smoked, stank.

This is Brown's trademark travelling back and forth in time, marked by the stark contrast between descriptions of the ancient and the modern ships, offering new slants on the topics.

In *Orfeo, A Masque* (1995) Brown placed the Greek legend in a contemporary Shetland context in thirteen stanzas. 'I imagine Orfeo, the fiddler, as a kind of part time fisherman, infatuated with the important farmer's daughter Maurya; himself (Orfeo) tended by a fishing lass whom he ignores.' The two impossible relationships proceed inexorably until Maurya, released from the Underworld by

Orfeo's marvellous fiddling, 'wanes, frail flame,/Drowned in torrents of noon.' Left to drag out his days, old, crippled, penniless and without status, Orfeo is 'torn to death, slowly/By the tongues of the women of Voe.' There is one survivor: the nameless, grey-eyed, undemanding and uncomplaining woman who has worked thanklessly to keep the man fed and warm, remains faithful to him:

> A girl came to cover his face,
>> Last look of the leal gray eyes.

As a masque, *Orfeo* has the potential to be performed, but it impresses more by its poetry which breathes the life into legend and gives it a new setting in time and place. An important by-product of this sympathetic but unsentimental work is the meditation on the role of art in society and of the poet in particular in 'A Search for Symbols', later reprinted in *Northern Lights*: 'It is the task of poets, perhaps, to keep the symbols in their purity and power . . . This sweet compulsion of art, the pattern, must have operated from very ancient times.' *Orfeo* is Brown's response to this compulsion.

Water (1996), a laminated pamphlet accompanied by prints, is a five-stanza poem on the quest for the narrator's role in life, linked by the theme of water: years at sea, domestic happiness beside a well, exile in the frozen north and retirement to drink and gossip with old men who have turned water to their advantage, until the nature of what he is destined to pursue is revealed.

In each phase of his experience he has a visitor who on each occasion has, for him, a different aspect, moving from threat to friend: 'the intruder . . . that stranger . . . the face like a star . . . the destroyer of peace . . . the guardian . . . the friend'. This character directs him to leave each place in search of a more beneficial form of the element of water. Whatever the uses and attractions of the form he finds, he is always ordered to move on:

> You have met the masks . . .
> Element and essence are further on.

At last the man's intended occupation is disclosed as he becomes 'Brother Doorkeeper' beside the holy water font at a church door.

Archaic vocabulary, 'Birth binds breath to glebe and quern till cess of hunger', frequent ellipses and dwelling on the Arctic exile make this a sober piece, lifted by effective imagery, offering glimpses of the end of his quest:

> I sought continually
> The one syllable that might
>   lock purity in the
>   ultimate crystal.

The literally brighter imagery here conveys his impression of what lies beyond 'the masks'. There is a different pursuit of perfection here, although in this context the narrator is directed, even pushed, to seek it out, rather than responding to some inner vision or purpose. In fact, the narrative voice does not seem to recognise perfection, but has to have it pointed out to him.

In Brown's work there are a number of voices seeking perfection in different forms. This poem plots the path, a gradual leading towards the goal, showing misconceptions and wrong turnings, along the way. What could be disturbing, or neurotic, about this path is the effect of making 'masks' of other aspects of life and landscape, leaving them shadowy and insubstantial, yet these are necessary stages along the way.

The Sixth Station (1996) in the fourteen Stations of the Cross is 'Veronica wipes the face of Jesus', one of the pauses in Jesus Christ's journey, with His cross, to Calvary and His death. Veronica is the woman who offers Christ comfort, by wiping sweat and blood from His face. An impression of Christ's face is left on the cloth. Having dealt with this episode in several fourteen-stanza Stations of the Cross poems, one of them devoted entirely to Veronica, Brown presents it here in yet another mode, a short story of almost two thousand words. Oddly, Brown's use of language at first seems so simple as to be flat. There is neither drama nor psychological depth to the characters of Pilate and the ambitious young civil servant sent to spy on him:

> There was a coming and going in the palace all that night, and in the city streets.
>
>   I slept poorly. There were so many hurried footsteps and urgent

whispers along the corridors that I barred my door.
    I heard cock-crow; then I drowsed for an hour or two.
    At breakfast time Pontius Pilate was not at the board.

Lacking the energy and concentration of Brown's poetry, this story labours unsuccessfully after the narrative and emotional effects Brown achieved in two lines of 'Stations of the Cross: The Good Thief' in *Following a Lark*:

> Veronica, seamstress. No napkin ever
> Soaked up such blood and sweat.

Yet, the flat, matter-of-fact prose does convey something of Pilate's notorious disengagement. In Brown's story, while Pilate is, in fact, agitated, he takes the indifference of those around him as a signal that he must not act: he has been 'given a task to do' and must simply get on with it, whether he agrees with it or not. What is chilling about this story is the lack of emotion. This is what makes Veronica's action of simple compassion so dramatic; by contrast, Pilate's inaction is even more striking. When, finally, he does express emotion in this story, it is too late. Christ is dead.

After the long flashback to Christ's 'Passion', Brown added a short conclusion, whose monosyllables – 146 in 175 words – convey the exhaustion of the vastly changed narrator, the civil servant, now an old man hunted for becoming a Christian:

> An old sailor has told me that the holy face is stored in a secret place in the holy city, and is brought out to be seen by the faithful on Good Friday, every year.
> And now they are saying that Veronica's act of love was done at the Sixth Station of the Cross.

Focusing on this man's – rather than Christ's – end and final reckoning is distinctive and characteristic of Brown's interest in the apparently minor characters and their surprisingly important or revealing roles.

Rockpools and Daffodils (1992)

I have long thought it a good thing to keep in touch with my fellow islanders by means of a small weekly essay in the *Orcadian*. There are treasures enough to rummage among, childhood memories and contemporary happenings and, as well, the turning wheel of the seasons and the astonishing weather in the north that can wear four different coats in a single day.

In this Introduction to *Rockpools and Daffodils* Brown reaffirms his commitment made in *Letters from Hamnavoe* (1975) and adhered to in *Under Brinkie's Brae* (1979), his two earlier collections of *Orcadian* columns, to keep in touch with fellow islanders. This book contains three hundred short essays, recording Brown's recollections of his childhood, changes in the street, local personalities, literary work in hand, visitors and excursions. There are also reflections on authors, praise for his favourites and generous tributes to new writers.

Domestic tragedies are described: his black refuse bag bursts; the toaster expires; there is a power cut; the tin opener for his tin of Spam loses the thread; and the dreaded rats return. These horrors are treated with far greater seriousness than his spells in hospital.

'Just a bit of fun', he used to say of these columns, but he was always pleased when someone's memories were awakened by reading one of them about Stromness's past, or contemporary developments in the town. People meeting him on the street would chat about the weather, or changes in the appearance or function of Stromness buildings or some other local event that had caught their eye and would subsequently find their words and views 'translated' into Brown's column. Whenever he was 'challenged' about this he would chuckle: 'I loved writing those paragraphs. What more can any journalist ask?'[14] He also said that these columns contained more of himself than any of his other works.

The rockpools and daffodils of the title are literal – not just figurative – subjects, showing Brown's personal observation: 'We probed among the little triangular rockpools left in interstices of the reef by the ebb, and found the kind of seaweed that went "pop" when you pressed it, and tiny semi-transparent crabs, and shells that when you held one to the ear brimmed with the songs of all the seven seas.' There is a light, bright tone and immediacy about these columns:

16—7—87

Under Brinkie's Brae

Funny, how we neglect the winter-time friend, television, in high summer... There it sits in the corner, blind and silent, unless to watch a single news bulletin or a piece of a Wimbledon final... Who wants, on a lovely summer evening, to watch 'Dallas' and 'Coronation Street'. There must be millions watching such ephemera — not for us!... But last night we did watch a film that TV does superbly well, one about the waterways of Britain: the springs, rivers, waterfalls, lakes, under-earth limestone surgings — and all the fish, plants, insects, and creatures too small to see, who live in and about them... But all are changing, the clean fresh cold waterways and the creatures who live in them... And man in his ignorance and arrogance and greed has been interfering with that delicate web for a long time... 'Generations have trod, have trod, have trod': lamented a century ago that great poet Gerard Manley Hopkins!

'Under Brinkie's Brae'. First page of unpublished article, 16 July 1987.

Suddenly the daffodils are everywhere, the indomitable ones, the flowers spun from light.

They sleep all winter along the roadside ditches, underground, hoarding their strength and beauty for spring. Then they turn in their sleep – 'Time to be up and about. The first lambs are on the hillside. We thought we heard a lark singing the day before yesterday.'

Brown gave the collection the subtitle 'An Orcadian Diary' and we can read this as a diary, not in the sense that it is in strict chronological order, but in the sense that it features the whole Orkney year. There were, in fact, readers who looked forward to his treatment of whatever annual event was coming up. Brown himself said of some of the subjects that 'we have been this way before', but even when he was revisiting well trodden ground the little essays are fresh and absorbing. He did have what almost amounted to an annual calendar of subjects, but these do not come across as predictable reflections; instead, they punctuate the year, with a pattern of feasts, celebrations, reminiscences and, above all, the intense drama of the weather.

The columns did not stop with this collection; Brown continued to write them till the week of his death, showing his genuine commitment to and enjoyment of writing them. If the remaining 500-word-plus pieces were collected in a new volume, they would add up to well over 100,000 words. That he also produced a second novel in this period is an indication of his continuing productivity.

Beside the Ocean of Time (1994)

'I have picked up a few curious things from the shore of the great ocean of time.' This statement is a minor character in the novel's modest refusal to make much of his discoveries as an amateur archaeologist, but it can serve as an understated assessment of Brown's sixth novel. Published less than two years after the long, well received novel *Vinland*, *Beside the Ocean of Time* was to be his last.

In this novel 'curious things' are events and relationships affecting the inhabitants of an Orkney island, seen through the eyes of the main character, Thorfinn Ragnarson, a crofter's son, as he voyages in his imagination from the Broch period, to the Crusades, to the Battle of Bannockburn, to World War Two. At the same time, the pattern of everyday life on the island of Norday, between young Thorfinn's daydreams, has its own tension and beauty. Brown's themes and preoccupations are transposed into the mind of the child who is the hero of his imagined adventures, but what is interesting is that the boy is the one who sees connections – or makes them up – between historical event and legend. In fact, when he started writing it, Brown intended this to be a book for children: 'When I began to write it, I rather thought of it as a boys' book, a child's book, but as often happens, it got out of hand. After a chapter or two it began to expand and grow, and I knew it wasn't a boys' book in the end.'[15]

This unplanned expansion happened frequently when Brown was writing a novel; it was the same with Mrs McKee's story in *Greenvoe*, and *Vinland*, which started as a boys' short story, but, as he described in three *Orcadian* columns, spiralled into a full-length novel. Certain aspects of a story took on a life of their own. In *Beside the Ocean of Time* there is a focus on the child, but it mutated from a story for children to a story exploring the child's world view: 'That Wordsworthian thing – childhood as the time of greatest and purest wisdom.' In conversation with Rowena Murray on 11 October 1994, Brown described the main character, 'on a kind of composite mythical island in Orkney. He's a bit of a dreamer, at school and elsewhere, and his imagination takes him back to the roots of time.'

In an account of how a crew of Swedish Vikings find their way to Byzantium, the episode in which they turn the tables on a treacherous host has the grim humour, brutality and stylistic terseness characteristic of the Norse sagas. There is a description of how the prestige of serving in the 'Varingers' (the Varangian guard) quickly turns to boredom and disenchantment, as the Vikings are left to pose in their fancy uniforms with very little to do. Recalled from these fantasies to be condemned as lazy and useless, Thorfinn's next imaginative participation in historical events is triggered by the 'village parliament's' debate in the smithy. As the voices drone on, he is off, in his imagination, to relive the battle of Bannockburn.

Meanwhile, in the real time and place in which Thorfinn lives, there are descriptions of the landscape, capturing its physical features, the associations that accumulate around places and the rhythms of the natural world, at once separate from and bound up with lives of the islanders:

> There was a very old ruin on the side of the hill, neglected but for an occasional amateur archaeologist.
>
> The ruin seemed to have some religious root; the remains of a round arched window could be seen, and two indecipherable tombstones were sunk in the floor. (In summer the place was lost in nettles, thistles, hogweed.)
>
> The shepherd Will Simpson was going home late one evening, under the first star, from seeing to a weakling lamb, when he thought he saw a glimmer among the broken walls. Occasionally a tramp visited the island, and slept under a dyke or in a cave in summer. Will Simpson thought he should look in.
>
> It was a windless night. The lappings of ebb on shore, the hush in the shallows, the distant Atlantic sonorities, rounded out the silence. The sun was down, every hollow was brimming now with shadows. The light in the ruin shone like a ruby.
>
> William looked carefully inside. A candle was burning in a niche. A shadow stood in the near corner, turned away, folded in silence.
>
> A new sound came from the sea, like a struck harp. The ebb-tide had reached its mark, some time ago, and made a pause. And now with this harp stroke, the flood-tide was beginning.[16]

This is a complex set of effects: evoking a scene, its atmosphere, the accumulated feelings of generations about it; the concrete evidence of its history, half-remembered, but still there; the comings and goings, in some loose pattern, of contemporary people; the vivid, sudden break in the pattern of everyday activities and assumptions. This is one of Brown's strengths as a prose writer, creating this complex weave of both collective and individual internal and external worlds.

Although Brown said there was nothing of himself in this novel (in an interview with Tom Morton), it is difficult not to see or hear his voice, particularly at the end of the novel. Thorfinn, having had some success with writing a historical novel, returns 'home' to strive for poetry:

> After the moderate success of the two novels . . . Ragnarson attempted something more special, a novel that yearned towards

poetry, a biography of an islander he remembered from his childhood, the pure inexorable graph from birth to death, but it was a complete failure with the reviewers and the public. Who nowadays is interested in the life of a poor islander, who has been here and there about the world and is not very popular with his neighbours and has no particular insights or skills, and has achieved nothing worthwhile?[17]

The final pages of the novel are autobiographical in specific details: the pattern of 'parties, pub-crawls, quarrels, love affairs and jealousies . . . hangovers'; the 'three-hours-a-day stint' of writing; the money-lending incident, which we know from conversations did happen. Brown also summed up what sounds like the writing and reception of his first novel, *Greenvoe*, though still in the guise of Thorfinn's writing. Yet the end of the book is very different from Brown's own life: Thorfinn has found a partner and she is to have a child. This significant difference may be why Brown denied *any* similarity with his own life. A more striking difference is Thorfinn's acceptance that he would never be a poet, while Brown made explicit his striving for the 'perfect' poem.

If we do read insights into Brown's life, we can understand why the proposed visits of Stella Cartwright to Orkney would have been difficult for him; apart from any difficulties he might have had with the relationship itself, it would have presented him with a clash of two worlds: memories of his chaotic life in Edinburgh would clash violently with his solitary existence in Orkney. Each place had a quite different role in shaping his identity as a writer. That he wrote about this, indirectly, in this novel perhaps indicates how intense his time in Edinburgh was and how destructive it could have been had he stayed.

There are similarities between *Beside the Ocean of Time* and *Greenvoe*: characters' daydreams, the islands' history, the impact of civilisation, a writer's view and vision and a blend of myth and realism in mode and matter. Yet *Beside the Ocean of Time* focuses much more sharply on the development of one boy. In fact, it has more in common with Thomas Mann's *The Magic Mountain*, Chapter Seven of which is titled 'By the Ocean of Time':

Can one tell – that is to say, narrate – time, time itself, as such, for its own sake? That would surely be an absurd undertaking. A story which read: 'Time passed, it ran on, the time flowed onward' and so forth – no one in his senses could consider that a narrative. It would be as though one held a single note or chord for a whole hour, and called it music . . . For time is the medium of narration, as it is the medium of life. Both are inextricably bound up with it.[18]

Given Brown's preoccupation with time, it is almost as if he took Mann's statement as a challenge. Mann had identified an intriguing theme, which Brown decided to take up; Brown 'held a single note' and used time as the element bound up with narration and life itself. Mann described a factor in our experience of time: 'a hermetical magic, a temporal distortion of perspective reminding one of certain abnormal and transcendental experiences in actual life'. This is very like what Brown was doing in *Beside the Ocean of Time*: describing both young Thorfinn's complete absorption in his imaginings and absorbing the reader in Thorfinn's imaginative journeys, bringing together different experiences of time.

In the essay called 'The Making of *The Magic Mountain*', Mann explained what he set out to do and, again, focused on the nature of narrative time:

I return to something I spoke of before: the mystery of the time element, dealt with in various ways in the book. It is in a double sense a time-romance. First in a historical sense, in that it seeks to present the inner significance of an epoch . . . And secondly, because time is one of its themes: time, dealt with not only as a part of the hero's experience, but also in and through itself. The book itself is the substance of that which it relates: it depicts the hermetic enchantment of its young hero within the timeless.[19]

Mann's words closely echo Brown's whenever he wrote about his desire to achieve perfection in his writing: 'to give perfect consistency to content and form, to the apparent and the essential'. Brown appears to have been very deeply affected by the last section, not just by the images Mann used, but also by his ideas about time. There are so many echoes of *The Magic Mountain* in *Beside the Ocean of Time* that it is almost as if he had been using it as a kind of source book. (For example, *The*

Magic Mountain, pp. 355, 371, 541; descriptions which could be by Brown himself, 429, 502, and many echoes of Brown's stories, 536, 577.) There are some very close similarities, as in Brown's use of the 'worn metaphor' of a river, in *Time in a Red Coat*, or 'The weeks, the months, the seasons, the years passed, as the waves fell incessantly on the wide bay' (*The Golden Bird*, p. 22), compared with Mann's 'That would surely be an absurd undertaking. A story which read: "Time passed, it ran on, the time flowed onward"' (p. 541), with its similar tone and image. There are many more of these resonances, which bring out how far Brown had understood and assimilated Mann's work, while pursuing his own agenda.

In the final section of *Beside the Ocean of Time* Thorfinn's boyhood imaginative freedom, at the start of the novel, is compared with the desperate casting about of his older self, now an established writer, for meanings and subjects. While the boy was immediately and totally lost in his imagination, the man is not even sure that he has either the motivation or the ability to realise his ideas in writing. There is a direct comparison between the boy's unrestrained imagination and his much more self-conscious adult view:

> As a matter of fact, Thorfinn at that very moment was on a Swedish ship, the *Solan Goose*, anchored off a port in the Baltic. The skipper, Rolf Rolfson, was making plans to meet the prince of Rus, with a view to trading with his people and establishing good relations.
>
> It should be said that Thorfinn was actually in the barn of Ingle, lying curled in the bow of his father's fishing yole, with the collie Stalwart sleeping in the stern. But in his imagination he was walking up a beach in the eastern Baltic, along with six other Swedish vikings, to meet a troop of envoys from the court of Rus.[20]

> To make something of what was left . . . There were enough fragments to see his time out, folk memories, legends, the seal people, the trows that loved music and lived under the green hill. But to write that kind of novel, a man needs to be a poet, and the stones he had broken up to then showed no least trace of ore.[21]

The physical, emotional and existential stresses of writing are the subject of this section. The older writer calculates that what he has gained in his 'spiked and marinated' stories, does not compensate for the loss of the 'innocent poetry of the first imagining'. There is a growing note of despair, not mitigated by the story of his success with one novel, only the hollowness of the 'fake epic'. There is a tragic note in his endless, pointless pursuit of perfection.

Yet the ending is life-enhancing: Thorfinn steps off the 'treadmill' of his city existence, returns to the island and takes what he sees as his last chance of recovering what he has lost, the true voice of childhood, the prospect of a child, the possibility of poetry. Whether or not we read this novel as a thinly disguised account of Brown's writing life, it offers fascinating insights into the writer's delicate negotiations with himself, carefully balancing his strengths and his weaknesses in order, above all, to keep writing, not simply immersing himself in free imaginings, but always, always 'toiling at the unattainable poem'. Brown's obsession was played out in the lives of his characters.

Winter Tales (1995)

It was in winter that the islanders gathered round the hearth fire to listen to the stories.

Harvest was gathered in. The ears that had listened only to necessary farming and fishing words all the year of toil and ripening were ready for more ancient images and rhythms.

A tongue here and there was touched to enchantment by starlight and peat flame.

In another of Brown's brilliant prefaces to his work, we see what he aimed to achieve in this collection of eighteen stories: to capture that moment in the year when people turn from outdoors to indoors, from the day-to-day to the imagination and from the humdrum to the magical or spiritual. Brown regarded such stories as part of a long tradition of story-telling, which, as ever, he was striving to keep alive, the enemy this time taking the form of modern media.

An apparently dour, backward-looking farmer narrates 'The Lost Sheep'. Seeming to set his mind against innovations designed to improve comfort and communication, he reflects on a deserted island's population, many of whose achievements were celebrated for generations beyond their shores. Out of sympathy with his time he may be, but his solitary musings on 'the spirit of the island' make him an interesting, distinctive character whose integrity is touched with pathos.

If Brown's insistence on the entertainment and spiritual value that narrative brings to a society is echoed by this farmer, another illustration of how technological advances do not give universal satisfaction is offered by 'The Paraffin Lamp': Thomas 'lived entirely in the past. He disliked all the fruits of progress that his fellow-islanders were beginning to splurge in.' His story demonstrates an adherence to old habits that verges on the perverse, as he switches off the electric light after priming his old lamp. All the characters in this story are only selectively anti-progress.

'Lieutenant Bligh and Two Midshipmen', the longest story by far in this collection, describes a visit the future celebrity pays to a prosperous merchant in Hamnavoe. Before this, Bligh's brusque tone, abrupt, unfinished sentences and awkward syntax bring out the gruffly caring nature of a man who shrinks from the display of feeling at the same time as being a shrewd observer of others' emotions. Throughout the evening, as the host pursues his own agenda, Bligh's meditation on the rise of the merchant class, his own slow advancement in the Navy and the potentiality of George Stewart, son of the house, is punctuated by a bitter-sweet relationship between Midshipman James Brisco and little Elizabeth Stewart. Meanwhile, George Stewart's contemplation of his 'inner landscape' parallels Bligh's own aspirations at the same age, while the engagement of Peter Linklater as carpenter and the lieutenant's 'punishment' of Brisco highlight other facets of his character.

This is a finely integrated story, which works on several levels of motivation and relationship. There is not a page in this collection without an image or extended pictorial passage bringing locations and people before us: 'the great star-wheel was beginning to brighten winterwards . . . behind every wet clay furrow was a madhouse of wheeling gulls.'

Orkney: Pictures and Poems (1996)

This was a reversal for Brown: instead of having his work illustrated by artists, he was to write poems to accompany Gunnie Moberg's photographs of Orkney. It was a closer collaboration than for previous illustrated volumes of his poetry; the photographs literally sat on an easel in his living room, so that he could see them constantly, as he thought and wrote.

Brown decided early on to focus on what lay behind the scenes depicted. Even when looking deep into the past, he searched for a new angle, acutely aware of the subjects he had treated thoroughly in earlier works: 'Oh, I don't know. I could do some romantic one about "the Venice of the North", on Brinkie's Brae clinging between the granite and the sea. I've done that so often. People are fed up with things like that,' he confessed to Brian Murray on 28 January 1995.

He started with his response to photography itself in the first poem:

> The eye of the camera seeks patterns
> On shore, on hill, in fields and lochs,
> And at all seasons.

His imagination, stimulated by the photographs, looked beyond the moment in time that they represented:

> We may note, page by page, the new
> And the old works of time.

What Brown made of the photograph that might have been 'the Venice of the North' is shown on page 77 of this beautiful book: the poem 'Waterfront, Hamnavoe', alongside a photograph of Stromness from the sea. Early islanders and their activities have a place in the 'turning of the stone pages of time', but a pointer to the future draws a parallel between the poet and his successors: 'The hills consider/Sagas unwritten yet, austere and beautiful'. The landscape is a constant, amid all the comings, goings and writings of people. Brown's interest lay in the human aspects of the town whose houses cram the photograph as they climb straight from sea to skyline, rather than in its scenic charm.

Similarly, 'Storm in Hoy Sound: Kirkyard', his response to what is perhaps the most evocative photograph in the book devotes a single memorable line to the dramatic weather it depicts: 'The Sound today scrolled with black music'. Brown said that, when writing about the graveyard, he imagined 'all the people lying there and what they say to each other. Like Thomas Hardy.'[22] Among voices from the grave is the ubiquitous Ikey's:

> Ikey, tinker: 'I rest better here
> Than under the lee of a dyke at snow-time
> Whistling
> To stop the clatter of my teeth.'

While Brown could show mastery of description without social comment in poems on plants and creatures, most often he was 'withdrawn to contemplation:/The inner vision'. Brown ponders the effects of time and technology on human beings' attempts to secure and enhance life and property. The Churchill barriers, causeways linking the islands, a triumph of engineering, put an end to people's way of viewing life there, 'In an island, time is a simple pure circle', raising new questions for them:

> Will the stars shine over islands again?
> Will sails fly from shore to shore to shore?

'Flotta Flare', symbol of Orkney's oil age, is shown as contending with natural light: 'See this tall finger of science/Scratch the stars out!' 'Martello Tower', built from locally quarried stone to stand against invaders who never came, proved to be a 'useless giant,/A Samson blinded' with an offensive visual impact on its setting. Meantime, poems describe how traditional sea-forts and egg-shaped shelters continue to protect sheep, one species of which, confined to the shore, is part of 'the ancient salt pastoral'. Brown had not changed his views on technology in all his years; he did not tire of warning us about it, or – what is often ignored by critics – of marvelling at it.

Partly because the poems in this collection are mostly short, surrounded by plenty of white space on the page, and partly because they sweep across vast swathes of time, there is a sense of vertiginous telescoping of time, from the 'oldest house in Europe', the 'Knap of Howar, Papay', to the oil age. Having imagined what it would have been like to live in the house in ancient times, with the photograph showing the house still intact, Brown placed two final lines, quite separate from the rest of the poem:

> A million bungalows will rot like mushrooms
> And this house be rooted still.

Brown was not simply criticising modern builders – though that is a reasonable interpretation of these lines – but prompting us actively to reflect on what else is likely to last as long, what else is likely to 'rot' away. Poignantly, Brown included songs, language and poetry in this process; very few remain 'rooted' in time. This can be read as another expression of Brown's sense of futility in searching for the perfect poem.

Following a Lark (1996)

Just days after Brown's death a collection of forty new poems was published. He had been fully involved in the production and provided an Introduction, written in December 1995: 'These poems are written mainly in praise of the light, and to glorify in a small way the Light behind the light.' Again, there is perhaps a sense of *memento mori*, a late surge of religion coming into the last writing. Certainly, natural illumination and spiritual radiance are described time and again, coming together in the short important poem 'Lux Perpetua':

> A star for a cradle
>
> Sun for plough and net
>
> A fire for old stories
>
> A candle for the dead

Each line has its own distinctive resonance and associations, before Brown's conclusion identifies the cycle of birth, work and death with a common striving for grace – significantly, the quality Edwin Muir applied to Brown's first book more than forty years earlier:

> Lux Perpetua
>
> By such glimmers we seek you.

The gnomic syllables suggest a universal truth that Brown was working to convey; the story of how an individual might pursue such truth is the subject of several other poems in this collection.

The title poem tells of a small boy on his way to school, struggling with increasing agitation to recall his homework:

> (Sixteen ounces, one pound. Fourteen pounds, one stone.)
> A sack of corn's a hundredweight.
>> I think a whale must be bigger than a ton . . .
>
> ('I wandered lonely as a cloud . . .' Oh where? What then?) . . .
>> A quarter of a mile to run.
>> My bare feet
>> Have broken three daffodils in the field.

This clever interlocking of half-remembered homework and the world he sees around him is measured out in contrasting short lines, suggesting his breathing as he runs. The boy does remember what he learned, but cannot yet recite it by rote. Instead, he translates the impersonal weights and measures into personal, meaningful equivalents.

Scenes in and around Stromness were still the subject of many poems, but Brown took a new angle in 'To a Hamnavoe poet of 2093'. In this poem he postulated continuity of subject, from the Skara Brae dwellers, via broch-builders and Vikings, up to his own day and beyond. Appropriately, he looked to future poets to keep alive 'the gentle ups-and-downs', as he did in a description of the stream running near his home:

> Rain-trail from hill to hill, a hushing;
>> Mayburn a penny whistle
>> Lilting from Croval, lingering
>>> (Tinker-boy) under my window.

In a familiar vein, he warned them that they would have to protect poetry, 'maimed more and more/On the grid of numbers', and made a final plea to 'guard/The pure source, silence'. This suggests that he was entrusting the poet of the future with his muse, concerned that someone should continue his task. It sounds as if he were passing on the pen to the next generation of poets. Yet, at this time, he was still working away on many other writings. While hindsight makes us read these poems as his valediction, he was far from giving up.

Conclusion

Still the 'scribe' overlaps with the 'sagaman'; the urge to record and document competed with the urge to renew and revive. In many of Brown's works the journalist was writing alongside the creative writer, as in *Magnus*, where he used a form of modern journalese to tell part of the story.

In so many ways, Brown was forced to stand outside his own community, by his vision, his illness and his religion. He found it difficult to find his place in it, or in the world in which he saw no work or lifestyle for himself. Did he, consciously or not, take up this separate position in order to protect his privacy? His isolation does not appear to have limited his productivity; he seems to have needed the silence it created.

Our last chapter, 'Epilogue', rounds off the story of Brown's work, including the growing list of posthumous publications.

Epilogue

It is all over. He is dead. The world-wanderer who never set foot outside his island has put a coin into the hand of the dark ferryman; he has found another shore, where there is no need (as I believe) of song or story; for all who set foot there are enclosed within a horizon of pure silence; and are content that it should be so.[1]

Since the most prolific period of Brown's writing life was his last three years, he left a huge amount of unpublished work behind. For example, there is a large quantity of unpublished poetry manuscripts in Edinburgh University Library. We know from his weekly *Orcadian* column that his writing régime had become even more productive:

> I have lived for years in a wilderness of paper, that has been getting wilder and wilder.
>
> Of course this happens when you write for a certain time every morning, and letters come winging in on almost every post . . . in the end the chaos of papers were there in ordered piles, in envelopes and folders neatly annotated.[2]

Written in 1990, after friends helped him put his papers in order, this gives us a glimpse of how much material is still to be published. The 'papers' he referred to were not simply old letters and drafts, but completed works, some much revised, in typescript, and many all but ready to go to print.

This creates, for those responsible for Brown's work, a backlog ready for posthumous publication. Two editors, Archie Bevan, Brown's literary executor, and Brian Murray, both friends of Brown, have arranged twelve new collections since his death. Since much of this new writing is finished material, they are not publishing work-in-progress; for every typescript they selected Brown had completed all the final steps in his writing process: signing it off, putting it to one side and planning no further changes. All but one of the posthumously published stories had been revised by Brown over a long period. He was satisfied with the exception, 'Paddy Crowsnest and the Elements', written in 1995.

Moreover, the editors were aware of Brown's intentions for the works: the work they had done to organise Brown's papers – during his lifetime – had led to discussions of his preferred format. This was a particular talking point for them because the late stories are, surprisingly, much longer than Brown's earlier ones. For example, they knew that Brown was interested in presenting certain stories in separate volumes and they have been faithful to his design. In the posthumous volumes brought out, they have tried to be true to Brown's vision and to create unity in each collection.

To begin this Epilogue, there is one book that sits between those published in Brown's lifetime and the posthumous publications, his autobiography, *For the Islands I Sing*.

For the Islands I Sing

Written in 1985, this autobiography was set aside until Brown could add a brief appendix, updating it, in November 1993. The book was published in 1997.

While the autobiography is, in places, almost too domestic, it does show how Brown saw himself. We have not seen this from him before. Appropriately, the publishers chose the title, the opening line of his first volume of poems, *The Storm*. It fills in some of the gaps in our knowledge of Brown, but his reticence will raise new questions for some readers.

Douglas Gifford questioned the fairness of producing works that an established author had not prepared for publication. It is an interesting question, particularly since what the newspapers chose to highlight in the autobiography was Brown's relationship with Stella Cartwright, serialised in the *Scotland on Sunday* newspaper in 1997. In the case of the autobiography Brown had always intended it to be published and had all but seen it into print. It was important to publish the book in which he appeared to want to set the record straight. Brown himself emerges slowly, diffidently, as an apparently frank character.

For the Islands I Sing is a treasury of information and stimulus whose poetic treatment of themes is illustrated by the excellent acrostic poems that break up the prose, including one to Stella Cartwright:

Stella Cartwright (for her birthday 15 May 1982)

So, once in the 50s
There was this crazy chap, high among clouds,
Edinburgh-bound.
Laurel-seeking he was, out of Orkney,
Long and salt his throat
Among the stanzas that starred the howffs of Rose Street.

Could he not bide forever in that beautiful city?
A sweet girl, one day,
Rose, a star, to greet him.
To him, she spoke sweeter than rain among roses in summer,
While poets like columns of salt stood
Round the oaken Abbotsford bar.
I, now
Going among the gray houses and piers of Stromness,
Hear that voice made of roses and rain still; and see
Through storm-clouds, the remembered star.[3]

This echoes 'The Poet': when the dancers withdraw he is left alone.

Brown's previous autobiographical writings were formulaic and impressionistic. Perhaps he was reticent about revealing his temperament. Parts of his autobiography are confessional, as he regrets moments of cruelty and pettiness. There is less of his characteristic healing or meaningful ritual patterning in his own story.

The Island of the Women and Other Stories (1998)

These stories, written over thirty years, were selected by the editors on the basis, firstly, of their completed state, and, secondly, because they could establish links between them:

... the first two take us into Orkney's remote past; another spans more than 300 years of life in a small island; a fourth traces the fortunes of a local story-teller from his youth in Hamnavoe through the foreign adventures he recounts ... and the four elements of water, air, fire and earth are shown to affect another islander from boyhood to old age .. . the last one ... explores the nature and practice of poetry.[4]

Although the selections for posthumous publications were not Brown's own, we can see his typical range of subject and technique. His careful management of the writing and revising processes was also clear from manuscripts (MS) and typescripts (TS) of the stories in this collection:

		Writing and revising
'The Island of the Women'	TS	Winter 1972, Spring 1976, Autumn 1977, Autumn 1979, Autumn 1988, Summer 1995
'The Fortress'	TS	January/March/October 1977–July 1989
'The Lairds' Story'	MS	Summer 1977–Summer 1978, Summer 1995
'The Wanderer's Tale'	TS	Summer 1982
'Paddy Crowsnest and the Elements'	TS	1995
'Poet and Prince'	TS	Winter 1985–86, September 1995

Northern Lights (1999)

This substantial collection was organised by the editors to reflect Brown's developing interests and personality over fifty years. It is clear from his comments and extensive revisions that he intended much for publication. In this book he did for Shetland what he did for Orkney in *An Orkney Tapestry*. The two final sections, 'Shetland: A Search for Symbols' and 'Shetland Diary', provide Brown's most sustained and valuable piece of writing on his craft. It is a fascinating opportunity to witness the writer at work, sharing his thoughts on his art, the psychology of inspiration, his habits of composition and, vividly, his personality.

On his Shetland holiday he wrote notes during the day and worked on them in the evenings, and then again when he returned to Orkney. For example, his diary notes his reading of a story that later became a poem:

Shetland Diary

One bleak day in May 1988 – just a month before we went to Shetland – I turned the pages of a book that almost froze the heart. Two whaling ships in the late autumn of 1836 – venturing too far after the whales (for the whale-masters must have their profits, and the skippers their bounty) – were caught in the ice, winter closed the gates upon them with groanings and clangours. The whalers' long agony began, with increasing scurvy and black depressions, lost for months. Almost daily, another body was lowered into an ice fissure, to the sun's eye. Two ships, thinly crewed by skeletal sailors, who had managed to keep the thread of breath unbroken, just, till the sun's loom kept faith with them in the south, limped into Stromness in Orkney.[5]

Brown took the well-known story and gave it a first-person narration by the skipper of the whaling ship, in a prose poem of six stanzas, revealing his vanity and greed:

Whalers

Now we are alone, but for the ship broken in the ice-jaws, *Leviathan*, that yet tilts a prow, a frail line athwart the stars, five miles to north . . . The men have made a fire on the ice and they warm themselves playing at football. The fiddle is silent, the fiddler is sick with bleeding at the gums, but a month more will take us to cabbage stalls in Dundee, and to ale and oranges. Gold cures all in the end.

It is interesting that Brown chose to make more of the skipper's deluded risk-taking, or misplaced confidence, in disregarding the advice of the other skippers who turned for home, than of the ordeal they subsequently suffered.

There are also insights into the sheer labour of writing poetry, as Brown described getting bogged down and persevering with a poem:

> I sit in the car and begin to write a dark prose-poem . . . No good – the images petered out in a marsh . . .

> What I wanted to write was a lilting lyrical piece about the first fiddle in Shetland, that land of fiddlers. Nothing came right: the images tangled with one another and, tugged this way and that, became hard knots . . .

> The wrecked poem about the first fiddler: why can't I let it rest in peace? Note in diary: 'May yet save yesterday's prose poem'.[6]

There are other examples, interesting glimpses into Brown's imagination at work on the raw material, revealing what he chose to highlight and make the focus of a poem.

Limited editions

Since Brown's death, Archie Bevan, the literary executor, has been approached with requests for new writing for further illustrated limited editions, continuing a strand of work that had flourished in earlier years: *Stained Glass Windows* (1998), *The Rose Tree* (2001) and *The Son of the Fisherman* (2002) are three of a dozen issued to date.

Stained Glass Windows is a collection of poems and prose poems over which Brown had editorial control. It has vitality, bringing to life saints often held static in church images. These are not essays in hagiography. What might be seen by some as purely religious lives are humanised. The book is a meditation on the qualities that make saints of people with very different backgrounds and characteristics. He captures the intensity of their thinking and the courage with which they faced the challenges to their faith and, ultimately, to their lives.

The Rose Tree, written February 1990, is a short story expanding an earlier Passiontide poem, 'The Gardener: Easter', published in *The Wreck of the Archangel*, and extending it to almost ten times its length. The main story-line is the household having to respond, at no notice, to the need to bury Christ. All the characters we usually see following Christ's death are included, but from a surprisingly uninformed angle, since Adam cannot know what is really going on. His kindness to Christ's family and followers is rewarded by a miracle, when his favourite tree is restored to full health.

The Son of the Fisherman (2002) is an Epiphany story written on 18 December 1991, but Brown's abundance of material about the festive season meant that it was left unpublished till 17 December 1999 (in the *Sunday Herald*). A beautiful edition of 165 copies with wood engravings by Rosemary Roberts was issued by the Celtic Cross Press in 2002.

Travellers (2001)

All but one of the eighty poems in this collection were printed from unpublished manuscripts or typescripts, or from the newspapers, periodicals and anthologies in which they appeared. Only 'December Day, Hoy Sound', long out of print and much sought after, was taken from a volume issued in Brown's lifetime. The editors noted in their introduction:

> Considerations of space and thematic variety resulted in the exclusion of many fine poems from George Mackay Brown's numerous collections . . . well over half the material . . . was produced in the last ten years of the poet's life: an indication that his delight in writing was undiminished.
>
> This book makes available many poems on topics familiar to those who know Brown's work, at the same time as it demonstrates the poet's response to important issues in the modern world.

The *Collected Poems* (2005) made the work available again in a volume demonstrating Brown's extensive output.

Endnote

Brown's view of his life was that it was rather a 'gray thing', with nothing dramatic happening. Yet his delight in writing never left him and he was prepared to acknowledge that he had succeeded in some of it. Although he repeatedly mentioned writing as an aptitude he happened to have, he clearly saw writing as an active 'task'. His ultimate ambition was 'some day to leave one or two really good poems behind'.[7] He certainly achieved that.

The tension that he seems never to have fully resolved, either in his life or in his work, between longing for change and horror at what it might bring, was perhaps the root of his internalised interrogation. For all that Brown's writing is about patterns across the generations, there are always individuals who stand apart from the patterns. These are the characters whose very presence and nature interrogate the patterns. This is true of Magnus, who knows that he goes to his death by going to meet his cousin in peace, rather than waging war on him. It is true of Walls, who searches for his dead friend, braving the disbelief and abuse of those he meets. It is true of the Skarf who writes the history of his community, even as it is falling apart.

The distance Brown travelled, particularly as a poet, can be measured by the contrasting techniques in his first, published in *The Orkney Herald*, 14 June 1939, and last published poems: the first showing his early engagement with the Orkney setting and the second his final arrival at contented 'silence':

The Hills of Hoy at Sunset
Sonnet

Blue swelling hills! O, never shall I see
    A picture more magnificent and still,
    An evening scene so peaceful and tranquil,
As when I see them now! Where can there be
Such lofty grandeur? Towering o'er the sea,
    And in the sunset bathed each rill.
    One day like this the Norsemen climbed yon hill,
And viewed the wond'rous Isles of Orcadie.

> Only to see the redd'ning sun, that fills
>   The western sky with glory unsurpassed,
>   Fade dim behind those rugged age-slopes.
> To see the evening clouds with gilded frills,
>   To hear the crisping wavelets, shoreward cast,
>   Stirs music in the mind, and new-born hopes.

'A Work for Poets'[8] was written for his seventieth birthday (1991):

> Here is a work for poets –
> Carve the runes
> Then be content with silence

Appropriately, there was no full stop at the end of the last line . . . as if in testimony to the writer's search for excellence of thought, form and expression. It is now fifty-four years since Edwin Muir's Introduction to *The Storm* (1954) recognised how Brown deserved admiration, 'not only as an Orkney poet . . . He has the gift of imagination and the gift of words: the poet's endowment.' Celebrating historical and contemporary Orkney and moving far from it in content and relevance, George Mackay Brown was a writer who merited and received what Muir wished him – 'all the recognition which he so truly deserves.'

George Mackay Brown (GMB) Chronology

Year (Age)	Event	Writing/Publications
17 Oct. 1921	GMB born	
c. 1925/26 (4/5)	Sister teaches GMB Scottish ballads	
1926–40 (4–18)	School	
1929 (7)		*The Celt* magazine
1931–32 (9–10)		First poem (now lost)
1934 (13)	Scores four goals in Orkney Lifeboys' Cup Final	
1935 (14)	Discovers Penguin books	
1936 (15)	Father retires without pension. GMB introduced to Romantic poetry	
1937 (16)		Writes first surviving poem 'The Island'
1937–39 (16–18)	Scottish Leaving Certificate (three sittings)	
1939 (17)		First published poem 'The Hills of Hoy at Sunset', *The Orkney Herald*
1940 (18)	Father dies. GMB serves in Local Defence Volunteers. Works in Post Office	

1941 (19)	Tuberculosis diagnosed at Forces Medical. Enters Eastbank Sanatorium. Discharged (not cured)	
1942 (21)	Literary Brains Trust panel member	
1943 (21)	Illness	Two poems in *The Orkney Herald*
1944 (22)	Francis Scarfe, poet, billeted with Browns	Stromness Correspondent of *The Orkney Herald.* Begins 'Ecclesiastical Episodes'
1945 (23)	Scarfe leaves	
1946 (24)	Meets Ernest Marwick	
1946–48 (24–27)		Notebook: reading, ideas and writing
1947 (25)		Begins 'Island Diary' column. Published in *The New Shetlander*. 'Memoirs of a Stromness Home-guardsman'
1948		Orkney guide book
1949 (27)		Three poems in Marwick's *An Anthology of Orkney Verse*
1950 (28)		GMB play performed, *The Wheel o' Fortune*
1951–52 (29–30)	Newbattle Abbey College	Edits college magazine *The Sun*
1952 (30)	Newbattle Abbey College Oct.–Christmas. Withdraws for health reasons	

1953 (31)	Eastbank Sanatorium (15 months)	Edits sanatorium magazine *Saga*
1954 (32)		First volume of poems, *The Storm.* Back to journalism
1955		Orkney guide book
1956 (34)	Newbattle, summer term. Brother Hugh dies at 43	Elegy poem: 'The Shining Ones'
1956–60 (34–38)	Edinburgh University	
1957 (35)		'A Seat by my Bed' broadcast
1959 (37)	Prize in Burns Bicentenary Competition	*Loaves and Fishes*
1960 (38)	Graduates English Language and Literature	
1960–61 (39–40)	Teacher Training (incomplete). Baptised in Roman Catholic Church	
1962–64 (40–42)	Edinburgh University Research on G. M. Hopkins	
1963 (41)		Orkney guide book
1965 (43)	Scottish Arts Council grant for poetry	*The Year of the Whale*
1966 (44)		*The Five Voyages of Arnor*
1967 (45)	Mother dies	*A Calendar of Love* and *Per Mare. A Spell for Green Corn* broadcast
1968 (46)	Society of Authors Travel Award	*Twelve Poems*
1969 (47)	Scottish Arts Council Literature Prize	*A Time to Keep* and *An Orkney Tapestry*

1970 (48)		*A Spell for Green Corn*
1971 (49)	Katherine Mansfield Menton Short Story Prize	3 stories broadcast: 'Play for Today'. *Fishermen with Ploughs, Lifeboat and Other Poems, Poems New and Selected*
1972 (50)	Scottish Arts Council Prize	First novel: *Greenvoe*
1973 (51)		'Oilscene' article. *Magnus*
1974 (52)	OBE	*Hawkfall* and *The Two Fiddlers*
1975 (53)		*Letters from Hamnavoe, Edwin Muir: A Brief Memoir*
1976 (54)	Honorary MA Open University Joint winner Cheltenham Poetry Festival	*The Sun's Net* and *Winterfold*. Starts 'Idylls'; returns to poetry
1977 (55)	Honorary Doctor of Laws, Dundee University. Elected FRSL	*Pictures in the Cave* and *Selected Poems*
1979 (57)		*Under Brinkie's Brae*
1980 (58)		*Six Lives of Fankle the Cat* 'Sanatorium, 1941' essay (unpublished)
1981 (59)	Hospital	*Portrait of Orkney*
1982 (60)		'The Way of Literature' essay
1983 (61)		*Andrina and other Stories* and *Voyages*

1984 (62)		*Time in a Red Coat, Three Plays,* and *Christmas Poems*
1985 (63)	Honorary D Litt, Glasgow University	*The Hooded Fisherman* and *Christmas Stories*
1986 (64)		*The Scottish Bestiary, Keepers of the House*
1987 (65)		*Stone, The Golden Bird, A Celebration for Magnus.* Edits Edwin Muir's *Selected Prose*
1988 (66)	Cataract operation James Tait Black Memorial Prize Shetland holiday	*Portrait of Orkney,* 2nd edition. 'The Cleansing of the Eye' essay (unpublished). *Songs for St Magnus Day* and *Two Poems for Kenna*
1989 (67)	Visit to London	*The Wreck of the Archangel, The Masked Fisherman and Other Stories* and *Tryst on Egilsay*
1990 (68)	Hospital	*Letters to Gypsy*
1991 (69)		*The Sea-King's Daughter: Eureka!, In the Margins of a Shakespeare* and *Selected Poems 1954–1983*
1992 (70)	Scottish Arts *Council Award*	*Rockpools and Daffodils, Brodgar Poems, The Lost Village, Foresterhill* and *Vinland*

1993 (71)	Scottish Arts Council Award	
1994 (72)	Booker Prize Shortlist Scottish Saltire Book of the Year	*Beside the Ocean of Time* and *The Sea and the Tower*
1995 (73)		*Winter Tales, Orfeo: A Masque*
1996 (74)	Died 13 April, Balfour Hospital, Kirkwall	*Water, Following a Lark, Selected Poems 1954–1992, Orkney: Pictures and Poems* and *The Sixth Station*
1997		Autobiography: *For the Islands I Sing*
1998		*Stained Glass Windows* and *The Island of the Women and Other Stories*
1999		*Northern Lights*
2001		*The Rose Tree, Travellers*
2002		*The Son of the Fisherman*
2004		*The Poor Man in his Castle*
2005		*Collected Poems, Island Wedding*
2006		*The First Wash of Spring*
2007		*The Fairground Poet*

Notes

Introduction: 'Interrogation of Silence' (pp. 1–8)

1. *Selected Poems 1954–1992*, p. 24.
2. 'Brig-o-Dread', *The Sun's Net*, 1976, p. 108.
3. 'The Lairds' Story', *The Island of the Women and Other Stories*, 1998, p. 191.
4. 'A Writer in Orkney', unpublished TV interview script, August 1970.
5. 'The Silent Pool' in *The Golden Staircase: Poems and Verses for Children*, chosen by Louey Chisholm, Nelson, n.d., Preface 1928, p. 391.
6. *The MacDiarmids: A Conversation – Hugh MacDiarmid and Duncan Glen*, with Valda Grieve and Arthur Thompson, Akros, Preston, 1970 [p. 60].
7. *Winterfold*, 1976, p. vi.
8. 'Nine Poems of Rognvald Kolson', *Scottish Poetry 6*, 1972, p. 11.
9. 'To a Hamnavoe Poet of 2093', *Following a Lark*, 1996, p. 13.
10. 'The Fortress', written January/March/October 1977–July 1989, *The Island of the Women and Other Stories*, p. 127.
11. 'The Wanderer's Tale', 1982, *The Island of the Women and Other Stories*, p. 221.
12. 'Poet and Prince: A Fable', Winter 1985–1986, revised September 1995, *The Island of the Women and Other Stories*, p. 269.
13. 'Shetland Diary', *Northern Lights*, 2 June 1988, p. 316.
14. 'Chinoiseries, Small Songs for the Beginning of Lent' (section 6), *Travellers*, 2001, pp. 99–100.

Part One

Chapter 1: 'A seeker after images': Childhood and Adolescent Writing (pp. 11–28)

1. 'Childhood in Orkney', *Scottish Field*, August 1968, p. 20.

2. 'A Hamnavoe Man', *Travellers*, 2001, p. 64.

3. 'A Work for Poets', *Following a Lark*, 1996, p. 86.

4. 'Childhood in Orkney', *Scottish Field*, August 1968, p. 19.

5. 'Living in Orkney', *Saltire Review*, 2(6), 1955, p. 54.

6. *Rockpools and Daffodils*, 1992, p. 71.

7. 'Sanatorium 1941', unpublished essay, 1980, p. 13.

8. ibid., p. 16.

9. Brown's Introduction to *Witch and Other Stories*, Longman, 1980 edition, p. x.

10. *Northern Lights*, 1999, p. 149.

11. *For the Islands I Sing*, 1997, p. 26.

12. *Travellers*, 2001, p. 13.

13. *Northern Lights*, p. 132.

14. *For the Islands I Sing*, p. 46.

15. *Scottish Educational Journal*, 17 October 1975, p. 969.

16. *The Orkney Herald*, 19 February 1946, p. 4.

17. 'Sanatorium 1941', p. 15.

18. Commonplace Book, April 1947, p. 15.

19. ibid., May 1947, looking back to his mid-teens.

20. 'Imagination taking wing with a flightless bird', *Weekend Scotsman*, 31 August 1985, p. 3.

21. 'Living in Orkney', *Saltire Review*, 2(6), 1955, pp. 54–60.

22. 'Oilscene', *Scotland*, January 1973, pp. 50–3.

23. *Scottish Educational Journal*, 17 October 1975, p. 969.

24. 'Writer's Shop', *Chapman* IV, (4), Summer 1976, pp. 21–4.

25. 'An Autobiographical Essay' in *As I Remember: Ten Modern Scottish Writers Recall How Writing Began for Them*, ed. M. Lindsay, Robert Hale, 1979, pp. 9–21.

26. 'John Brown – Tailor and Postman', *Northern Lights*, pp. 143–50.

Chapter 2: The Stromness Correspondent: Journalism, Poems and Stories (pp. 29–44)

1. 'This scarf became a symbol', *The Orkney Herald*, 19 April 1960, p. 9.

2. 'Working on *The Orkney Herald*', Radio Orkney, 1983.

3. Letter to Ernest Marwick, 5 May 1946, The Orkney Library.

4. *For the Islands I Sing*, p. 78.

5. 'Island Diary: History of a Column', *The Orkney Herald*, 2 November 1948, p. 4.

6. ibid.

7. *The Orkney Herald*, 19 May 1953, p. 4.

8. 'Island Diary: History of a Column', op. cit.

9. ibid.

10. 'Island Diary', 25 June 1946, p. 7.

11. 'Island Diary', 2 July 1946, p. 7.

12. 'Rackwick', *Northern Lights*, p. 90.

13. 'The Waning Year', 'Stromness News', *The Orkney Herald*, 16 August 1949, p. 6.

14. Letter to Ernest Marwick, 5 May 1946.

15. Letter to Ernest Marwick, 24 October 1946.

16. ibid.

17. *For the Islands I Sing*, p. 59.

18. Letter to Ernest Marwick, 27 April 1946.

19. Letter to Ernest Marwick, 5 May 1946.

20. 'Orkney', August 1944 (unpublished).

21. 'The Last Words of St Magnus', 1944–6, The Orkney Library.

22. '*The Orkney Book*: A New Estimate', *The Orkney Herald*, 9 January 1945, p. 5.

23. 'This scarf became a symbol', *The Orkney Herald*, 19 April 1960, p. 9.

24. ibid.

25. ibid.

Chapter 3: Closed Societies of Island, College and Hospital: *The Storm* (pp. 45–63)

1. 'Island Diary: Edinburgh in Three Hops', *The Orkney Herald*, 15 May, 1956, p. 4.

2. Interview dated 10 April 1984. Isobel Murray, ed., *Scottish Writers Talking*, 1996, p. 7.

3. Letter to Ernest Marwick, 23 October 1956.

4. *Contemporary Authors: Autobiography Series*, Gale Research Co., Detroit, MI, 1988, p. 70.

5. ibid.

6. 'Newbattle Abbey: By One Who Was There' by Hjal [George Mackay Brown], *The Orcadian*, 16 July 1953, p. 2.

Notes

7. *Contemporary Authors*, p. 70.
8. *The Sun*, Summer Term 1953, p. 25.
9. 21 October 1953, Marwick's unpublished Newbattle diary, The Orkney Library.
10. *The Sun*, June 1956 [p. 16] (pages not numbered).
11. *Saga*, 1, Summer 1953, pp. 8–9.
12. 'A Seat by my Bed', pp. 3, 16.
13. ibid., p. 18.
14. Letter to Ernest and Janette Marwick, 30 April 1952.
15. Letter to Ernest Marwick, 24 November 1953.
16. Introduction to *The Two Fiddlers*, 1974, p. 9.

Chapter 4: 'A swarm of symbols': *Loaves and Fishes* (pp. 64–78)

1. 'The Masque of Bread', *Loaves and Fishes*, 1959, p. 13.
2. *Edinburgh Evening News*, 23 April 1983, p. 5.
3. Letter to Ernest Marwick, 18 July 1952.

Part Two

Chapter 5: 'The Way of Literature': *The Year of the Whale* (pp. 81–96)

1. Letter to Ernest Marwick, 12 October 1962.
2. Letter to Ernest Marwick, 15 February 1963.
3. Letter to Ernest Marwick, 14 September 1964.
4. 'The Poet Speaks', RG 456, Argo Record Company Ltd, 1965, recorded 13 October 1964.
5. 'Fisherman and Boy', *The Year of the Whale*, 1965, p. 45.
6. Letter to Ernest Marwick, 1 September 1965.
7. ibid.
8. 'The way of literature: An apologia', *The Tablet*, 12 June 1982, pp. 584–5.
9. Letter to Ernest Marwick, 27 February 1969.
10. *The Year of the Whale*, p. 45.

Chapter 6: 'The Orkney gift of narrative': (pp. 97–123)

1. 'The Old Man and his writing desk', *The Scotsman*, 12 October 1991, p. 9.

2. 'The Art of Narrative', in H. T. Robertson, ed., *Snakes and Ladders*, 1988, Unwin, p. 69.

3. Introduction to *Orkney Short Stories*, Orkney Press, 1983, p. 10.

4. 'Scottish Writing', 'George Mackay Brown – The Orkney Saga Man', BBC Scotland Radio 4 programme by Alexander Scott, broadcast, 29 September 1972; quoted in Brian Murray, 'Turning back the calendar for reissue of GMB short stories', *The Orcadian*, 7 December 2000, p. 20.

5. Brown's interview notes, 27 February 1969; quoted in Brian Murray, ibid.

6. 'A Calendar of Love', 'April', *A Calendar of Love*, p. 15.

7. ibid., 'March', pp. 12–13.

8. ibid., 'July', p. 20.

9. ibid., 'November', p. 33.

10. Foreword dated July 1986 to the 1987 Vanguard (New York) edition of *A Time to Keep and Other Stories*, p. ix.

11. 'Stone Poems', *A Calendar of Love*, pp. 143–4.

12. 'The Art of Narrative', pp. 68–9.

13. *Northern Lights*, 1999, p. 295.

14. *The Orcadian*, 1 December 1966, p. 1.

15. *The Orcadian*, 15 June 1967, p. 1.

16. Seamus Heaney, 'Celtic Fringe, Viking Fringe', *The Listener*, 21 August 1969, p. 254.

17. *For the Islands I Sing*, p. 170.

18. Maurice Lindsay, *Modern Scottish Poetry: An Anthology of the Scottish Renaissance*, Faber and Faber, 1966, p. 19.

19. *The Scottish Literary Revival: an anthology of twentieth-century poetry*, Collier-Macmillan, 1968, p. 5.

20. R. Bell, ed., *The Best of Scottish Poetry: An anthology of contemporary Scottish verse*, Chambers, 1989, p. v.

21. A. T. Turner, ed., *45 Contemporary Poems: The Creative Process*, Longman, 1985, p. 20.

22. 'Writer's Shop', *Chapman*, Summer 1976, p. 23.

Chapter 7: Confronting the Twentieth Century: Ruin and Regeneration (pp. 124–164)

1. 'The Art of Narrative', in H. T. Robertson, ed., *Snakes and Ladders*, Unwin, 1988, p. 68.
2. ibid.
3. ibid.
4. 'The Black Horseman' in *A Scottish Poetry Book*, compiled by Alan Bold, Oxford University Press, 1983, p. 32.
5. *Letters from Hamnavoe*, November 1971, Gordon Wright, 1975, p. 26.
6. Quoted in Jack Webster's 'Portrait of a Natural Man', *Scottish Daily Express*, 26 June 1973.
7. *For the Islands I Sing*, p. 171.
8. *Scottish International*, 1971, 14, pp. 11–21.
9. 'Scottish Writing', 'George Mackay Brown – The Orkney Saga Man', BBC Scotland Radio 4 programme by Alexander Scott, broadcast, 29 September 1972.
10. *Greenvoe*, p. 14.
11. ibid., p. 246.
12. *Northern Lights*, pp. 124–42.
13. 'A Christmas Holiday: A Short Faction', 9 December 1991, unpublished manuscript.
14. Ernest Marwick, *The Folklore of Orkney and Shetland*, Batsford, 1975, pp. 66–8.
15. Letter to Ernest Marwick, 15 June 1971.
16. Quoted in Satish Kumar, 'George Mackay Brown: Orkney Oracle', *Resurgence*, 122, May/June 1987, pp. 6–10.
17. ibid.
18. *The Scotsman*, 23 April 1977.
19. *For the Islands I Sing*, pp. 178–9.
20. ibid.
21. *Times Literary Supplement*, 28 September 1973, p. 1101.
22. 'A new translation of Orkneyinga Saga', *The Orcadian*, 12 January 1978, p. 4.
23. Rowena Murray, 'The Influence of Norse Literature on the Twentieth-Century Writer George Mackay Brown' in *Scottish Language and Literature: Medieval and Renaissance*, eds. D. Strauss and H. W. Drescher, Proceedings of the Fourth International Conference 1984, Frankfurt am Main, 1986, pp. 547–57.

24. Letter to Stewart Conn, Edinburgh University Library, 16 July 1967.

25. ibid.

26. Letter to Ernest Marwick, 19 February 1965.

27. *An Orkney Tapestry*, p. 54.

28. 'Shetland Diary', 2 June 1988, *Northern Lights*, p. 316.

29. Letter to David Morrison, 22 February 1969.

30. 'An Autobiographical Essay', in Maurice Lindsay, ed., *As I Remember*, Robert Hale, 1979, p. 15.

31. *For the Islands I Sing*, p. 33.

32. Letter to Ernest Marwick, 5 May 1946.

33. *The Two Fiddlers*, 1974, p. 10.

34. Bernard MacLaverty, *The Educational Times*, 12 December 1974, p. 23.

35. 'The Eye of the Hurricane', *A Time to Keep*, p. 167.

36. *For the Islands I Sing*, pp. 186–7.

37. Questionnaire completed for Ernest Marwick in Orkney Library, 27 February 1969 for a Radio Orkney broadcast.

38. Alexander Scott, 'George Mackay Brown' in James Vincent, ed., *Contemporary Novelists*, second edn., St James Press, 1976, pp. 193–5.

39. *For the Islands I Sing*, p. 179.

Part Three

Chapter 8: 'Through the eye of the needle of Orkney': Experiment and Consolidation (pp. 167–190)

1. Introduction to *Rockpools and Daffodils*, 1992, p. v.

2. Alasdair Maclean, 'Cavemen', *The Times Literary Supplement*, 25 March 1977, p. 347.

3. Seamus Heaney, the cover of Brown's *Selected Poems 1954–1983*, John Murray, 1991.

4. J. E. C., *Princeton Encyclopedia of Poetry and Poetics*, 1974, p. 362.

5. 'The Wanderer's Tale', *The Island of the Women*, 1998, pp. 216–17.

6. 'The Scholar', *The Masked Fisherman*, 1989, p. 169.

7. 'Hunters, An Idyll', *Scottish Short Stories*, 1981, Collins, p. 127.

8. 'The Winter Song', *The Masked Fisherman*, pp. 190–1.

9. 'Italian Chapel', *Orkney: Pictures and Poems*, 1996, p. 106.

10. 'The Seven Poets', *The Sun's Net*, 1976, p. 268.

11. Introduction to *Witch and Other Stories*, dated December 1975, Longman, 1977, pp. viii and x.

12. ibid.
13. *A Time to Keep and Other Stories*, new Introduction written July 1986, published 1987, for the American Vanguard edn., pp. vii–ix.
14. Alan Bold, *George Mackay Brown*, Oliver & Boyd, 1978, p. 74.
15. *Hawkfall*, p. 81.
16. *The Sun's Net*, p. 10.
17. ibid., p. 11.
18. *Under Brinkie's Brae*, 30 December 1976, Gordon Wright, 1979, p. 48.
19. Alasdair Maclean, op. cit.
20. Alexander Scott, 'The Orkney Saga Man', BBC Scotland, Radio 4, broadcast, 29 September 1972.
21. Ernest Marwick, 'Looking Around', *The Orcadian*, 24 October 1974, p. 3.
22. 'The First Letter', *Letters from Hamnavoe*, p. 1.
23. *Northern Lights*, p. 333.
24. *Letters from Hamnavoe*, p. 41.
25. Conversation, 20 November 1994, with Brian Murray.

Chapter 9: The Recurring Journey (pp. 191–234)

1. 'The Art of Narrative', 1988, p. 67.
2. ibid., p. 68.
3. Isobel Murray, ed., 'A Sequence of Images: George Mackay Brown', *Scottish Writers Talking*, Tuckwell Press, 1996, pp. 49–50.
4. *Time in a Red Coat*, Chatto & Windus, 1984, p. 39.
5. ibid., pp. 31–2.
6. ibid.
7. *The Orkney Herald*, 2 July 1946, p. 2.
8. *Time in a Red Coat*, pp. 240–3.
9. *The Wreck of the Archangel*, John Murray, 1989, p. ix.
10. ibid., p. 46.
11. ibid., p. 53.
12. ibid., p. 60.
13. ibid., p. 62.
14. ibid., p. 12.
15. *Selected Poems 1954–1983*, John Murray, 1991, p. 67.
16. ibid., p. 73.
17. ibid., p. 93.
18. Seamus Heaney's Introduction to *Poetry in Manuscript, an exhibition of poets' work sheets*, February 1970, Queen's Art Gallery, pages unnumbered.

19. Isobel Murray, 'Orkney isles', *The Financial Times*, 26 February 1983 and 'When small is beautiful', *The Scotsman*, 19 February 1983.

20. *The Masked Fisherman and Other Stories*, 1989, Introduction, p. ix.

21. ibid., p. 104.

22. ibid., p. 126.

23. ibid., p. 151.

24. ibid., p. 174.

25. ibid., p. 193.

26. *Orkneyinga Saga*, trans. Hermann Pálsson and Paul Edwards, Hogarth Press, 1978, 'Poetry and Fishing' chapter, pp. 142–3.

27. *Winterfold*, pp. 40–2.

28. *Andrina*, p. 21.

29. *A Celebration for Magnus*, Attic Records, Finstown, Orkney, 1987.

30. 'Sara', in *The Seventh Ghost Book*, Barrie & Jenkins, 1971, p. 32.

31. 'The Masque', *Stone*, p. 12.

32. 'Song of the Stone', ibid., p. 20.

33. David Annwn, 'Correspondences: An Interview with George Mackay Brown', *Poetry Wales*, 27, 2, September 1991, p. 19 [pp. 18–21].

34. Donald Campbell, 'The Drama, "Greenness in Every Line"', *Spear*, 2000, p. 65 [pp. 63–73].

35. Morag MacInnes in *St Magnus Festival, A Celebration*, compiled and ed. by Pamela Beasant, 2002, p. 164.

36. Notes for a recorded conversation with Ernest Marwick, March 1971, The Orkney Library.

37. Unpublished notes for an interview by Ernest Marwick, August 1972.

38. Preface to *Three Plays*, p. ix.

39. Unpublished notes for an interview by Ernest Marwick, August 1972.

Chapter 10: 'Perfect Silence' (pp. 235–264)

1. Introduction to 'Brodgar Poems', *Selected Poems, 1954–1992*, p. 166, written in February 1996.

2. 'To a Hamnavoe Poet of 2093', *Following a Lark*, p. 13.

3. *Selected Poems 1954–1983*, p. 24.

4. *New Statesman*, 17 May, 1974, p. 700.

5. *For the Islands I Sing*, p. 184.

6. 'Under Brinkie's Brae' column, 29 November 1990, *Rockpools and Daffodils*, p. 248.

7. *Vinland*, pp. 98–9 and 103.

8. ibid., p. 185.

9. ibid., p. 232.

10. 'Under Brinkie's Brae', *The Orcadian*, 2 March 1989, p. 4.

11. ibid.

12. ibid.

13. *Voices at the Door, An Anthology of Favourite Poems*, ed. Owen Burt and Christine Jones, Shelter Cymru, University of Wales Press, 1995, p. 204.

14. 'This scarf became a symbol', *The Orkney Herald*, 19 April 1960, p. 9.

15. Tom Morton interview, 'The Norse star shines', *The Scotsman*, 7 October 1994, p. 17.

16. *Beside the Ocean of Time*, pp. 121–2.

17. ibid., p. 213.

18. Thomas Mann, *The Magic Mountain*, translated by H. T. Lowe-Porter, Vintage Classics, 1999, p. 541.

19. ibid., p. 725.

20. *Beside the Ocean of Time*, p. 4.

21. ibid., p. 215.

22. Conversation with Brian Murray, 7 February 1995.

Epilogue (pp. 265–73)

1. 'The Wanderer's Tale', *The Island of the Women and Other Stories*, 1998, p. 221.

2. 'A Wilderness of Paper', *Rockpools and Daffodils*, 1992, p. 242.

3. *For the Islands I Sing*, pp. 140–41.

4. Brian Murray, 'Inspiration and craft: new GMB collection', *The Orcadian*, 24 September 1998, p. 19.

5. 'Shetland Diary', *Northern Lights*, p. 292.

6. ibid., pp. 310, 314, 318.

7. Letter to Ernest Marwick, 5 May 1946.

8. 'A Work for Poets', *Following a Lark*, p. 86.

Bibliography

(1) Poems

The Storm and Other Poems, Kirkwall: Orkney Press, 1954.

Loaves and Fishes, London: Hogarth Press, 1959.

The Year of the Whale, London: Chatto & Windus/Hogarth Press, 1965.

The Five Voyages of Arnor, Falkland, Fife: K.D. Duval, 1966.

Twelve Poems, Belfast: Queen's University Festival Publications, 1968.

Lifeboat and Other Poems, Bow, Crediton: Richard Gilbertson, 1971.

Fishermen with Ploughs: A Poem Cycle, London: Hogarth Press, 1971.

Poems New and Selected, London: Hogarth Press, 1971.

Penguin Modern Poets 21: Iain Crichton Smith, Norman MacCaig, George Mackay Brown, Harmondsworth: Penguin, 1972.

Winterfold, London: Chatto & Windus/Hogarth Press, 1976.

Selected Poems, London: Hogarth Press, 1977.

Seven Poets, ed. C. Carrell, Glasgow: Third Eye Centre, 1981.

Voyages, London: Chatto & Windus/Hogarth Press, 1983.

Christmas Poems, Oxford: Perpetua Press, 1984.

The Scottish Bestiary, Edinburgh: Paragon Press, 1986.

Stone, Verona: K. D. Duval and C. H. Hamilton, 1987.

Four Poets for St Magnus, Orkney: Breckness Press, 1987.

Songs for St Magnus Day, The Seven Jars of Sorrow and Comfort, Oxford: Perpetua Press, 1988.

Two Poems for Kenna, Dorset: Words Press, 1988.

Tryst on Egilsay: Hakon and Magnus, Wetherby: Celtic Cross Press, 1989.

The Wreck of the Archangel, London: John Murray, 1989.

Selected Poems 1954–83, London: John Murray, 1991.

Brodgar Poems, Oxford: Perpetua Press, 1992.

Foresterhill, Schondorf: Babel, 1992.

The Lost Village, Wetherby: Celtic Cross Press, 1992.

The Sea and the Tower, Calgary, Canada: Bayeux Arts, 1994.

Orfeo: A Masque, Lastingham, York: Celtic Cross Press, 1995.

Following a Lark, London: John Murray, 1996.

Orkney: Pictures and Poems, Grantown-on-Spey: Colin Baxter Photography, 1996 (with Gunnie Moberg's photographs).

Selected Poems 1954–1992, London: John Murray, 1996.

Water, Twickenham and Wakefield: North and South, 1996.

Stained Glass Windows, Lastingham, York: Celtic Cross Press, 1998.

Travellers, London: John Murray, 2001.

Collected Poems, London, John Murray, 2005.

Island Wedding, Lastingham, York: Celtic Cross Press, 2005.

(2) Short Stories

A Calendar of Love and Other Stories, London: Hogarth Press, 1967.

A Time to Keep and Other Stories, London: Hogarth Press, 1969.

Hawkfall and Other Stories, London: Hogarth Press, 1974.

The Sun's Net, London: Hogarth Press, 1976.

Witch and Other Stories, London: Longman, 1977.

Andrina and Other Stories, London: Chatto & Windus/Hogarth Press, 1983.

Christmas Stories, Oxford: Perpetua Press, 1985.

The Hooded Fisherman, Pitlochry: K. D. Duval and C. H. Hamilton, 1985.

The Masked Fisherman and Other Stories, London: John Murray, 1989.

The Sea-King's Daughter: Eureka!, Nairn: Balnain Books, 1991. *Eureka!* is a story.

In the Margins of a Shakespeare, Monmouth: Old Stile Press, 1991.

Winter Tales, London: John Murray, 1995.

The Sixth Station, Holybourne: Clarion, 1996.

The Island of the Women and Other Stories, London: John Murray, 1998.

The Rose Tree, Lastingham, York: Celtic Cross Press, 2001.

The Son of the Fisherman, Lastingham, York: Celtic Cross Press, 2002.

The Poor Man in his Castle, Lastingham, York: Celtic Cross Press, 2004.

The Fairground Poet, Lastingham, York: Celtic Cross Press, 2007.

(3) Novels

Greenvoe, London: Hogarth Press, 1972.

Magnus, London: Hogarth Press, 1973.

Time in a Red Coat, London: Chatto & Windus/Hogarth Press, 1984.

The Golden Bird: Two Orkney Stories, London: John Murray, 1987.

Vinland, London: John Murray, 1992.

Beside the Ocean of Time, London: John Murray, 1994.

(4) Plays

A Spell for Green Corn, London: Hogarth Press, 1970.
Three Plays, London: Chatto & Windus/Hogarth Press, 1984.
The Loom of Light, Nairn: Balnain Books, 1986.
A Celebration for Magnus, Nairn: Balnain Books, 1987.
The Sea King's Daughter: Eureka!, Nairn: Balnain Books, 1991.

(5) Non-Fiction

Let's See the Orkney Islands, Fort William: William S. Thomson, 1948.
Stromness, The Orkney Islands: the Official Guide, ed. L. Horton Bone, Cheltenham and London: J. Burrow & Co., 1955.
Stromness, In the Orkney Islands: Official Guide, Stromness: Stromness Town Council, 1963.
An Orkney Tapestry, London: Victor Gollancz, 1969.
Letters from Hamnavoe, Edinburgh: Gordon Wright, 1975.
Edwin Muir: A Brief Memoir, West Linton: Castlelaw Press, 1975.
Under Brinkie's Brae, Edinburgh: Gordon Wright, 1979.
Edwin Muir: Selected Prose, London: John Murray, 1987.
Portrait of Orkney, London: Hogarth Press, 1981; revised edition London: John Murray, 1988.
Rockpools and Daffodils: An Orcadian Diary 1979–1991, Edinburgh: Gordon Wright, 1992.
For the Islands I Sing: An Autobiography, London: John Murray, 1997.
Northern Lights: A Poet's Sources, London: John Murray, 1999.
The First Wash of Spring, London and Edinburgh: Steve Savage, 2006.

(6) For Children

The Two Fiddlers: Tales from Orkney, London: Chatto & Windus, 1974.
Pictures in the Cave, London: Chatto & Windus, 1977.
Six Lives of Fankle the Cat, London: Chatto & Windus, 1980.
Keepers of the House, London: Old Stile Press, 1986.
Letters to Gypsy, Nairn: Balnain Books, 1990.

(7) Essays and columns (Selected)

'Stromness News', *The Orkney Herald*, 5 September 1944 (fourteen years, weekly).

Bibliography

'Ecclesiastical Episodes', *The Orkney Herald*, 24 October 1944–16 April 1946 (74 items).

'Island Diary', *The Orkney Herald*, 25 September 1945–23 October 1956 (425 columns).

Focus (of the week), *The Orkney Herald*, 21 March 1950–25 September 1951.

'Mansie' series, The Orkney Herald, May 1953–6 October 1953 (19 essays).

'The Orkney Common Reader', *The Orcadian*, 6 August 1953–22 April 1954 (19 essays).

'What the Pierhead is Saying', *The Orkney Herald*, 24 August 1954–25 September 1956 (weekly).

'Living in Orkney', *Saltire Review*, 2(6), 1955, 54–60.

'What the Pierhead is Saying', *The Orcadian*, 9 November 1961–2 July 1970 (weekly).

'The Last Ballad – George Mackay Brown considers that radio and television have done harm to the Orkney Islands', *The Listener*, 20 June 1968, pp. 800–1.

'Childhood in Orkney', *Scottish Field*, August 1968, pp. 19–20.

'Letter from Hamnavoe', *The Orcadian*, 18 February 1971–27 March 1975 (weekly).

'Oilscene', *Scotland*, January 1973, pp. 50–3.

'Writers and Education', *Scottish Educational Journal*, 17 October 1975, p. 969.

'Under Brinkie's Brae', The Orcadian, 5 February 1976–11 April 1996 (weekly).

'Writer's Shop', *Chapman*, 16, IV, 4, Summer 1976, pp. 21–4.

'An Autobiographical Essay' in M. Lindsay, ed., *As I Remember: Ten Modern Scottish Writers Recall How Writing Began for Them*, London: Robert Hale, 1979, pp. 9–21.

'Newbattle: Early Days – Second Chance', *Newbattle Abbey College Journal*, Spring, 1982, pp. 6–7. (Reprinted from 'Friends of Newbattle Abbey Association Bulletin 7', Spring 1977.)

'The way of literature: An apologia by George Mackay Brown', *The Tablet*, 12 June 1982: 584–5.

'George Mackay Brown remembers', [Edinburgh] *Evening News*, 23 April 1983, p. 5.

Introduction to *Orkney Short Stories*, Stromness: The Orkney Press, 1983, pp. 9–11.

'Orcadian perspectives on life and literature', *Glasgow Herald Weekend*, 15 June, 1985, p. 9.

'The Seven Ages of George Mackay Brown', *Weekend Scotsman*, 30 August 1986, pp. 1–2.

'George Mackay Brown', *Contemporary Authors: Autobiography Series*, Detroit, MI: Gale Research Company, 1988, pp. 61–76.

'Keeping the Flame Alive', *Spotlight*, February 1988, pp. 47–9.

'The Art of Narrative' in H. T. Robertson, ed., *Snakes and Ladders*, London: Unwin Hyman, pp. 67–9.

'Et in Orcadia Ego', *The Independent Weekend*, 3 August 1991, p. 25.

'The Old Man and his writing desk', *The Scotsman*, 12 October 1991, p. 9.

(8) Criticism of George Mackay Brown's work (Selected)

Annwn, D. (1984) *Inhabited Voices: Myth and History in the poetry of Geoffrey Hill, Seamus Heaney and George Mackay Brown*, Frome, Somerset: Bran's Head Books.

Annwn, D. (1991) 'Correspondences: An Interview with George Mackay Brown', *Poetry Wales*, 27(2), September 1991, pp. 18–21.

Annwn, D. (1991) 'The Fresh Echo, The Recent Poetry of George Mackay Brown', *Poetry Wales*, 27(2), September 1991, pp. 21–4.

Annwn, D. (1995) '"The Binding Breath": Island and community in the poetry of George Mackay Brown' in H. W. Ludwig and L. Fietz, eds., *Poetry in the British Isles*, Cardiff: University of Wales Press, pp. 283–310.

Beasant, P., ed. (2002) *St Magnus Festival: A Celebration*, Kirkwall: *The Orcadian*.

B[evan], [A.] (1954) 'The Storm: A Book of Poems by George Mackay Brown', *The Orcadian*, 1 July, p. 4.

Bevan, A. (1996) 'Orkney Story in Pictures and Poetry', *The Orcadian*, 20 June, p. 15.

Bevan, A. (2003) 'George Mackay Brown: Poet and storyteller' in D. J. Waugh, ed., *The Faces of Orkney: Stones, Skalds and Saints*, Aberdeen: Scottish Society for Northern Studies, pp. 33–45.

Blythe, R. (1998) 'Going to See George: A visit to George Mackay Brown', *Books and Company* 1, pp. 33–46.

Bold, A. (1978) *George Mackay Brown*, Edinburgh: Oliver & Boyd.

Bold, A. (1983) 'George Mackay Brown: Elemental Rhythms' in *Modern Scottish Literature*, London: Longman, pp. 241–8.

Bruce-Watt, J. (1983) 'George Mackay Brown', *The Scotsman Magazine*, 11 February, pp. 14–15.

Butter, P. H. (1987) 'George Mackay Brown and Edwin Muir', *The Yearbook of English Studies*, 17, pp. 16–30.

Cambridge, G. (1996) '"A Thread Too Bright for the Eye": an appreciation of George Mackay Brown', *Chapman*, 84, pp. 36–41.

Campbell, I. (1975) 'Modern Scottish Writers', *Northern Studies*, 5, pp. 24–9.

Bibliography

Campbell, I. (1996) 'Beside Brown's Ocean of Time' in S. Hagemann, ed., *Studies in Scottish Fiction: 1945 to the Present*, Frankfurt am Main: Peter Lang, pp. 263–74.

Coe, J. (1992) 'Sydney's Inferno', *The London Review of Books*, 24 September, p. 22.

Conn, S. (1966) 'Poets of the Sixties', *Lines*, 22, pp. 10–17.

Conn, S. (2001) *Distances: A Personal Evocation of People and Places*, Dalkeith: Scottish Cultural Press, pp. 77–85.

Craig, C. (2000) *The Modern Scottish Novel: Narrative and the National Imagination*, Edinburgh: Edinburgh University Press.

Craig, C., ed. (1987) *The History of Scottish Literature, Vol. 4*, Aberdeen: Aberdeen University Press.

Craig, P. (1987) 'Getting On', *Times Literary Supplement*, 17 September, p. 925.

Crossley-Holland, K. (1972) 'Hoy: The Supreme Sacrifice' in *Pieces of Land: Journeys to Eight Islands*, London: Gollancz, pp. 43–51.

Cruickshank, M. (1991) 'Interrogation of Silence', *Times Educational Supplement*, 6 December, p. 25.

D'Arcy, J. M. (1996) 'George Mackay Brown' in *Scottish Skalds and Sagamen: Old Norse Influence on Modern Scottish Literature*, East Lothian: Tuckwell Press, pp. 242–83.

Drever, D. (2003) 'The Literature of Orkney' in D. Omand, ed., *The Orkney Book*, Edinburgh: Birlinn, pp. 263–67.

Dunn, D. (1974) '"Finished Fragrance": The Poems of George Mackay Brown', *Poetry Nation*, 2, pp. 80–92.

Fergusson, M. (2006) *George Mackay Brown: The Life*, London: John Murray.

Fraser, R. (2001) 'George Mackay Brown and the Orkney Islands', *Sewanee Review*, Autumn, pp. 565–73.

Garriock, N. D. (1990) 'George Mackay Brown: Juvenilia to Loaves and Fishes', *Chapman*, 60, pp. 1–7.

'Geremy' (1969), Gerald G. A. Meyer, 'From My Journal/George Brown – A Profile', *The Orcadian*, 6 November 1969, p. 4.

Gifford, D. (1994) 'The never-ending story', *The Scotsman Weekend*, 26 March, p. 13.

Gifford, D. (1996) 'Appreciation: George Mackay Brown', *The Scotsman*, 15 April, p. 9.

Gifford, D. (1999) '"Out of the World and into Blawearie": The Politics of Scottish Fiction' in E.J. Cowan and D. Gifford, eds., *The Polar Twins*, pp. 284–303, Edinburgh: John Donald.

Gifford, D., Dunnigan, S. and MacGillivray, A. (2002) *Scottish Literature in English and Scots*, Edinburgh: Edinburgh University Press.

Gifford, T. (1993) *Green Voices: Understanding contemporary nature poetry*, Manchester: Manchester University Press, pp. 33–39.

Gillman, P. (1989) 'A Cold Northern Light', *Sunday Times Magazine*, 3 September, pp. 56–9.

Gray, A. (2000) *Circle of Light: The History of the Catholic Church in Orkney since 1560*, Edinburgh: John Donald.

Heaney, S. (1969) 'Celtic Fringe, Viking Fringe', *The Listener*, 21 August, p. 254.

Herbold, T. (1974) 'Four Imports', *Parnassus*, 3, pp. 65–76.

Huberman, E. (1977) 'Mackay Brown's *Greenvoe*: Rediscovering a Novel of the Orkneys', *Critique*, 19(2), pp. 33–43.

Huberman, E. (1981) 'George Mackay Brown's *Magnus*', *Studies in Scottish Literature*, 16, pp. 122–34.

Kumar, S. (1987) 'George Mackay Brown: Orkney Oracle', *Resurgence*, 122, pp. 6–10.

Loppert, M. (1977) 'Orkney, St Magnus Festival: The Martyrdom of St Magnus', *Opera*, 28, pp. 46–8.

MacDonald, F. J. (1968) 'Poets' Places', *Akros*, 3(8), pp. 24–25.

MacGillivray, A. (1989) 'George Mackay Brown's *Greenvoe*', Scotnotes No. 6, Aberdeen: The Association for Scottish Literary Studies.

MacInnes, M. (2002) 'Finding a Voice in the Forties', *The New Shetlander*, 221, pp. 30–6.

Manlove, C. (1994) 'George Mackay Brown, *Magnus* (1973) and Others' in *Scottish Fantasy Literature: A Critical Survey*, Edinburgh: Canongate Academic, pp. 182–96.

Marwick, E. (1975) *The Folklore of Orkney and Shetland*, London: Batsford.

Marwick, E. (1977) 'North East Review: George Mackay Brown', *Leopard Magazine*, pp. 23–6.

Morton, T. (1994) 'The North Star Shines', *The Scotsman*, 7 October, pp. 17–18.

Murray, B. (1996) 'Vintage GMB – as his legacy lives on with new volume of poems', *The Orcadian*, 20 June, p. 14.

Murray, B. (2000) 'Turning back the calendar for reissue of GMB short stories', *The Orcadian*, 7 December, p. 20.

Murray, B. and Murray, R. (2004) 'Remembering GMB's first volume of poems, 50 years on', *The Orcadian*, 7 July 2004, pp. 20–21.

Murray, I. and Tait, B. (1984) 'Voyages Around George Mackay Brown', *Weekend Scotsman*, 8 December, p. 1.

Murray, I. and Tait, B. (1984) 'George Mackay Brown: *Greenvoe*' in *Ten Modern Scottish Novels*, Aberdeen: Aberdeen University Press, pp. 144–67.

Bibliography

Murray, I., ed. (1996) *Scottish Writers Talking*, East Lothian: Tuckwell Press, pp. 1–54.

Murray, R. (1986) *Style as Voice: A Reappraisal of George Mackay Brown's Prose* (unpublished PhD thesis), State College: Pennsylvania State University.

Murray, R. (1986) 'The Influence of Norse Literature on the Twentieth-Century Writer George Mackay Brown' in D. Strauss and H.W. Drescher, eds., *Scottish Language and Literature: Medieval and Renaissance*, Proceedings of the Fourth International Conference, 1984, Frankfurt am Main, 1986 pp. 547–57.

Nicholson, C. (1992) 'Unlocking Time's Labyrinth' in *Poem, Purpose and Place: Shaping Identity in Contemporary Scottish Verse*, Edinburgh: Polygon, pp. 96–113.

O'Driscoll, D. (1978) 'Poems from a Small Island: An Introduction to the Poetry of George Mackay Brown', *Poetry Australia*, 68, pp. 49–54.

O'Driscoll, D. (2001) 'George Mackay Brown' in *Troubled Thoughts, Majestic Dreams: Selected Prose Writings*, Oldcastle, Ireland: Gallery Books, pp. 225–7.

Orr, P. (1964) *The Poet Speaks* (recorded interview with George Mackay Brown), London: British Library National Sound Archive.

Pacey, P. (1976) 'The Fire of Images: The Poetry of George Mackay Brown', *Akros*, 32, pp. 61–71.

Parham, M. (1992) 'Master of an Island Universe', *The Times Saturday Review*, 25 July, pp. 10–11.

Parham, M. (1998) 'From Orkney, the World Lies at Your Feet', *Literary Review*, May, p. 23.

Perryman, K. (1990) 'Babel Questionnaire: George Mackay Brown', *Babel*, 6, pp. 58–9.

Reino, J. (1984) 'George Mackay Brown', in W. B. Sherry, ed., *Dictionary of Literary Biography*, vol. 27, Columbia, SC, pp. 31–9.

Robb, D. S. (1992) '*Greenvoe*: A Poet's Novel', *Scottish Literary Journal*, 13(1), pp. 47–60.

Roberts, J. G. (1983) 'Tradition and Pattern in the Short Stories of George Mackay Brown' in D. Hewitt and Spiller, M., eds., *Literature of the North*, Aberdeen: Aberdeen University Press, pp. 176–88.

Roberts, N. (1973) 'George Mackay Brown', *Cambridge Quarterly*, 6(2), pp. 181–9.

Schmid, S. (2003) *Keeping the Sources Pure: The Making of George Mackay Brown*, Oxford: Peter Lang.

Schoene, B. (1995) '"I Imagined Nine Centuries . . .": Narrative Fragmentation and Mythical Closure in the Shorter Historical Fiction of George Mackay Brown', *Scottish Literary Journal*, 22(2), pp. 41–59.

Schoene, B. (1995) *The Making of Orcadia: Narrative Identity in the Prose Work of George Mackay Brown*, Frankfurt am Main: Peter Lang.

Sharpton, W. (1996) '"Hamnavoe Revisited": An Interview with George Mackay Brown', *Chapman*, 84, pp. 20–7.

Spear, H. D., ed. (2000) *George Mackay Brown – A Survey of his Work and a Full Bibliography*, Lampeter: Edwin Mellen Press.

Stafford, F. (2000) 'Starting Lines' in *Scottish, Irish and English Poetry, From Burns to Heaney*, Oxford: Oxford University Press, pp. 29–33.

Turner, A. T., ed. (1985) *45 Contemporary Poems: The Creative Process*, London: Longman.

Wallace, G. and Stevenson, R., eds. (1993) *The Scottish Novel Since the Seventies: New Visions, Old Dreams*, Edinburgh: Edinburgh University Press.

Welham, H. (1990) 'Brown's Fiction for Children', *Chapman*, 60, pp. 13–18.

Whyte, C. (2004) *Modern Scottish Poetry*, Edinburgh: Edinburgh University Press, pp. 165–73.

Yamada, O., Spear, H. D. and Robb, D. S., eds. (1991) *The Contribution to Literature of Orcadian Writer George Mackay Brown: An Introduction and a Bibliography*, Lampeter: Edwin Mellen Press.

Zagnoli, M. (1988) '*Story* and *Fable* in the Purgatorial Ghost Stories of George Mackay Brown', *Studies in Scottish Literature*, 23, pp. 77–86.

*

Three recent surveys treat Brown's work as part of the writers' comprehensive surveys of Scottish literature:

Brown, I., Clancy, T. O., Manning, S. and Pittock, M., eds. (2007) *The Edinburgh History of Scottish Literature*, vol. 3, Edinburgh: Edinburgh University Press.

Crawford, R. (2007) *Scottish Books: The Penguin History of Scottish Literature*, London: Penguin Books.

Watson, R. (2007) *The Literature of Scotland: The Twentieth Century*, 2nd ed., Palgrave Macmillan.

Index

Index

Index

Index